FOLEY

Also by Michael Smith

ODD MAN OUT (with Peter Elphick)

OLD CLOAK, NEW DAGGER

FOLEY

The Spy Who Saved 10,000 Jews

Michael Smith

Hodder & Stoughton

For Hayley

British Library Cataloguing in Publication Data
A CIP catalogue record is available from the British Library

ISBN: 0 340 71850 1

Typeset by Palimpsest Book Production Limited,
Polmont, Stirlingshire
Printed and bound in Great Britain by
Clays Ltd, St Ives plc

Hodder and Stoughton
A division of Hodder Headline PLC
338 Euston Road
London NW1 3BH

Acknowledgements

I am grateful to all those who agreed to be interviewed during the research of this book and to the families of Frank Foley and Margaret Reid for allowing me access to, and use of, material they had written. I should particularly like to thank the following individuals for the help they gave me: Batsheeva Arian; Hugh Astor; Chanan Baram; Dean Beeby; Irene Berlyn; Kenneth Benton; Desmond Bristow; Catherine Charlton; Ross Davies; Charles DeSalis; Patricia Dunstan; Richard Dunstan; David Eppel; Gwenda Evers; Marilyn Ferris; Dennis Foley; Margaret Foley; Ann Forbes-Robertson; Vincent C. Frank-Steiner; Dr J. A. Harding; David Higgs; Arnold Horwell; Rev John B. Kelley; William Lee Kelley; Sabine Komberti; Werner Lachs; Elisheva Lernau; Batia Leshem; David List; Gaby Loewidt; Geoffrey Maslen; Susanne Meyer-Michael; Martin Middlebrook; Ruth Moiret; Ze'ev Padan; Arnold Paucker; Tristran Pointon; Miriam Posner; Ohniel Preis; Paula Quirk; John and Sally de Renzy Martin; Heinz Romberg; Ernest Ruppel; John David Sainsbury; Shlomo Shpiro; Jimmy Thirsk; Oleg Tsarev; Simon Wertheimer.

I must also thank Roland Philipps and Angela Herlihy at Hodder and Stoughton, and the staff of the following libraries and archives for their assistance: the Public Record Office; the

Central Zionist Archives in Jerusalem; Yad Vashem; the Imperial War Museum; the KGB Archives; the Regimental Museum of the Staffordshire Regiment; Stourbridge Library; the Wiener Library; the Leo Baeck Institute; Caversham Library; and last, but by no means least, the *Daily Telegraph* Library.

Contents

List of Illustrations   ix
Prologue   1
1   The First War   3
2   On Secret Service   17
3   Hunting for Bolsheviks   29
4   A Rule of Terror   39
5   The Jonny Case   51
6   Not Strictly Passport Control   63
7   A Catch-22 Situation   77
8   'Only a Fool Will Grumble'   89
9   'Like Vultures Swarming Down'   101
10   Jews and Dogs Not Wanted   111
11   The Night of Broken Glass   121
12   'An Active Little Man'   131
13   All the Fault of England   143
14   Looking for a Final Solution   153
15   Into the Camps   163
16   The Oslo Report   173
17   The Foley Mission   185
18   The Shetland Bus   197
19   The Hollowed-Out Tennis Racquet   207

20	Rudolf Hess	217
21	Meeting Philby	227
22	The Twenty Club	237
23	Like a Spider Spinning His Web	249
24	Hunting for Nazis	261
	Postscript	275
	Author's Note	278
	Notes	279
	Bibliography	345
	Index	349

List of Illustrations

Hamburg in the early 1900s
Inns of Court OTC training at Berkhamsted (*Imperial War Museum*)
Officers of the Inns of Court OTC (*Imperial War Museum*)
Inns of Court OTC on parade at Berkhamsted (*Imperial War Museum*)
Frank Foley's parents, Isabella and Andrew Wood Foley
Kay with her sister, Jane, around the time she became engaged to Foley (*William Lee Kelley*)
Frank and Kay's marriage certificate
Foley on his balcony in Berlin, 1923
Kay and her sister, Jane, attending a German Foreign Ministry dinner at which they were received by Hitler (*The Rev John B. Kelley*)
Wilfred, Herbert and Amy Israel
Hubert Pollack
Foley and Ursula on holiday in England, July 1933 (*William Lee Kelley*)
Josef Goebbels
Hermann Göring
Rudolf Hess
Wolfgang Meyer-Michael

Leopold and Adele Wertheimer (*Simon Wertheimer*)

Willi Preis (*Ohniel Preis*)

August Weber

Foley's letter to the Fehr family, telling them to come and collect
their passes

Gunther Powitzer in Sachsenhausen (*Ze'ev Padan*)

Foley in London, 1939

Margaret Reid

Foley and Leslie Mitchell in Oslo, 1939

Oluf Reed Olsen and Kaare Moe (*Oluf Reed Olsen*)

Paul Rosbaud (*Lotte Meitner-Graf*)

Foley's letter to Dr Fehr's wife after Oskar Fehr's internment

Foley photographed before going to Buckingham Palace, 1941

Foley's medals

Ursula Foley with a neighbour's daughter in Stourbridge

Adolf Eichmann

Benno Cohn

All photographs courtesy of private collections unless otherwise stated

Prologue

On Friday, 19 June 1959, a small group of men and women gathered on the edge of a windswept forest near Kibbutz Harel, just outside Jerusalem. A grove of trees had been planted there to commemorate a remarkable Englishman. Each of the 2,200 pines had been paid for by someone he saved from the Nazi concentration camps. Contributions for more trees were coming in each day.

The speakers at the ceremony included some of the most eminent members of the Jewish community in pre-war Berlin. Benno Cohn, former chairman of the Zionist Organisation of Germany, reminded those present that they had gathered to pay tribute to a British official who saved tens of thousands of Jews from the Holocaust. 'He was the Pimpernel of the Jews,' Cohn said. 'Day and night, he was at the disposal of those who sought help. In those dark days, he restored to many of us our faith in humanity.'

A memorial stone placed in front of the grove read simply: 'Major Francis Edward Foley, England, Memorial Grove'.

Chapter 1

The First War

Frank Foley was born on 24 November 1884 in a two-up, two-down terraced house close to the railway station in the small Somerset town of Highbridge. His father, Andrew Wood Foley, was from Tiverton in Devon, but had moved first to Swindon to take a job on the Great Western Railway, working as an engine fitter in the company's locomotive works. It was here that he met and married Isabella Turnbull, a local girl of Scottish extraction, and where their first two children, Andy and Bert, were born.

Some time around 1883, the Foleys and their two young sons arrived in Highbridge. Andrew Wood Foley was to be one of the 250 workers at the 'extensive locomotive works' which the Somerset and Dorset Joint Railway Company had just built to maintain their blue-engined locomotives. The family lived at 7 Walrow Terrace, one of a row of terraced houses built for the railway workers, and it was here, little more than a year after their arrival in Highbridge, that Isabella gave birth to her third son, christening him Francis Edward. By the time he started school, his parents had had two more children: George, and Margaret – Isabella's longed-for daughter and the youngest member of the family.

Highbridge lay at the mouth of the River Brue in the centre

of an area of reclaimed marshland known as the Somerset Levels which extended for many miles inland and was frequently flooded during the autumn and winter. The Levels were criss-crossed by long narrow drainage ditches known locally as rhynes. By the late nineteenth century, the town was dominated by the railway, which served a long, narrow harbour at which coasters from South Wales unloaded cargoes of coal and iron, replacing them with local timber, bricks, corn, cider and Cheddar and Caerphilly cheese.

The Foleys' home faced west, looking out across open meadows towards the Bristol–Exeter line of the rival Great Western Railway. There were no houses on the opposite side of Walrow Terrace, just a bullrush–lined rhyne that flowed underneath the main road to Wells before skirting around the locomotive works and draining into the River Brue about a hundred yards south of Frank's house. About the same distance to the north was Pitt's Brickyard, the other major contributor to the local economy.

Isabella Foley was a devout Catholic and insisted that all her children be sent to St Joseph's Roman Catholic School in Burnham, run by the French La Retraite order of nuns. It was here that Frank acquired a devotion to the Church, telling his parents that, when he grew up, he wanted to be a priest.

For some reason, at the age of nine, Frank changed schools. Possibly his father had become concerned that the nuns were having an undue influence on his children. His daughter Margaret, who would eventually become mother superior of a convent school in Bristol, already harboured childhood ambitions of becoming a nun while Frank was always his favourite son, the clever child on whom he pinned his hopes for the future. Whatever the explanation, Frank was taken out of St Joseph's and placed in St John's Church of England Elementary School on the borders between Highbridge and Burnham.

Andrew Wood Foley was studying to become a civil engineer, and that determination to improve the lot of both himself and his family seems to have extended to his ambitions for Frank. His son had the ability to make something of his life; he should not waste it on the Church.

But Isabella was clearly equally determined that if her son wanted to become a priest, he should get his chance. Nor had the nuns forgotten their young protégé. They arranged for him to obtain a scholarship to Stonyhurst College, a Jesuit-run school in Lancashire. Then, at the age of eighteen, Frank was sent to St Joseph's College, a Catholic seminary in the French city of Poitiers, to be trained as a priest.

After three years at St Joseph's, Frank went to the Université de France in Poitiers to study classics. But the freedom and excesses of student life made him reconsider his suitability for the priesthood and he decided instead on an academic career. He set off to travel around Europe, through Austria, Holland, Denmark and Germany, taking teaching jobs to pay his way and intending eventually to return to England to try to find an academic post at Oxford or Cambridge.

When Britain declared war on Germany in August 1914, Frank was in Hamburg studying philosophy. A short, slim young man with a thin face, a pointed nose and a slightly earnest look, he was now fluent in German as well as French, and had made many friends in the city. But with British citizens resident in Germany being rounded up and at best interned, he needed to get out quickly or face an uncertain fate. Borrowing a military uniform from a colleague, he set off by train, claiming to be a Prussian officer on his way to the front.

Realising there was little chance of getting out across the French or Belgian borders, where the German Army was locked in battle with the Allied forces, Frank decided to head for East Frisia and the border with northern Holland. Leaving the train at Bremen, where the line turned south towards the Rhineland, he set off on foot, taking refuge along the way wherever he could, mainly in the homes of sympathetic clergymen who didn't ask too many questions and who appeared to assume he was a conscientious objector fleeing the war.

By now the meadows and woodland of the north German plain had given way to windswept marshland riddled with dykes and canals that were reminiscent of the rhynes which drained the levels around Burnham and Highbridge. Frank had exchanged the officer's uniform for an ill-fitting set of civilian clothes, but 'spy fever' was rampant and there had already been a number of cases of suspicious strangers being lynched on the spot. The only safe way of travelling was to avoid public transport and proceed on foot, and it took him some time to reach the North Sea port of Emden.

Making his way to the city's Moederkerk, the Great Church of the Dutch Reformation, he found a sympathetic Lutheran *domine*, a descendant of the sixteenth-century refugees who had fled from religious persecution in the Spanish Netherlands. The cleric put Frank in touch with shrimp fishermen from the small Dutch village of Termunten who were prepared to ferry him, no questions asked, across the Dollard Lagoon, which provided the bulk of their catch and separated Germany from neutral Holland.

Arriving back in Britain, Frank took the train to Burnham, where his father's new career as a civil engineer had brought a move up the social scale and a small degree of affluence, allowing the family to buy a large house in the centre of the town. Uncertain of what he should do next, Frank took a job as an assistant master at Bengeo Preparatory School in Hertford.

At the end of 1915, he decided to join the army and applied to the Inns of Court Officer Training Corps based in the nearby town of Berkhamsted. The original rules preventing the corps from taking any recruits other than barristers had been relaxed to include those who had attended university or public school, and it was now fully occupied training officers for the Territorial Army.

Frank was sent to corps headquarters in Stone Buildings, Lincoln's Inn, where an elderly barrister wearing the blue dress uniform, boots and spurs of a cavalry major took his details and told him to report the next day for initial training. One of his fellow recruits recorded his impressions of the first day of his army service.

> Parade at ten in Lincoln's Inn Gardens. About 100 recruits, all looking rather lost and most unmilitary in 'civvies' with every sort of hat. Several earnest and warm-looking NCOs push us into some kind of formation and we are then sorted out into squads. An ardent corporal takes us in hand and drills us vigorously, with an interval for luncheon, until 4 o'clock when we are dismissed for the day and I retire to my club for a much needed drink feeling as if I had never worked so hard in my life.

After two weeks of this, and having been issued with old uniforms to replace their 'civvies', the new recruits were sent to join the rest of the corps at Berkhamsted.

'We camped out in "Kitchener's Field" near the railway station in summer and in winter were billeted in different houses throughout the town,' said one young man who trained at the same time as Frank.

> We messed in sheds in Key's Timber Yard. Lectures were given in the ruins of the Old Castle in which the Black Prince had kept King John of France a prisoner. Cooper's Dip Works fixed up hot baths where we had plenty of boiling water.
>
> We exercised on the Common and in Ashridge Park with its beautiful beech trees and had route marches to such places as Chesham, Tring, Boxmoor, Great and Little Gaddesden and Ivinghoe Beacon. On Fridays we had 'night operations' which were not popular and I fear we learned little or nothing from them. Indeed, the rank and file knew little or nothing of the purpose or result of any operation, whether by day or night, in which we were exercised.

Saturday afternoons saw a mass exodus for home until Sunday evening, except for those unfortunate enough to be placed on guard duty.

At the start of the war, Inns of Court trainees could have expected to have received their commission within six weeks. But for some time, the War Office had not needed to take officers from the corps. As a result, the number of trainees had risen to around four thousand, four times the normal strength.

In order to help keep control of such a large body of men, selected trainees, Frank among them, were given the rank of lance-corporal and placed in charge of a section. It was not until 25 January 1917, at the relatively late age of thirty-two, that Frank was commissioned into the Hertfordshire Regiment, as a lowly second lieutenant. He was immediately seconded to the 2/6th Battalion, the North Staffordshire Regiment, and dispatched to France.

His new unit, made up mainly of conscripts from the Burton-on-Trent area, had been in Ireland helping to restore order in the wake of the 1916 Easter Uprising. They had crossed to Liverpool a week before Frank was posted to the battalion and were now encamped at Codford, near Salisbury, awaiting the orders sending them to France. Frank was given leave and told to meet them at Folkestone on 25 February 1917, when – their training still incomplete – they were to assemble prior to crossing the Channel headed for the Somme.

By now, the major battles that were to make the area infamous were over, and as a result of the outcry at home, conditions in the trenches had improved. Nevertheless, the journey through the north French countryside devastated by the first Battle of the Somme could not have been more demoralising for young soldiers with so little experience of action.

One of those moved up to the front line recorded his own account of their surroundings in his diary. 'Nothing but desolate wastes, villages wiped out, and now the ruins all overgrown with grass until it was barely possible to see any trace. Roads all churned up; slush and brick dust; old barbed wire; old dugouts; broken wagons; pieces of rifles; shattered tree stumps; wooden crosses, with here and there a rifle or a helmet hanging on them; and now and again a roadside crucifix, marvellously intact.'

The period in transit was spent completing the battalion's training, and by September, when they were finally sent to the front, Frank had been promoted to acting captain in charge of one of the companies. At first, there were a number of gas attacks and occasional small-scale raids on enemy trenches, but little in the way of real action.

'Things were fairly quiet and comfortable, the only nuisance being the rats,' said Private Frank Beardsall, one member of the battalion. 'We spent most of our time shooting these pests and at night stood on sentry with rifle in one hand and entrenching stick in the other, more intent on killing rats than Germans.'

The reason for the lack of action was simple. The 2/6th were part of the 59th (North Midland) Division, one of the so-called 'Conscript Divisions'. The '2' in their title designated them as second-line Territorials rather than members of the more professional New Army. Neither the generals nor the first-line troops trusted them. 'We weren't taken very seriously,' said Beardsall. 'If they wanted anything special doing, they didn't send for us.'

Frank was heavily aware of his lack of height – he was just five feet four inches tall – and in what appears to have been an attempt to compensate for this he had a tendency to bark orders at his men. But coming from a relatively poor background and having been educated in France, rather than at one of the English public schools that produced so many of his fellow officers, he enjoyed an easy rapport with the troops and seems to have been genuinely well liked. That popularity was soon to be tested to the hilt.

Throughout the early part of 1918, rumours swept the British lines of a 'final' German offensive intended to roll the Allies back to the Channel before the American entry into the war could begin to take effect. Frank's men had spent the early part of March in front-line trenches to the north of the small French town of Bullecourt. On 11 March, they were relieved and sent back to the village of Mory for what was supposed to be a period of rest and recuperation.

'Before we had been at Mory many hours we found everyone in a state of "wind-up" that the expected German offensive was very near,' said Beardsall. 'We became infected and the following eight days were a perfect nightmare. Our time was completely taken up with digging extra trenches and strong points. The chaps were getting very fed up when we had a diversion by way of visiting the cinema at Benagnies and an issue of a pint of beer per man. We thought this too good to last and we were right.'

A day later, on the evening of Tuesday, 19 March 1918, they were pushed back up to the front. They relieved a battalion of the Lincolnshire Regiment at around seven o'clock that evening. The poorly entrenched positions, only recently taken over from the French, lay around the small village of Ecoust-St-Mein, to the west of Bullecourt and on the southern edge of a large ridge known as the Hog's Back.

The front line ran along the main railway line from Cambrai to Arras. 'Our quarters were holes dug in the railway embankment,' said Beardsall. 'The ground in front was a Royal Engineers' dump, one mass of railway construction material. One side was bounded by the village of Ecoust, the railway embankment on another, a road on the third side, and behind the ground seemed to be a mass of barbed wire entanglements. Truly a happy position in which to be caught.'

During the early evening of the next day, Wednesday, 20 March, a ground mist began to rise over the whole area, turning within hours into a thick fog. An uneasy silence fell along the British front, broken only occasionally by the noise of horse-drawn transport being moved around behind enemy lines and German officers ordering troops into position. Patrols sent out into no-man's-land encountered few enemy, but those prisoners that were taken were extremely keen to be moved swiftly to the rear of the British lines, confirming their claims that the *Kaiserschlacht* – the Kaiser's battle, as the Germans had dubbed their so-called final offensive – was about to begin.

Shortly before 5 a.m. on Thursday, 21 March, the German guns opened up, bombarding the British artillery positions 'with shells of every calibre' including phosgene gas, while trench mortars concentrated their fire on the infantry positions. 'I saw this colossal flash of light,' one officer recalled. 'I heard nothing for a few seconds and for a moment I wondered what it was. I think I just managed to hear the gunfire itself before the explosions as the shells arrived all around us.' The British generals immediately ordered 'Bustle', the planned move to battle stations.

Along with the 5th North Staffordshires, the 2/6th South Staffordshires and three battalions of Sherwood Foresters, Frank's battalion was defending a narrow front extending from Hendecourt, just north of Bullecourt, to Noreuil, a mile south of Ecoust, now little more than a collection of ruined buildings and rubble.

Against them were massed two full-strength divisions of crack German storm troops. As the Staffordshires staggered through the darkness and the 'heavy, nauseating mixture of fog and gas' to their battle stations, 'holding on to each other like blind men', the German artillery switched its fire to the infantry for ten minutes, completely disorientating the Tommies, before reverting to gassing the British gunners for a further hour or more.

Then for two hours the barrage was concentrated again on the British front-line troops, softening up the infantry for 'Michael I', the first part of the assault, and ensuring that the barbed wire that blocked the German's route across no-man's-land was cut to shreds.

'So heavy was the fire that the very air seemed to vibrate with shell bursts,' the official historian records. It ripped the British front line apart, throwing up large clouds of smoke and dust that worsened the already poor visibility. As the sun rose, it could be seen faintly from the higher ground, but even there the British troops, wearing gas masks and peering through the fog, dust and smoke, could rarely see further forward than about ten yards.

Shortly after half past nine, there was a brief lull in the bombardment. No doubt the more experienced of Frank's NCOs would have warned him that this was an indication that the German offensive was about to begin. Then, with a series of tumultuous explosions, the artillery opened up again, first targeting the front line before moving forward in an inexorable *Feuerwalz*, a 'creeping barrage' designed to fall just in front of the advancing German infantry, thereby minimising the British resistance.

At precisely 9.40 a.m., the German troops went over the top, crawling though prepared gaps in the barbed wire and making their way unseen towards the British front-line positions, most of which were swept away in the initial rush. For many of the waiting troops, the first sign that the enemy had broken through their lines was the sight of a German soldier, wearing the characteristic 'coal scuttle' steel helmet and with bayonet fixed, appearing out of the fog a few yards in front of them.

'Under cover of heavy mist, Jerry was pouring thousands of bullets from his machine-guns,' Beardsall said. 'To add to the general discomfort, an enemy aeroplane commenced low flying and swept us with a machine-gun. At one time, I could see the occupants quite distinctly and even see the gunner pressing his buttons.'

All morning, small groups of German troops attempted to scale the railway embankment and break through the battalion's lines, without success. The 2/6th Battalion of the South Staffordshire Regiment, on their right flank, was not doing so well. It had been practically obliterated by the enemy artillery barrage, and at midday the two companies of North Staffordshires based in Ecoust itself were ordered up as reinforcements.

Just as they prepared to move out, the enemy attacked in force. The North Staffordshires came under fire from what was virtually the full force of the forward German division, the 111th. What should have been a relatively strong defensive position, on high ground overlooking the valley along which the Germans were attacking, was rendered useless by the heavy fog.

'There seemed to be thousands of Jerries swarming down the slopes behind us and we retired to a refuge behind a barricade of sandbags,' said one of Frank's men. 'I've not the slightest idea whether I was hitting anything. I certainly never saw anyone fall. I'd been in France ten months and this was the first time I'd fired at the enemy. I wasn't frightened; it seemed to be something that was happening outside of me.'

Among the German troops advancing on their positions was Ernst Jünger, later one of Germany's most influential authors but now a subaltern in the 73rd Hanoverian Fusiliers. 'The task assigned to the regiment was to break through between the villages of Ecoust-St-Mein and Noreuil,' he said.

> We crossed a battered tangle of wire without difficulty and at a jump were over the frontline. The attacking waves of infantry bobbed up and down in ghostly lines in the white rolling smoke. The great railway embankment in the line Ecoust-Croisilles, which we had to cross, rose out of the mist.
>
> From loopholes and dug-out windows built into the side of it, rifles and machine-guns were rattling merrily. The English held two terraced trenches on the slope. I jumped down into the first trench and fired off my cartridges so fiercely that I pressed the trigger ten times at least after the last shot. Above us everyone was going for it over the top. For the first time in the war, I saw large bodies of men in hand-to-hand fighting. Below us lay a strongly-held position in a sunken road. In front of it were two machine-gun nests, one on each edge of the hollow. The enemy seemed to have recovered. At any rate, he was pouring out lead as fast as it would leave the barrels. After a pause for breath we went over the top. It was a fight to the death.

The first wave of enemy troops was beaten off. But as the fog started to lift, the British resistance began to crack. 'A lot of our chaps put up their hands and surrendered,' one soldier said. 'But we decided to fall back to our reserve positions, a decision which I am afraid cost many of our men their lives because we were under shell and machine-gun fire as we fell back.'

There was a desperate struggle for Ecoust, with hand-to-hand fighting along the railway line and around the village cemetery. But the Germans swept round the southern flank, aiming for the western end of the Hog's Back to cut the battalion off. Frank was hit in the chest and fell to the ground. The bullet had penetrated his left lung before coming out through his armpit, and he was losing a lot of blood.

Although by now it had become virtually a case of every man for himself, he was carried clear of the fighting and back with his retreating troops to the prepared fallback positions in Mory. Had he been left behind, as many an unpopular officer was, Frank would almost certainly have been killed. The retreating forces took very few of their wounded back, and with food, water and, perhaps more importantly, medical supplies low, the Germans were not overly inclined to take prisoners.

Many of those who surrendered were shot anyway. 'No quarter was given,' Jünger recalled. 'To kill a defenceless man is baseness. On the other hand, the defending force, after driving their bullets into the attacking one at five paces distance, must take the consequences. A man cannot change his feelings again during the last rush with a veil of blood before his eyes. He does not want to take prisoners but to kill.'

The official history records that just one officer from Frank's brigade survived the fighting of 21 March. In fact, even in his own battalion, he was not alone in getting out. The 2/6th's war diary lists those killed in action as Lt-Col. T. B. H. Thorne, the commanding officer, and just three other ranks, while the known wounded are limited to Capt. F. E. Foley and eight ordinary soldiers.

But these apparently low casualty figures totally underestimate the effect of the fighting. The battalion had been ripped apart. A total of 22 officers and 586 men were listed as missing, only later to be presumed dead or captured. The unit strength had been cut by two-thirds within the space of little more than a couple of hours. The much-derided second-liners of the 59th North Midland had lost all of their positions, but only after putting up some of the stiffest resistance of the whole British lines and suffering the highest casualties of any division.

Frank said later that the things he saw, during what was by any standards one of the most savage battles in a war characterised by horrific and senseless loss of life, led him to question his belief in God. For some time, the young man who had once dreamed of becoming a priest described himself as an atheist. There was no way that the God he had believed in would have allowed such terrible things to occur.

He was mentioned in dispatches for his part in the defence of Ecoust and was evacuated back to England for medical treatment. After a six-week stay in the London Hospital and a period of recuperation at a hotel turned auxiliary hospital in the Cornish town of Fowey, he appeared before a medical board.

His left lung had been damaged by the German bullet, leaving him occasionally short of breath. The board ruled that he was no longer fit for front-line action. He was told to apply for the £125 'blood money' all subalterns were entitled to for such injuries and sent on leave. By the time he reported back for duty, someone at the War Office had noted his language skills, and the daring escape from Germany, and he was encouraged to apply for 'secret service' with the Intelligence Corps.

Chapter 2

On Secret Service

It was some time in July 1918 that Frank reported back to the War Office. He was tested in French and German and sent to Harrow-on-the Hill, Middlesex, where the army had a 'spy school'. At the end of a two-month course, he was ordered to report to Major Ernest Wallinger, who ran the army's secret service offices at 7 Basil Street in Knightsbridge. There he was taken up three floors in a lift and ushered into a drawing room.

After a short while, Wallinger, a former artillery officer who had lost a foot earlier in the war, limped in, introduced himself and took Frank through a private flat and into a small office where a couple of other Intelligence Corps officers and a secretary were working.

Wallinger explained that it was his role to control the various intelligence networks in France, Belgium and Holland through a series of outstations, one of which Frank was to join. Among the most productive networks were the train-watching units which monitored the movement of German troops towards or away from the front.

'From the composition of the train, it could be seen if it was a leave train, a freight train or a train carrying what we called a "constituted unit",' wrote Ivone Kirkpatrick, one of Frank's colleagues. 'About forty trains of constituted units were required to move a division. So a study of these traffic returns could show how many divisions were moving along the Belgian and French railways and in which direction.'

Perhaps the best of the networks was La Dame Blanche, an extensive train-watching system named after the legendary White Lady of the Hohenzollerns whose appearance was supposed to signal the dynasty's downfall. It was run by Henry Landau, an Intelligence Corps officer attached to the Secret Service whose motto of 'a little but good' was to make a lasting impression on Frank.

The other networks included Felix, a group of Belgian prostitutes run by Kirkpatrick from a small house in Rotterdam and paid for the information they garnered from their German clients with drugs smuggled in from London. There was also a train-watching network based in Luxembourg which passed on its intelligence in coded knitting patterns published in a local newspaper, a plain stitch for a coach carrying men, a purl for a wagon full of horses.

Frank was taught the techniques of the Secret Service, among them how to recruit an agent. 'Try to exchange conversation with the object of finding out what type of man he is, i.e. talkative, indifferent, or an enthusiast on any particular subject,' the instructions suggested. 'Going very gently, see if he accepts small offers of cigarettes or beer and ask him casually for a little information, some harmless questions but of such a nature that will cause him to show by his answer if he is likely to become an agent or not.'

He was also introduced to the various 'toys', employed by the agents and their runners – the hollow coins, pencils and even broomsticks used to conceal messages, and the various invisible inks. Scientists at London University consulted by the British Secret Service, or MIic as it was then known, on what was the best invisible ink available, had replied that it was semen, since it failed to react to iodine vapour or an open flame.

After a few weeks, Frank was given the qualification of 'Agent

2nd Class' and sent to France, where his colleagues included a former Guards officer, Major Stewart Menzies, who was to have a important influence on his future career. It was here, while debriefing Belgian refugees, that he first became aware of the extent of anti-Semitism on mainland Europe. Several thousand Belgian Jews had been forced out of their homes, mainly in Antwerp, where they were involved in the diamond trade, as the civilian population looked for someone to blame for the deprivations of war.

Frank had barely had time to get used to his new role when the devastating German losses of August 1918 brought the fighting to an end. After the signing of the Armistice in November of that year, Frank, now promoted to 'Agent 1st Class', was posted to the Inter-Allied Military Commission of Control in Cologne, from where the occupied Rhineland was administered.

Officially, the main role of the Intelligence Corps officers stationed there was to monitor military and political activity on both the extreme left and right, as well as German compliance with the terms of the Versailles Treaty. But they soon found much of their time taken up with countering French attempts to set up a separatist movement that would espouse the cause of a buffer state, a so-called independent Rhineland Republic.

'The British Intelligence Service in Cologne was proving a thorn in the side of its former ally,' Landau wrote. 'It was no use for France to pretend that she was not sponsoring the separatist movement, for all her intrigues and plans were being uncovered by British agents.'

One of the officers working in the Control Commission was a young RAF flight lieutenant, Owen Lee. He invited his twenty-three-year-old sister Kay over to Cologne for a holiday and introduced her to one of his fellow officers, Frank Foley. Kay was tall, pretty and extremely outgoing, almost the complete opposite of Frank. But something about the small, quiet, thoughtful man appealed to her, and they agreed to write to each other and to meet up when Frank next came to England on leave.

Landau had meanwhile been recalled to London, where Mansfield Cumming, the head of the Secret Service, or 'C' as he was known, offered him a plum job as a reward for his successful handling of La Dame Blanche. 'I was informed by the Chief that in recognition of my services, he had awarded me the best of his appointments abroad in the post-war re-arrangement of the Secret Service. I was to open an office in Berlin.' With Bolsheviks causing mayhem and threatening a German revolution to match that in Russia, Berlin was expected to be the service's most important overseas station.

He bought an old hunting lodge on the edge of Berlin's Tiergarten as the service's German headquarters. Originally the hunting preserve of the dukes and electors of Brandenburg, the Tiergarten had been transformed into an English-style public park and was now Berlin's favourite recreation area, dotted with restaurants and tented bars.

The Tiergartenstrasse, which ran along its southern edge, had become a popular residential area for the rich and famous. But in the wake of the war, the price of property had fallen through the floor, and Landau had picked up his plush new offices for a song.

He struggled to come to terms with his new posting and in particular the cover as Passport Control Officer adopted by Secret Service station heads in all the major capitals.

Anyone seeking a visa to come to Britain or anywhere in the Empire had to be vetted by the local passport control officer. This allowed British Intelligence to keep track of Bolsheviks and anarchists. But it also involved heads of station in a lot of monotonous paperwork.

Landau, used to the excitement of running a wartime network, swiftly became bored and resigned. Asked to find his own replacement from among his wartime colleagues, he went to Cologne, to the Kölner Hof, the requisitioned hotel that was the officers' mess for the Control Commission, where he offered the job to his old friend Frank Foley.

The Intelligence Corps presence in Cologne was being run

down rapidly, and Frank jumped at the chance of the new job. After bidding farewell to his friends and colleagues in the Military Control Commission, Frank returned to England to be briefed on what he was to do.

The headquarters of MI1c was in Whitehall Court, just off Trafalgar Square. The building had been extended upwards to cope with the service's wartime expansion and was likened by one postwar agent to a rabbit warren. Frank was to report to Lt-Col. Freddie Browning, the deputy head of MI1c, who took him in a lift up several floors to a maze of passages through which they made their way until they came to the offices of C, the Chief of the Secret Service.

Browning ushered Frank in to see Cumming. 'From the threshold the room seemed bathed in semi-obscurity,' said Paul Dukes, another MI1c officer, describing his own first meeting with C around the same time.

> Against the window everything appeared in silhouette. A row of half-a-dozen extending telephones stood at the left of a big desk littered with papers. On a side-table were maps and drawings, with models of aeroplanes, submarines, and mechanical devices, while a row of bottles suggested chemical experiments. These evidences of scientific investigation only served to intensify an already overpowering atmosphere of strangeness and mystery.
>
> But it was not these things that engaged my attention as I stood nervously waiting. My eyes fixed themselves on the figure at the writing table. In a swing desk chair, his shoulders hunched, with his head supported on his hand, sat the Chief. This extraordinary man was short of stature, thick-set with grey hair half covering a well-rounded head. His mouth was stern and an eagle eye, full of vivacity, glanced – or glared as the case may be – piercingly through a gold-rimmed monocle.

The Chief, as his men called him, had lost the lower part of one leg in a car crash that killed his son, and his eccentricities included using a child's scooter to get around the maze of passages in 2 Whitehall Court and a predilection for writing all his correspondence in green ink.

'At first encounter, he appeared very severe,' said Dukes. 'His manner of speech was abrupt. Yet the stern countenance could melt into the kindliest of smiles, and the softened eyes and lips revealed a heart that was big and generous. Awe-inspired as I was by my first encounter, I soon learned to regard "the Chief" with feelings of the deepest personal admiration.'

Cumming explained the origins of the passport control system Frank would help to operate and the situation in postwar Berlin. As Chief Passport Control Officer, he would be on the staff of the ambassador, Lord Kilmarnock. But as head of MI1c's Berlin station, he would be completely denied should he be uncovered. The Foreign Office had taken a rather sniffy attitude to secret service work and had refused to give the Passport Control Officers diplomatic status. If he fell foul of the authorities he would have to fend for himself.

For this reason, in theory at least, he would not be able to operate against Germany under what was to become known as the Third Country Rule. His German counterpart had already approached Landau, pleading poverty and asking if the two sides might not collaborate to produce intelligence on the French. The offer had been politely declined. But some form of co-operation with the German police would be essential if Frank were to carry out his passport control role properly.

The Passport Control Offices had developed from the military border controls introduced during the war and served a number of purposes. Firstly, they acted as 'a fine-meshed sieve' through which the stream of foreigners attempting to come to Britain could be filtered. They also provided a useful cover for British Secret Service officers abroad and saved MI1c a considerable amount of money, since the wages of the PCOs were paid out of Home Office funds. But most critically, in the dangerous postwar period, they provided Cumming with 'an all important intelligence service on the movements of international revolutionaries'.

Russia was the new threat, and as head of Berlin station, Frank could expect to be at the centre of things. There were those, particularly in the Foreign Office, who, in the wake of the Armistice, were arguing that intelligence budgets should be cut. They would be happy to be rid of the passport control system. But with strong support from Sir Basil Thomson, Director of Intelligence at Scotland Yard, Cumming had managed to fight them off.

The avowed intention of the Soviet Government was to provoke a world revolution, and it had large sums of gold which it was prepared to lavish on this objective, Cumming told Frank. In a situation where communism was making great strides across western Europe, including Britain, the abolition of the passport control system would have been 'an act of suicide'.

Germany was at the centre of these Russian attempts to provoke world revolution, Cumming said. In the immediate aftermath of the war, it had been expected to be the scene of the next communist revolution. Berlin swarmed with demobbed soldiers and deserters, many of them starving. There was little food for the poor, while the rich and war profiteers lived the life of Riley. It all provided a fertile breeding ground for communism. An attempted revolution, led by the left-wing Spartakus League, had been put down in January 1919, and its leaders, Rosa Luxemburg and Karl Liebknecht, brutally murdered.

But support for the communists remained high. Red Army intelligence officers were making hay of all this, and there had been frequent attempts to infiltrate Russian spies and professional agitators into Britain through Berlin. It would be Frank's main job to keep track of these Soviet agents and to prevent them getting into Britain.

For this he would have the assistance of junior officers based in Hamburg and Munich and would be paid the sum of £800 per annum free of tax. But, Cumming stressed, if anything went wrong, he could not promise there would be any support from the government. The Foreign Office was not prepared to sully its hands with such an ungentlemanly pursuit as espionage or to be seen to offer support to spies.

Frank was sent off to the Home Office where he was given his instructions, which were largely taken up with warnings of the dangers posed by 'Bolshevik agents or other persons whose object is to assist in spreading Bolshevik propaganda'.

But there was also a need to protect British jobs, and under no circumstances should a visa be granted to any German who might possibly try to gain work in England. All other applicants should be weeded out as strictly as possible, and only after a thorough investigation had found them to be 'people of good faith' who would not take British jobs or cause trouble should they be allowed to come to Britain, at a cost of the equivalent of one gold franc for a transit visa and ten for a visitor's visa.

Having received these final instructions, Frank took the train to Burnham-on-Sea for a few weeks with his parents. Andrew Wood Foley was particularly proud of his son. After a worrying period when he had seemed unable to find any roots, and then the uncertainty of the war, Frank had really made something of his life. He was now a respectable civil servant with a striking title – Director of the Passport Control Office of the Royal British Embassy at Berlin – and an identity card in French, German and English to prove it. What was more, he appeared to have found a young lady. At the age of thirty-five, he might finally be settling down.

Frank had already warned them that he had been invited to visit Kay to meet her parents. He was anxious to renew his acquaintance with the lively, bright-eyed young woman who had made such an impression on him in Cologne. Her father, William Lee, owned the King's Arms Hotel in Dartmouth, and he intended to take up the Lees' offer to spend some time with them.

The feeling of closeness that had existed between Frank and Kay during her brief visit to Cologne was still there. They spent a lot of time together, taking long walks out on Gallant's Bower, overlooking Start Bay, and it seems to have been during this time that they both became certain of their love for each other.

One afternoon, as the sun was setting and it was close to time to walk back to the King's Arms for supper, Frank proposed marriage and Kay accepted. After seeking William Lee's permission, he took her to meet his parents and then left her in Dartmouth as he went off to Berlin to start his new job.

The German capital was centred around the Brandenburger Tor, a neo-Grecian archway built in the late seventeenth century and topped by a sculpture of four horses drawing the chariot of the Goddess of Victory.

To the east, along the wide lime-tree-lined avenue Unter den Linden, were the massive square stucco-coated official buildings constructed by the Kaisers: the Reich Chancellery; the State Opera House; and the Imperial Palace. To the west, Unter den Linden became the Charlottenburger Chaussee before sweeping through the Tiergarten, past the zoo and the wealthy shopping district of the Kurfürstendamm, or Ku'damm as it was popularly known, and out to the palatial new villas of the rich and famous in Grünewald.

But outside the affluent centre of the city, in the working-class suburbs, the poor lived in row upon row of depressing grey tenement buildings. The city was filled with men still wearing military uniform. These were not the impressively disciplined soldiers Frank had come across during the war; they were scruffy, dirty and had neither work nor money with which to support their families.

The Berlin authorities could do little for them other than dish out frost-bitten potatoes at communal kitchens set up around the capital. Even for many of those with jobs, the situation was desperate. Much of the standard diet was ersatz – produced from cheap substitutes. Coffee was made from ground acorns, cakes were cooked with potatoes, and the so-called Havana cigars sold in many of the bars were rolled from cabbage leaves steeped in nicotine and dried.

But for those who had money, anything was available. The black marketeers, or *Schieber*, who had made fortunes from the war, were cornering the market in foodstuffs and the ordinary necessities of life to make new fortunes. At the big hotels and in the better restaurants, the rich could live like kings. Unashamedly flaunting their furs and expensive clothes, they wandered along the Unter den Linden and the Kurfürstendamm by day, and by night filled the expensive hotels and nightclubs. The *Schieber* were not the only ones to do well out of all of this. The communist agitators were hard at work and the working-class districts like Wedding and Neukölln had become completely 'red'.

Not all the working class had turned to communism. Many former soldiers, hankering after the order, camaraderie and respect they had enjoyed during the war, had joined the Freikorps, the volunteer military force used by the Social Democrat president Friedrich Ebert to put down the Spartakist revolution. They saw the Treaty of Versailles which had ended the war as a humiliating stab in the back by the German politicians who agreed to sign it.

Germany had lost large tracts of land to its neighbours and was forced to pay crippling reparations. The Allies were to occupy the Rhineland for fifteen years. The air force was to be disbanded; the army limited to a hundred thousand soldiers and the navy to just six battleships and no submarines. When Ebert, under pressure from the Allies to comply with the treaty, sought to disband the Freikorps, it mounted a coup attempt that was only thwarted by a general strike in support of the Social Democrat-led government.

Key leaders of the putsch received only light sentences while others escaped arrest altogether. Nor was the Freikorps disbanded. It had too much support from within the German establishment. Right-wing businessmen supplied funding while the army surreptitiously provided weapons. Once bitten, the government left the Freikorps alone. It was a dangerous policy. Many of its members were addicted to violence. They spent much of their time beating up 'Bolsheviks' on the streets. But for most of the Freikorps, the definition of a Bolshevik was broad enough to include not just communists, but socialists, democrats and Jews.

The violence was executed to the accompaniment of marching

songs like that of the Ehrhardt Brigade which had led the coup attempt.

> *Wir sind kein Judenknechte,*
> *In Deutschland soll immer nur ganz allein*
> *ein Deutscher unser Führer sein.*

> We are no slave of the Jews,
> Forever and ever in Germany
> Only a German should our leader be.

Chapter 3

Hunting for Bolsheviks

The stucco-covered hunting lodge on the Tiergartenstrasse that Landau had bought as his offices was an imposing building. A wide set of stone steps led up from the outer courtyard to the main entrance on the middle of three storeys. It was on this floor that the Passport Control Office was located. Downstairs was the commercial secretariat. The top floor was occupied by the Consulate-General's office and the military attachés, whose role also included gathering intelligence and who had already irritated Landau by treading on his toes.

There was a great deal of 'competition and overlapping', Landau said. 'Every member of the allied missions was making reports, with the general sense that everybody was encroaching on important work that everybody else was doing.'

Having introduced Frank to the office staff, Landau briefed him on the Secret Service work. For security reasons, Head Office coded the countries in which it had stations numerically. Germany was '12-Land', which meant that Frank's designation would be 12000. His deputy would be 12100, the next man down the chain 12200 and so on. Any agents they recruited would be given similar codes; thus Frank's first agent would become 12001.

Landau had not had time to develop many agents, but the trick was to get a number of main people who could be highly trusted and have them run their own subagents, thereby providing a cut-out that would protect Frank should something go wrong. These subagents might supply information for any number of reasons, money being the most obvious but by no means the only one. Civil servants and servicemen with a grudge against their superiors were often useful, and sex frequently had a role to play.

The system of agents and subagents meant that there would always be at least one person, or cut-out, and sometimes as many as three, between Frank and the agent supplying the information. Meetings, or 'Treffs', should be kept to the minimum. There were plenty of quiet park benches among the chestnut and lime trees of the Tiergarten itself where these could take place, but in the main a private flat was better than a public place if any information was to be handed over. Messages could be left in dead-letter boxes, agreed hiding places, or written in invisible ink on the back of innocuous letters sent to accommodation addresses.

A typical day would begin before 9 a.m. with encryption of the reports of the previous day's agent information for transmission to London by diplomatic bag. The Passport Control Office itself opened at 10 a.m. This whole side of the job was extremely tedious and was his main reason for leaving, Landau said. Much of his time had been taken up with PCO work. He had found himself turning down around twenty-five visa applications a day which, according to Head Office, represented more than half of the total refused worldwide.

Even after the office closed at 4 p.m. there was an inordinate amount of paperwork relating to visa applications before Frank would be able to get back to the real work, liaising with the German police and preparing reports on intelligence that had come in through the day. Only in the evening would Frank have time to cultivate the contacts that would be a vital part of his intelligence network.

But while the Passport Control role provided a useful cover, it also supplied vital intelligence. Anyone suspicious wishing to travel to Britain had to be thoroughly checked out, Landau said. The first stops were inevitably the MI5 blacklist of suspicious aliens and the files of the Berlin police.

'As to the traveller's purposes, and the usual commercial information, it was not only obtained through recognised business channels such as banks, but in many cases the applicant was watched for a long time by our agents. Every movement was followed. I often laughed over the indiscretions of some of the individuals. In the hands of their wives, the information would have been devastating.'

Once Landau had left, Frank found himself a flat at Sächsischestrasse 70, in Wilmersdorf, a largely Jewish middle-class district to the west of the city and just south of the Ku'damm, and set about building up his own network of contacts.

With the Bolsheviks the main target, the Russian community was likely to prove the most productive starting point. There were estimated to be at the very least fifty thousand Russians in Berlin, most of whom had fled to the German capital after the Bolshevik revolution. Wherever you went in Berlin, you were likely to hear Russian being spoken. Some of the émigrés wanted to return home to make their peace with the Bolsheviks. Others insisted there could never be reconciliation. The arguments between the two opposing sides were rehearsed repeatedly in Berlin's half a dozen Russian-language newspapers and in the host of Russian bars and restaurants.

The bulk of the Russian community lived on the other side of the Ku'damm from Frank in Charlottenburg, or 'Charlottengrad', as it had been dubbed. Their noisy arguments dominated the atmosphere in the Café Prager Diele, the Café Leon and the Café Landgraf, and in restaurants like the Coq d'Or, the Blauer Vogel, with its Russian cabaret, and in particular the Allaverdi.

Run by Ukrainians, the Allaverdi offered a wide variety of Russian dishes – *zakuski*, *blini*, *shashlik* and *borscht* – to the accompaniment of a whole orchestra of balalaika. Behind the bar, a spiral staircase led down to an after-hours club in the cellar where champagne and pickled mushrooms were served until dawn to the accompaniment of violins. The arguments in the Allaverdi either in favour of the Bolsheviks or against were not diminished by the introduction, after the German government recognised Lenin's government in 1922, of a *Stammtisch*, a regulars' table, reserved for Moscow's official emissaries, who include numerous intelligence agents.

The presence in the German capital of large numbers of Soviet spies was confirmed in an influential memo from the head of the foreign section of the Soviet intelligence service, advocating that the whole of the Russian intelligence operation across Europe be centred on Berlin. Post-war Germany was 'the object of a constant and bitter struggle by various anti-Soviet groups and parties to influence its foreign policy', he said.

> The cultivation and the elucidation of the activities of these anti-Soviet groups and parties inside Germany will undoubtedly always lead to the international centres (Britain, America, France) who are fighting us. Germany should be looked upon by our intelligence service as a litmus paper. This and the favourable conditions prevailing there for recruiting makes it imperative to concentrate our intelligence thrust on Germany.

Frank did not confine himself to the Russian bars and restaurants. The German capital was slowly beginning to recover from the war. During the day, Berliners drank coffee, read newspapers and exchanged gossip in Jostys, the Schiller, the Monopol or the Romanische Café, the legendary barn-like café just across from the Kaiser Wilhelm Memorial Church which had replaced the Café des Westens as the principal meeting place for the city's writers, artists and actors.

The nightclubs of Berlin were the most uninhibited anywhere in Europe. The darling of the cabaret audiences was Josephine Baker, but her naked dance performances were by no means unique. Couples desperate for cash made love live on stage. Outside on the Ku'damm, high-booted streetwalkers waved their umbrellas to stop every man who passed.

It was an exciting place to be for a young man in his thirties. The effects of Foley's injuries meant that he was far less fit than when he had trekked across northern Germany to escape internment. The First World War wounds had left a peppery scar under his left eye and he was beginning to fatten out as middle age set in. But Berlin's nightclubs made ideal meeting places with the contacts needed by the head of Britain's Secret Service in a major foreign capital.

'Frank was always sort of roaming around,' said one of his embassy colleagues. 'Berlin was a mass of nightclubs. There was an extraordinary atmosphere. You never seemed to go to bed. There were so many clubs, everybody seemed to stay up all night, and wherever you went, you met Frank having a good time. Not drunk or anything like that, but just merry and not a care in the world. Always very friendly, very jolly, that was Frank.'

His relationship with Kay had by now blossomed, and on Friday, 24 June 1921 they were married. 'A very pretty wedding was solemnized at St Saviours Church, Dartmouth, on Friday morning last,' the *Dartmouth and South Hams Chronicle* recorded. 'The service was conducted by the Rev J F V Lee, Rector of Cranford, Middlesex, and the uncle of the bride. While the guests were assembling, Mr W J Friendship, the organist, played Lied by Wolstenholme, Souvenir de Printemps by Holbrook and Salut d'Amour by Elgar. The processional hymn was Lead Us Heavenly Father Lead Us.'

Owen Lee was the best man and Kay's sister Joyce was the bridesmaid, the newspaper told its readers.

> The bride wore a beautiful dress of silver grey Crepe de Chine trimmed with kilted frills and embroidered medallions with a very becoming hat of Grey Georgette and carried a sheaf of Madonna's Lilies. During the service, the choir sang the hymn The Voice that Breathed o'er Eden. At the conclusion, Mr Friendship played Lohengrin's Bridal March and Mendelssohn's Wedding March while the bells of St Saviour's Church rang a merry peal.

After a reception and wedding breakfast at the King's Arms Hotel, Frank and Kay left to stay the night in Bournemouth before crossing the Channel to spend their honeymoon touring central Europe. The trip ended in Berlin, where Kay set about transforming Frank's Wilhelmsdorf flat into a family home, for both of them were keen to have children. Just over a year later, Kay proudly presented Frank with a daughter, Ursula Margaret.

Their Jewish neighbours had less cause to celebrate. Already the early signs of the impending assault on Germany's Jews were beginning to be evident. Under the Weimar Republic, the Jews had achieved success in both the arts and the professions. Many had gained fame as theatre directors, actors, playwrights, film producers, artists and musicians. There were many Jewish doctors, lawyers, scientists and academics and a good deal of resentment at their success.

Three months before Ursula was born, Walter Rathenau, an industrialist who had taken charge of raising funds for the Kaiser's war effort and had become the country's foreign minister, was assassinated by members of the Ehrhardt Brigade. His patriotic efforts on Germany's behalf both during and after the war were resented rather than praised. He could not be a German, he was a Jew. 'We are no slave of the Jews,' Rathenau's assassins sang. 'In Germany, only a German should our leader be.'

The country desperately needed the skills of men like Rathenau. It was struggling to pay the £6.6 billion bill for reparations imposed under the terms of the Treaty of Versailles. These difficulties came to a head in January 1923, when German failure, or more accurately inability, to pay its dues led to the French and Belgian armies occupying the Ruhr, Germany's main industrial region. The local population responded by refusing to work, which only served to exacerbate Germany's financial problems. Without any real financial resources to cover the loss to the German economy and the compensation it was paying industry, the Weimar government responded by printing more money. The result was rampant hyperinflation.

The value of the mark went into free-fall. Prices rocketed and people's life savings were wiped out overnight. Shops, restaurants and bars changed price tickets every night, some several times during the day.

'I dropped into a café to have a coffee,' one German recalled.

> As I went in, I noticed the price was 5,000 marks – just about what I had in my pocket. I sat down, read my paper, drank my coffee, and spent altogether about one hour in the café, and then asked for the bill. The waiter duly presented me with a bill for 8,000 marks. 'Why 8,000?' I asked. The mark had dropped in the meantime. So I gave the waiter all the money I had. He was generous enough to leave it at that.

Frank, who was paid in pounds, was unaffected by all this and used some of the stacks of valueless marks he was given to paper the lavatory of his flat. But for many Germans the effects were crippling. They directed their anger at the government for signing the Treaty of Versailles, and support for the extremists of both left and right grew. When Gustav Stresemann became Chancellor in September 1923, he decided that the only way out of the economic crisis was to revalue the currency, end the policy of passive resistance on the Ruhr and recommence reparation payments. To the nationalist right this was yet another humiliating betrayal.

On 8 November, the Bavarian-based National Socialist Party launched their own revolution from the Bürgerbräukeller, one of Munich's largest beer halls. The National Socialists had grown out of a small discussion group set up by a locksmith called Anton Drexler in March 1918 to counter left-wing pacifist propaganda. Drexler soon joined forces with Karl Harrer, a journalist, to form the German Workers' Party. This would no doubt have had as little chance of success as the discussion group from which it had been formed if the Bavarian military authorities, wrongly suspecting from the name that it must be a subversive left-wing group, had not sent a young army corporal called Adolf Hitler to monitor one of its meetings.

Initially, the young Austrian was unimpressed by the meeting, but recognising an opportunity to be in at the start of a new party and therefore influential in the way it developed, he decided to join. Soon he had become its most popular speaker, drawing large audiences to hear his mesmeric blend of calls for a return to the pre-war days of German domination of central Europe with virulent anti-Semitism. By April 1920, when Frank arrived in Germany, Hitler was playing a leading role in the party and had persuaded it to change its name to the National Socialist German Workers Party.

Both the title and the policies of the Nazi Party, as it swiftly became known, were aimed at appealing across the social classes and political beliefs. Despite the party's essentially right-wing make-up, socialists were wooed with calls for the nationalisation of large companies and the abolition of unearned income. But the essential focus of the party's twenty-five-point programme was the abrogation of the humiliating post-war treaties and the creation of a Greater German 'Nation', including ethnic German areas of neighbouring countries. 'None but those of German blood, whatever their creed, may be members of the Nation,' it read. 'No Jew, therefore, may be a member of the Nation.'

The two main groups attracted to the party were the middle classes, small businessmen and shopkeepers who saw the Jews as stealing their trade, and the young ex-soldiers who had drifted into the Freikorps when they discovered there was no work for them on their return from the front and who now found a new home in the Nazi Party's brown-shirted paramilitary wing – the Sturmabteilung or SA.

'This consisted largely of rootless ex-servicemen who, if not of the middle class, nevertheless clung, with a pertinacity that sprang from their qualifications, to the belief in their superiority to the working class,' one British observer noted. 'These were frustrated men, forever regretting the loss of the figure they had cut in the Army, the discipline that had relieved them of personal responsibility, and the security of regimentation.'

The financial crisis had dramatically increased the number of Nazi Party members, and Hitler, now a virtually all-powerful party chairman, decided the time was ripe to stage his own coup. He would march on Berlin, mustering support along the way, much as Mussolini had come to power in Italy the previous year. On the night of 8 November 1923, backed by six hundred members of the SA, Hitler hijacked a political meeting in the Bürgerbräukeller to announce that 'the national revolution has broken out'.

The next morning, accompanied by the war hero Field Marshal Erich Ludendorff and several thousand Nazis, he marched on Munich. But the police were waiting for them, blocking their path in the narrow Residenzstrasse. Shooting broke out, leaving sixteen Nazis and three police officers dead. Hitler cowered behind the body of one of the fallen and then fled, but Ludendorff marched on defiantly before being arrested.

Hitler was captured and put on trial for high treason. Given a nationwide platform, he turned the court case into a denunciation of the government for having failed the German people, attracting immense publicity for himself and his party. His five-year prison sentence was extremely light given the charge against him, and he ended up spending only seven months in jail, a period which he used to outline his political doctrines, and in particular his hatred of the Jews, in a book written with the assistance of his political aide and fellow prisoner, Rudolf Hess.

'Was there any shady undertaking, any form of foulness, especially in cultural life, in which at least one Jew did not participate?' Hitler observed in *Mein Kampf* (My Struggle). The Jews were 'true devils with the brain of a monster not a man' whose hideous culture 'must finally lead to the breakdown of civilisation and the devastation of the world', he said. 'Should the Jew with the aid of his Marxist creed, triumph over the people of this world, his crown will be the funeral wreath of mankind, and this planet will once again follow its orbit through ether, without any human life on its surface, as it did tens of thousands of years ago.'

Germany needed a strong leader capable of saving it from the

Jews, Hitler claimed. 'There must be no majority decisions. The decisions will be made by one man, only he alone may possess the authority and right to command. I believe today that my conduct is in accordance with the will of the almighty creator. In standing guard against the Jews, I am defending the handiwork of the Lord.' There could be no compromise here, he said in an ominous portent of what was to come. 'There is no such thing as coming to an understanding with the Jews. It must be the hard-and-fast "Either–Or".'

Chapter 4

A Rule of Terror

Mein Kampf became a bestseller when it was published in 1925. But despite its success, Hitler remained the leader of a small and apparently insignificant party largely irrelevant to the politicians in Berlin. The Weimar government's policies had brought inflation under control, restoring economic confidence and launching '*die goldenen zwanziger Jahren*', the Golden Twenties, for the German capital.

With four million people, it was the world's third-largest city, after London and New York, and was fast laying claim to be the most modern in Europe. The first traffic light outside America had been erected on the city's Potsdamer Platz. The Bauhaus school was beginning to produce the latest ideas in design, and the UFA film studios were the European equivalent of Hollywood. Berlin was a major centre for both art and science, while its *avant-garde* lifestyle and nightlife were unrivalled anywhere in Europe.

But the glitter of the theatres, cafés and nightclubs could not hide the anger on the streets, where the private armies of the left and right frequently clashed. 'The feeling of unrest in Berlin went deeper than any crisis,' wrote Stephen Spender.

It was a permanent unrest. In this Berlin, the poverty, the agitation, the propaganda, witnessed by us in the streets and cafés, seemed more and more to represent the whole life of the town, as though there were almost no privacy behind doors.

Berlin was the tension, the poverty, the anger, the prostitution, the hope and despair thrown out on the streets. It was the blatant rich at the smart restaurants, the prostitutes in army top boots at corners, the grim, submerged-looking communists in processions, and the violent youths who suddenly emerged from nowhere into the Wittenbergplatz and shouted: '*Deutschland Erwache*'.

The Nazis had been banned in the immediate aftermath of the Beer Hall Putsch. But Hitler had learned the lessons of the abortive coup. If the Nazis were to come to power, they would need to do so with a strong electoral base and at least the tacit support of both the army and industry. On his release from jail, Hitler re-formed the party and began to change its tactics, reshaping it from an organisation obsessed with propagating extremist nationalism into a vehicle for achieving power.

Despite its fascist characteristics, there were many in the party who sincerely believed in the need for a socialist revolution, in particular Hitler's main rival, Gregor Strasser, and the young and ambitious Josef Goebbels. They stressed the more left-wing aspects of the Twenty-Five Point Programme, such as nationalisation of key industries, which risked alienating big business, and they represented a serious challenge to Hitler's authority.

Early in 1926, Hitler used a key party meeting to reassert his control. During a four-and-a-half-hour speech, he told delegates that the party was not a discussion group, its primary aim was the *Machtergreifung*, the seizure of power, and that could only be achieved by working through the Establishment. 'Instead of working to achieve power by armed coup, we shall have to hold our noses and enter the Reichstag against the opposition deputies,' Hitler said. 'If outvoting them takes longer than outshooting them, at least the results will be guaranteed by their own constitution. Sooner or later we shall have a majority, and after that – Germany.'

He then set about giving Strasser and Goebbels roles that would divert their energies away from developing socialist programmes objectionable to the big businessmen on whose support he depended. Goebbels was made regional party boss, or Gauleiter, of Berlin. Strasser was given charge of revamping the party's image as Reich Propaganda Leader, an appointment that led to the choreographed Nazi rallies which increased the party's profile and gave it an image that was attractive to many ordinary Germans.

The party began to build up a considerable base around the country by moulding its policies to fit the requirements of individual communities. Nothing in the Twenty-Five Point Programme was too sacrosanct to be played down if it meant winning more votes. Even the party's anti-Semitism, so central to Hitler's own beliefs, was often removed entirely from its propaganda in districts where it did not go down well. But in many areas, particularly among the working classes, it was seen as a guaranteed vote-winner.

In Red Berlin, the working-class vote was not easy for the Nazis to win. The party's strength in the German capital was among the *Mittelstand*, the middle-class small businessmen. It was the communists who dominated the working-class areas like Neukölln, Friedrichshain, Lichtenberg, Weissensee and Wedding. But Goebbels organised his SA Brownshirts like guerrillas making forays into enemy territory for small-scale skirmishes with their communist counterparts, attempting to conquer the working-class areas street by street.

The SA would take over a café or bar and turn it into a *Sturmzentrum*, establishing the local area as their 'territory'. They would then sell copies of their rabidly anti-Semitic newspaper *Der Sturmer*, collect party funds and wait for the inevitable challenge to their authority from the communists.

Frequently, the violence exploded without warning. Kozis confronted Nazis or vice versa. Knives, knuckledusters, leaded clubs, even guns, appeared from nowhere and disappeared as swiftly as their owners, leaving the victims lying in pools of their own blood.

In the confrontation between right and left, the Establishment tended to favour the right. SA men who appeared before the courts received lighter sentences than their communist counterparts. When the communists announced a march through Neukölln for May Day 1929, the police banned it. When the communists marched anyway, the police opened fire, killing thirty-one people.

Politically, the Nazis remained on the fringes of the Reichstag, winning just twelve seats in the 1928 election. But that was all to be changed by the 1929 Wall Street crash. The ensuing depression led American and British banks to recall their loans to German industry. Many businesses were forced to close and the number of unemployed rose dramatically.

The Weimar politicians, fearing a return of the rampant inflation that had dominated the early 1920s, implemented firm fiscal policies, increasing taxes while cutting wages and unemployment benefits. The Social Democrats, the largest party in the Reichstag, refused to accept such policies and withdrew from the government, fatally wounding it at a time when its popularity was already at an all-time low.

The Jews who 'controlled' the big banks of Britain and America were to blame for withdrawing the loans and causing Germany's economic woes, the Nazis claimed. On New Year's Day 1930, SA storm troopers turned their attention from the communists to the Jews, killing eight. In the run-up to elections called for September that year, attacks on Jews became increasingly frequent.

With many Germans regarding the government as weak and incompetent, Nazi propaganda projecting Hitler as the strong leader the country needed to make it great again was extremely attractive to many Germans. The party's highly efficient organis-ation allowed the Nazis to capitalise on this, increasing their vote dramatically in the elections to gain 107 seats in the Reichstag. As the support for the Nazis rose, so too did the number of attacks on the Jews and Jewish businesses, while more and more signs warning against buying goods from Jewish shops began to appear on the streets.

In rural areas, Nazi Party officials instructed that 'the natural hostility of the peasants against the Jews must be worked up to a frenzy'. In the cities and towns, Jews were already being dismissed from their jobs, even in some Jewish-owned businesses. Student protests against Jewish professors or fellow students became commonplace.

On 12 September 1931, Jewish New Year's Day, truck-loads of SA Brownshirts chanting 'Jews Out' and 'Beat the Jews to Death' began attacking Jews as they left synagogues across the capital. 'While three youths beat an elderly gentleman with their fists and rubber truncheons, five other young men stood around to protect them,' one eye-witness said. Jewish cemeteries and synagogues around the country were desecrated and attacks on Jews became routine.

'Crush the skulls of the Jewish pack and then the future is ours and won,' the Nazi storm troopers sang. 'Proud waves the flag in the wind, when swords with Jewish blood will run.'

While this thuggery horrified many Germans, Hitler himself managed to appear detached from it all, and more and more people saw him as an almost messianic figure who would lead the country out of the mire. When he stood in the 1932 presidential election, Goebbels chartered aircraft to fly him all over the country, allowing him to speak at several rallies a day.

Although Hitler lost the vote, both his profile and that of the party were considerably enhanced. In the July general elections, the Nazis became the largest party with 37.3 per cent of the poll and 230 seats, and Hitler demanded to be made Chancellor. President Hindenburg, who despised 'the little Bohemian corporal', declined, appointing Franz von Papen, a rich Catholic nobleman with little public support. But without the backing of the largest party, von Papen's government quickly collapsed.

Fresh elections in November 1932 brought signs of a backlash against the loutish behaviour of the storm troopers, with the Nazis losing 34 seats. Nevertheless, they remained the largest party in the Reichstag, and while the left and centre still held 353 seats to the 279 of the right – they were unable to form a workable coalition.

A series of attempts to form a right-wing government followed, first under General Kurt von Schleicher, an influential adviser to the President, and then again under von Papen, who eventually succeeded in persuading Hindenburg that if Hitler was not made Chancellor he was likely to seize power anyway, sparking a civil war.

After being appointed Chancellor in January 1933, Hitler moved swiftly to consolidate his position. He confiscated the property of all communist and socialist organisations and used an arson attack on the Reichstag building, allegedly carried out by a young Dutch communist, as an excuse to persuade Hindenburg to sign a 'Decree for the Protection of the People and the State', conferring wide emergency powers on the government and allowing anyone to be taken into 'protective custody' without the need for a warrant or a trial.

'A considerable number of people were arrested without any reason at all,' said Benno Cohn, a former Jewish leader in Berlin. 'Among them were a considerable number of Jews.'

The storm troopers, under the command of Ernst Röhm, an old colleague of Hitler's from the army, were co-opted as Feldgendarmerie or auxiliary policemen, giving their hooliganism virtually free rein. They instigated a rule of terror against anyone who dared to question the regime, opening *wild* or unofficial con-centration camps in cinemas and warehouses around the country.

'In February 1933, three prisons were built in the Hedemannstrasse, the General Palpe Strasse and the Lehrter Strasse in which the Feldgendarmerie tortured political prisoners to death,' wrote Hubert Pollack, one of those who helped the Jews escape.

> These prisons were the forerunners of the Gestapo prisons and the concentration camps. The personnel were among the most

depraved sadists to be found in the various SA, and later SS, formations. Trade unionists, social democrats, communists, socialists, pacifists and other left-wingers were abducted from their homes or from the street. After a while, the bodies could be collected from the hospital in the Scharnhorststrasse.

On Thursday, 9 March 1933, the first official camp was opened at Dachau, near Munich. The mass arrests of left-wingers and pacifists continued while Röhm's storm troopers ran riot on the streets settling old scores with their political opponents. Within a month, two more concentration camps had been built, at Esterwegen and Sachsenhausen.

'Once Frank and I drove our car along a road in the pine forests, looking for a picnic spot,' Kay Foley recalled. 'But we could not stop. Everywhere was marked with signs: "Forbidden to halt." Later we found out that it was a new concentration camp.' Increasingly, the inmates of such camps were not just political prisoners, communists and socialists, but 'non-Aryans' – gypsies and Jews.

Those more sensible members of the Jewish community who could afford to leave began to do so. By the end of 1933, some sixty-five thousand Germans had emigrated, the vast bulk of them Jews. Some had headed for neighbouring countries such as France and Holland, believing that soon the tide would change and it would be safe to return. But many looked for more permanent sanctuary and headed for the Jewish homeland in Palestine.

For a long time, Palestine had been controlled by the Turks as part of the Ottoman Empire. During the First World War, when Turkey was allied to Germany, Palestine was occupied by the British. In November 1917, Arthur Balfour, British Foreign Secretary, announced British support for the establishment of a Jewish homeland there, providing that the rights of the existing non-Jewish communities, almost entirely Arab, were safeguarded.

The so-called Balfour Declaration was incorporated into the League of Nations Mandate under which Britain administered

Palestine. The Mandate specifically urged the British to 'facilitate Jewish immigration under suitable conditions'. But in 1929, the Palestinian Arabs – who with good reason saw immigration as the means by which the *Yishuv*, or Jewish community, planned to take over the country – began to riot.

Thereafter, British policy on immigration was a constant attempt to appease the Arabs with strict limits on the number of Jews to be allowed in. The German Jews hoping to flee there to escape the Nazis therefore needed visas which had to be obtained from the British Passport Control Office.

In a dispatch to London dated 29 March 1933, Frank wrote: 'This office is overwhelmed with applications from Jews to proceed to Palestine, to England, to anywhere in the British Empire. Professional men of the highest standing, including some who were wounded in the German side during the war, have consulted me with regard to emigration.'

Three days later, on Saturday, 1 April 1933, the Nazis instigated a nationwide boycott of all Jewish businesses in retaliation for the growing international criticism of Hitler's policies which the Germans alleged was being orchestrated by the international Jewish community. Jews were stopped in the street by members of the SA and forced to wear yellow Stars of David.

'On every Jew shop was plastered a large notice warning people not to buy in Jewish shops,' wrote Lady Rumbold, the wife of the British ambassador. 'Often you saw caricatures of Jewish noses. To see people pilloried in this fashion, a very large number of them quite harmless, hardworking people, was altogether revolting, and left a very nasty taste in the mouth. I shall never forget it.'

International pressure forced Hitler to call off the boycott. But the Jews were left bewildered by the government's behaviour. 'They could not possibly believe that this cultured German nation, the one that was the most cultured of the peoples of the world since time immemorial, would resort to such an iniquitous thing,' said Benno Cohn. 'That Sunday I walked through the streets of Berlin. I saw a terrible picture. All the Jewish shops were marked

"Jew" and on their windows slogans were scrawled – "Drop dead Jew"; "Danger to Life – Jews Get Out"; "Go to Palestine".'

Robert Weltsch, editor of the *Jüdische Rundschau*, the country's main Jewish newspaper, urged the Jews to 'wear the yellow badge with pride'. Those made to wear the badge during the boycott had been forced to admit their Jewishness 'not out of an inner conviction, not out of loyalty to their people, not out of pride in a magnificent history and in the noblest human achievement', but because the Nazis were determined to humiliate them.

'For 24 hours, the Jews were put on the pillory of shame,' Weltsch wrote. 'They meant to dishonour us. But the Jews should take the Star of David and wear it with pride. Admit that you are a Jew.'

Sefton Delmer, a journalist later drafted into British Intelligence to produce anti-Nazi propaganda, had supper a few days later with leading members of the SA and its sinister rival, Heinrich Himmler's Schützenstaffel – the SS. He found them curiously downbeat about the effects of the boycott.

> That ominous stillness which marks the presence of armed SA and SS men had fallen on the Viktoriastrasse. Outside No 11, a few motor cars were standing. Smartly dressed gangsters in the black uniform of the SS, Himmler's personal bodyguard, and equally smart SA men in brown attending on Röhm scrutinised would-be visitors. Besides my host only four of the circus had foregathered when I arrived. Himmler, Röhm, Esser and Krauser, one of the chief pilots. They looked what they were, vigorous, intrepid and rather uncouth. I had never seen Röhm at close quarters before. He was even more repulsive than I had imagined.
>
> We sat down to supper. I found myself next to Himmler. He proved like Röhm to be more intelligent and reasonable than I anticipated. He was a trifle depressed. They had looked forward to victory to get even with their enemies, the Jews and Marxists, but every time they started to do something drastic somebody seemed to clutch at their sleeve. I agreed that they had all been made to look April Fools when the boycott was called off. He winced at this.

But even as they sat down to eat, the government was announcing more measures against the Jews. All civil servants 'who are not of Aryan descent' were to be retired.

It was to be the first of a series of laws aimed at excluding the Jews from all walks of German society, followed shortly by the law against 'the excessive number of students of foreign race in German schools and universities', limiting the numbers allowed to attend secondary schools and universities. The foreign race in question was of course the Jews. A non-Aryan was defined as 'anyone descended from non-Aryan, particularly Jewish, parents or grand-parents. It suffices if one parent or grandparent is non-Aryan.'

From this point on, the Nazis set about progressively forcing the Jews out of all walks of German life. For the next two years, this would be a relatively gradual process. The effect on the economy of the international reaction to the Jewish boycott forced Hitler to move slowly. But the Aryanisation of German society had begun. Jewish businesses were sold off to Nazis at knock-down prices. Jewish directors and managers were dismissed. No area of German society was to be tainted by the Jew. Business, the judiciary, the medical and dental professions, the universities and schools, the media, even the arts – especially the arts – were all to be cleansed of non-Aryans.

One Nazi official told a British visitor that this was understand-able. The Jews had been allowed to swamp various professions, he said. More than 90 per cent of the doctors in some hospitals in Berlin were Jews while three-quarters of the capital's lawyers were Jewish, he claimed. This meant that 'true German citizens' belonging to those professions were kept out and unemployed. The theatres had fallen almost entirely into the hands of the Jews under recent governments and had been used to promulgate 'the Jewish line' of decadent ideas and contempt for Christianity.

A series of regulations led to the dismissal of thousands of Jewish lawyers, scientists, teachers, lecturers and doctors. A special decree limited the number of Jewish doctors and dentists allowed to practise medicine. Secondary schools were ordered to restrict the number of non-Aryans to no more than 5 per cent of the number of pupils. Anyone who had been naturalised as German between the end of the First World War and 30 January, 1933, and whose naturalisation was now deemed to be 'undesirable', was stripped of their nationality, leaving thousands of the Jews who had fled persecution in eastern Europe without passports.

By the end of 1933, around fifty thousand Jews had left Germany. Those without papers found themselves unwelcome in many countries, regarded as illegal immigrants and liable to arrest and expulsion to a neighbouring state where they were then in exactly the same position.

Even those with papers found themselves in difficulties as country after country tightened its restrictions in the face of the exodus. The effects of the Depression were still keenly felt and there was great pressure to protect jobs. Certain types of skilled and agricultural labourers were the only workers who could be sure of a job. But the vast majority of those seeking to leave Germany were the professional people who had been worst affected by the Nazi ordinances. Their plight provoked some sympathy among the general population in Germany but little criticism of the regime that had implemented it.

Maurice Hankey, a senior British civil servant, toured Germany in the summer of 1933. 'I was interested to find that no one ever criticised Hitler,' he reported on his return.

> The whole country so far as I could judge is in a state of extraordinary exaltation. 'Hitler has put us on the up-grade again' was first said to me by a prominent lawyer at Bonn but was echoed wherever I went. Some of his actions such as the anti-Jewish campaign were obviously not acceptable to well-educated people but they were always excused. When driven into a corner, they would say: 'I am not a politician and I do not know all the details but Hitler has done so much for Germany and is so great a man that he must have very sound reasons for all he is doing.'

While Hitler undoubtedly enjoyed a great deal of support, not least among the reasons that nobody ever criticised him were the Nazi takeover of the secret police force, the Geheime Staatspolizei or Gestapo, and the presence of more than twenty-six thousand people held in 'protective custody' in concentration camps.

With party membership the only way of ensuring that you kept your job, Germany had swiftly become a nation of informers. 'The methods of the Nazis brought about a widespread terrorisation and intimidation of the population,' one observer noted at the end of 1933. 'Spying and denunciation became rampant.'

Even the most minor criticism of the state was likely to lead to a late-night knock on the door followed by, at best, a short sojourn in one of the camps. Most people, including the majority of the Jews, thought it better to keep their heads down. Things would not go on like this for ever. It could only get better.

But for the Jews in particular, the enforced Aryanisation of German society ensured that things only got worse. Only those who had served at the front during the war, the so-called 'Frontline Fighters', or those who had lost a parent in the war, were to be exempt from the new rules making the Jews outcasts from virtually every walk of life. But even this concession was frequently ignored and would soon be dropped.

Frank's colleague downstairs in the commercial secretariat told London that the actions against the Jews were being carried out with typical German thoroughness. 'To be a Jew in Germany at the present moment, whether merely by race or from religious conviction is equal to being a pariah.'

Chapter 5

The Jonny Case

Hitler's *Machtergreifung* and the repression of the Jews had little immediate effect on Frank's intelligence priorities, which remained dominated by the Bolshevik threat. The German authorities had fired the occasional shot across Frank's bows, demanding to know what his precise status was, but his main concern was not with Germany itself; it remained the detection of Soviet spies and agitators trying to get into Britain and the Empire.

During the 1920s, the Soviet secret services had decided that Germany, with its very strong Communist Party, was a convenient centre for espionage activities in Europe. The OGPU, the forerunner of the KGB, controlled what it called 'the Central European Sector' from its Berlin Rezidentura.

But the OGPU was far less of a threat than its military counterpart, the GRU, which based its activities partly on Russian-controlled companies and partly on the Comintern, the organisation set up to co-ordinate and control the work of communist parties around the world. A constant stream of agitators and spies were sent out by the Comintern International Relations Department to advise the various parties on a wide variety of issues, but the main areas of interest were espionage and subversion.

In order to disguise the purpose of visits abroad by its agents, or 'International Political Instructors', the Comintern set up a field headquarters in Berlin. The large Russian community in the German capital would make it harder for Western intelligence officers like Frank to work out who were genuine émigrés and who were spies.

'The laws of conspirative work demanded that the broad stream of international agitators in and out of Russia should be reduced to only the most necessary trickle,' wrote Jan Valtin, one of the GRU agents attached to the Comintern. 'It was decided to let all threads end in Berlin and to retain only a single line of communication between Berlin and Moscow. A western Secretariat of the Comintern was therefore established in Berlin, whose jurisdiction reached from Iceland to Cape Town.'

The Westbureau as it was known had its headquarters in the Führer Verlag bookshop and publishing house on the Wilhelmstrasse. It was also the sponsor for another MI6 prime target, the Indian Communist Party, which was based in Berlin.

'Its activities, which represent a combination of secret conspiracy and open propaganda, are directed by M N Roy an Indian seditionist of some notoriety and no resources of his own,' one British intelligence report noted. 'It is controlled and financed by the Communist International. Its policy is the creation and intensification of discontent in India as a prelude to violent revolution and the introduction of communism.'

After the Reichstag fire, when Hitler clamped down on the communists, the Westbureau dismantled its Berlin operations and the agents scattered, regrouping in the Danish capital Copenhagen. Yet despite the Nazis' open antipathy towards Bolshevism, and the apparent contradiction of the two creeds, a curious relationship continued between Moscow and Berlin.

For some time, British Intelligence had been aware that the Soviet Union was secretly allowing German troops to train on its territory, in defiance of the terms of the Versailles Treaty. This was to turn into a boon for MI6, providing it with a man who is still regarded within the service as one of its best agents.

Johann Heinrich deGraff, or Jonny X as he became known, was a walk-in, a Soviet agent who volunteered his services to Foley after the Nazis came to power, partly because of the continuing co-operation between the Red Army and the Reichswehr and partly because he had heard that his wife, a fellow GRU agent, had been purged.

Comintern agents were frequently paired together on the assumption that a married couple travelling abroad were far less likely to arouse suspicion than someone on their own. They were all specially trained at the International Division of Moscow's Lenin University, Valtin recalled. 'There was a special section – reserved for a strictly segregated and tight-lipped elite – where GRU officers were the instructors. Known to all were the classes in which large numbers of Russian girls worked tirelessly to acquire fluency in the languages of the West. These girls were political workers. They were the *Aktivisti* – a title of which they were proud.'

Foreign parties also put forward the names of young women prepared to serve the cause in this way, and they were all thoroughly trained by the GRU officers at the Lenin University in how to organise strikes and armed uprisings as well as espionage, subversion and sabotage. Although in theory the couples only existed for cover purposes, inevitably their relationships frequently developed into something more serious. So it was with deGraff and his wife.

On hearing that she had been purged, he walked into the Tiergartenstrasse offices and demanded to see the man in charge. Frank was busy, but he sent word that he would meet him later in one of the beer tents on the Tiergarten. He knew the minute that deGraff explained who he was that he ought to signal London and ask for instructions. But that could take time, and deGraff was only in Berlin for a while between missions. The Westbureau might send him anywhere at any time, and then the opportunity would be lost.

Over the next few days, Frank carefully debriefed deGraff, and it soon emerged that he would be of immeasurable value to the

British. Born in 1894 in Nordenham, a small town across the Weser from Bremerhaven, he had run away to sea at the age of fourteen. During the First World War, he had joined the German Navy, and in 1917 was one of the leaders of a communist-inspired mutiny on board the battleship *Westfalen*. He had been court-martialled and sentenced to death. But before the sentence could be carried out, a revolution broke out and he was freed.

DeGraff described how, in the wake of the abortive Spartakus revolution of January 1919, and the murders of Karl Liebknecht and Rosa Luxemburg, he had joined the Communist Party. He had worked his way up through the ranks of the Hamburg organisation where Richard Sorge, later famous as the leader of a successful Russian spy network in Japan, was in charge of training young party activists. With unemployment out of control, the communists found many willing recruits and began to build again for another attempt at revolution.

Senior Russian officials travelled to Germany on false passports to organise the uprising. It was to take place in 1923 on the anniversary of the Bolshevik revolution when the communists could take to the streets without anyone suspecting that something was amiss. Huge sums of money, supplied by the Russian State Bank in Berlin, were poured into the creation of the Red Hundreds, the groups that were to lead the uprising.

But at the last minute the Politburo in Moscow changed its mind. Couriers were sent to all the main communist strongholds with the message that the revolution had been called off. Unfortunately the news failed to reach Hamburg in time.

Throughout the second half of October, striking workers clashed with the police on the city's streets, deGraff said. On Sunday 21 October, with pressure building up, the Hamburg party activists decided that the time was already right for the uprising.

If it was begun in Hamburg now, it would spark a general uprising around the country. The city's Red Hundreds would take over key points – including the police and rail stations, the airport, the docks and the arms depots – in the early hours of

Tuesday morning. Railway workers were to be called out on strike to hamper the movement of police reinforcements.

DeGraff had been one of around eight hundred dedicated party members who were organised into Red Hundreds. Despite the Russian roubles poured into the planned revolution, they had only a few rusty weapons and no machine-guns with which to take on the heavily armed police, deGraff said.

Nevertheless, the authorities were caught by surprise and initially the uprising went well in a number of areas. But with the messages from Moscow having reached the other communist strongholds, there was little support elsewhere in the country for the Hamburg uprising. For three days, the Red Hundreds fought a bloody but hopeless battle with the police.

Frank listened sympathetically as deGraff described how the failed uprising had led to widespread disillusionment among party activists and explained that eventually he had decided he would follow his old mentor Richard Sorge to Moscow. He attended the Lenin University where he studied in the Comintern classes and then, like Sorge before him, was recruited by the GRU.

He had been sent to the Frunze Military Academy, graduating in 1930 as a major, a member of the élite group attached to the Comintern who travelled the world setting up intelligence networks and acting as political commissars, ensuring party activists followed the Moscow line and teaching them how to bring about world revolution.

One of his first missions had been to England, where the Communist Party had failed to capitalise on the rising unemployment and hunger marches and was under pressure from the Comintern leadership to reform. He could give Frank a complete breakdown of all Communist Party activity in Britain. He had helped to organise it.

Having heard deGraff out, Frank sent a coded letter to London. 'Am in touch with Johann, who is Comintern and can supply full breakdown of British and other communist parties.' The message caused consternation verging on panic at MI6 headquarters and urgent consultations between Admiral Hugh Sinclair, who had replaced Cumming as C, and Colonel Valentine Vivian, the head of Section V, the department that handled counter-espionage.

'Head Office sent Vivian to Berlin immediately to find out what was going on,' a former MI6 officer said. 'VV was much maligned as a fusspot, which he was. But he had a policeman's eye for detail and note-taking that proved immensely useful. Jonny had visited the UK in 1931 and 1932 and there was a lot of excitement about it all because of this. Details were passed to MI5 who took executive action on the basis of information supplied by Foley.'

DeGraff was persuaded not to defect. He should stay in place, obey the GRU's orders to the letter and let the British know what was going on at each step of the way. Shortly afterwards, Jonny X, as he was now known to the British, was sent back to London by the GRU, travelling on a false passport as a wine trader called Ludwig Dinkelmeyer, the alias he had used on his previous visits. During the trip, he spent a weekend at a country house being fully debriefed by Vivian.

Later that year, the Comintern sent Jonny to Shanghai. The city, the world's fifth largest behind Berlin, was dominated by the international settlements, controlled by the British, French, American and Japanese. It was China's most industrialised city and was famous for its scandalous nightlife dominated by White Russian women who, having fled the Bolsheviks, had settled in the French quarter of the city, turning Frenchtown, as it was known locally, into the city's red-light district.

Shanghai was also the centre for communist attempts to take over the country. The Chinese Communist Party had gone underground in the face of 'elimination campaigns' waged against it by the Nationalist leader Chiang Kai-Shek. Communist rebels, led most notably by Mao Tse-Tung, were out in the provinces fighting against the Nationalist troops. But the party's under-ground headquarters was in Shanghai. The Comintern had a very strong presence there, based around the offices of *Shanghai Life*,

a Bolshevik newspaper, and the Russian Cooperative Society –
Centro-Soyuz.

'The offices of *Shanghai Life* act as a meeting place and a cover for
the disaffected residents of Shanghai and the various agents that visit
the place,' said one British intelligence report, possibly based
on information provided by Jonny. Gregory Semeshko, who
was rumoured to be 'a former orthodox priest dismissed for
drunkenness', was seen as the most important Comintern agent in
Shanghai. He and other 'leading spirits in *Shanghai Life* are regularly
visited by Bolshevik agents from Vladivostok and Peking'.

Many of the Comintern's more famous members were in Shanghai at various times in the early 1930s, including Richard Sorge,
the prominent American communist Agnes Smedley, and Arthur
Ewert, a leading member of the German Communist Party.

GRU officers like Jonny and Sorge were sent into Shanghai
to advise the communist rebels both in political subversion and
military tactics. Jonny's own role in Shanghai is unclear. But at
the very least he would have been able to supply the British with
detailed information on the Comintern's operations there. Jonny
was apparently in contact with Harry Steptoe, the MI6 head of
station in the city, who was clearly speaking from experience when
he later advised the British police commissioner in Shanghai on
how to counter Comintern activity.

'I would point out that the members of the Comintern are all
highly trained and hand-picked men, sent out on their various
missions only after intensive training,' Steptoe said.

> Their number is not legion; the Comintern is concerned with
> guarding their identity and their functions. If their identity can be
> discovered, personal descriptions obtained (and photographs where
> possible) their value to the Comintern is lessened, in fact it may
> become nil. If their functions on the spot can be ascertained,
> then knowledge of their method of work becomes available, the
> ramifications of the apparatus known, and the chances of being
> able adequately to provide for internal security are enormously
> increased.

Over the next few years, Jonny X was sent to Austria, Romania, France, Czechoslovakia, the Netherlands, Belgium, Argentina, Brazil and back to Britain, assisting the various communist parties in setting up structures aimed at bringing down the state while at the same time providing MI6 with full details that could not only be incorporated into its own reports on communist activities but could also be traded with the security services in those countries for information the British needed.

Apart from the information Jonny X provided on the British and Chinese communist parties, perhaps his most spectacular success came during the aborted communist coup in Brazil in 1935. The Soviet leaders decided in the early 1930s that the experience gained in China could be transferred to Brazil. The establishment of a Soviet-style regime there would disrupt Anglo–American influence in South America and provide the stepping stone for a communist takeover of the United States of America.

Brazil was chosen not just because it was the largest country in South America but because it had a recent history of turmoil and a relationship between landowners and peasants that in many ways appeared to mirror that of China, where communism was taking a strong hold. Best of all, the Comintern controlled a Brazilian leader around whom the discontented masses would rally.

Luis Carlos Prestes, the so-called Knight of Hope, had become a national hero in Brazil after the failed 'Lieutenants' Uprising' of 1924. When the revolution failed he led a ragged band of little more than a thousand rebels on a fifteen-thousand-mile march through the country's impoverished heartland.

A few years later, the US government approached him, offering him the Brazilian presidency if he would back a coup aimed at installing a government more favourably disposed to the Americans. But Prestes, who was already secretly in contact with Moscow, declined the American offer.

Prestes went to Russia, where he was carefully groomed to lead a new communist-backed revolution in Brazil. His presence in Moscow was kept completely secret, Jonny told MI6. 'He studied intensively both military affairs and politics and became a committed member of the communist party.'

During the spring of 1934, a number of Comintern agents were infiltrated into Brazil. They included two men with direct experience of China. Arthur Ewert, travelling on an American passport under the name of Harry Berger, was appointed head of the South American Bureau of the Comintern and given the task of organising the revolution.

The other key figure with China experience was Jonny, who arrived from Germany under the name of Franz Paul Gruber. Jonny appeared to be just another member of the team. But in fact he was the political commissar, the man put there by Moscow to ensure everything went precisely to plan. He was accompanied by his latest Comintern 'wife', Erika, who was to act as the group's typist and driver.

The Comintern agents began setting up the so-called National Liberation Alliance (ANL), a coalition of socialists, liberals and communists that was to form the platform for the triumphant return of the 'Knight of Hope' to Brazil. In fact, Prestes had already been secretly brought back to Rio de Janeiro and was living in a safe house on the Rua Barao da Torre.

Under the Comintern plan, ANL supporters inside the Brazilian armed forces were to seize power in the north of the country on a popular mandate, carefully concealing the fact that the alliance was a communist front. Once the northern provinces were secured, the revolution would move to the capital.

The ANL, led by Prestes, was to remain in government until the situation had stabilised, at which point the country would be turned into a Soviet-style regime and Prestes would remove the non-communists from power.

'Next would come the Sovietisation and complete appropriation of the property of the landowners and bourgeoisie, then the distribution of land among the population,' Jonny told MI6. 'Once the northern provinces had been made Soviet, there would be a breathing space to allow communist influence to spread over the remainder of Brazil and the other states of south America. The process of Sovietisation would continue until it covered the whole of Brazil.'

The Comintern propaganda experts skilfully manipulated the media to portray Prestes as a liberator waiting for the right moment to return to rescue his countrymen. His letters from 'abroad' were read out at alliance meetings to rapturous applause and the movement grew rapidly.

The British tipped the Brazilian government off in early 1935. A few months later, clashes between ANL supporters and fascists gave the Brazilians the excuse they needed to ban the alliance and force it underground. The Americans were also brought into the picture, agreeing to fund Jonny's disruption of the Comintern operation to the tune of forty thousand dollars.

As the military expert on the team, Jonny was well placed to ensure that the carefully planned revolution failed. His main tasks for Moscow were to spread subversion among the junior army officers who would ostensibly lead the revolution and to train the local communist activists in revolution. 'It was my job to organise the Army for revolution and train party members accordingly,' he said. 'Through careful planning, I worked it so that half the army was in favour and half opposed.'

He succeeded in working those in favour of the coup up to such a pitch that they started the revolution ahead of orders, successfully taking over garrisons in the key northern cities of Natal and Recife. Prestes and Ewert brought forward the parallel revolution in Rio de Janeiro, but with Jonny having ensured that a majority of army officers in the capital were ANL opponents, it soon failed.

Officer cadets infiltrated into the army by the alliance took over an infantry barracks in the fashionable suburb of Orca, at the foot of the Sugar Loaf Mountain. The local population collected on the mountain to watch as troops loyal to Vargas assembled on the Copacabana beach before bombarding the barracks with artillery fire and retaking it with ease. More than one hundred people were reported killed and several thousand were taken into custody.

Ewert was arrested, along with the group's communications expert, while other members of the group, including Jonny, fled abroad. Prestes went on the run shortly before police raided the house on the Rua Barao da Torre. The safe containing all the documents detailing the Comintern plans should have been booby-trapped. As the team's explosives expert, Jonny was supposed to have rigged it up so that anyone attempting to open it without the combination would have been blown sky high together with all the team's secret documents.

But although Jonny constructed what the police later described as an 'infernal machine' inside the safe, he ensured that the impressive combination of TNT and dynamite would not blow up if the safe was opened. The police recovered documents, letters, maps and notes incriminating hundreds of people involved in the planned coup.

Following the failure of the Brazilian revolution, the Comintern radio networks buzzed with messages as an investigation was put in place. Jonny was recalled to Moscow and repeatedly questioned for fifteen months, but neither the GRU, the Comintern nor even the NKVD could shake his story that he had done his job as best he could.

Although his efforts had ensured that the revolution failed, he could argue quite honestly, as he did in his report to MI6, that 'the real causes of the failure were the lack of support from the civilian population and the disregard of certain Brazilian officials who in spite of their agreement to help sat on their hands'. Jonny was eventually cleared by Moscow of any blame, continuing with his role as a British agent-in-place.

Vivian would later tell new recruits to MI6 that the case of Jonny deGraff provided 'an example of the outstanding success of penetration of Russian secret organisations'. Jonny stayed in place inside the GRU until the outbreak of the Second World War. To this day, and despite the subsequent defections of a number of senior Soviet intelligence officers during the Cold War, he is regarded as one of MI6's best catches.

Chapter 6

Not Strictly Passport Control

The increase in Frank's workload caused by the recruitment of Jonny and the growing numbers of Jews seeking visas to travel abroad helped to keep his mind from two major tragedies in his own life. First his father died, and as executor of the will he had to return to Burnham to sort out the family's affairs.

Then his young daughter Ursula fell down the marble steps of the British embassy, a palatial building on the Wilhelmstrasse close to the Foreign Ministry and next door to the Adlon Hotel. The fall triggered off a fit. Ursula was diagnosed as having epilepsy. Frank and Kay were devastated by their daughter's illness. 'They decided not to have any more children,' their nephew John Kelley said. 'They could not take the risk that it would happen again.' Frank threw himself into his twin responsibilities of gathering intelligence and passport control.

The main burden of helping Jews who wanted to go to Palestine lay with the Jewish Agency's Palestine office. But the leaders of Germany's Jews were quick to set up their own welfare organisations to assist those suffering from Nazi persecution. Most came under the umbrella of the Reichsvertretung der Deutschen Juden, the Reich Representation of German Jews, led by Rabbi Leo Baeck.

The two largest groups were the Zentralausschuss für Hilfe und Aufbau, the Central Committee for Relief and Reconstruction, led by Werner Senator, an immigration official brought over especially from Jerusalem, and the Hilfsverein der Deutschen Juden, literally the Assistance Organisation for the German Jews. The Hilfsverein helped Jews to emigrate, advising on where immigration visas could be obtained, contacting relatives abroad who could sponsor refugees and where necessary finding the money for tickets.

One of the most prominent members of the Hilfsverein was Wilfred Israel, owner of a large Berlin department store and Christopher Isherwood's model for Bernhard Landauer in *Goodbye to Berlin*. Isherwood's first impression of Israel was of a tall, pale young man given to relaxing in a beautifully embroidered kimono.

> His over-civilised, prim, finely drawn, beaky profile gave him the air of a bird in a piece of Chinese embroidery. He was soft, negative, I thought, yet curiously potent with the static potency of a carved ivory figure in a shrine. I noticed again his beautiful English, and the deprecatory gestures of his hands, as he showed me a twelfth-century sandstone head of Buddha from Khmer which stood at the foot of his bed – 'keeping watch over my slumbers'.

Israel had known Frank since the early 1920s, when the British official had assisted him in getting his father Berthold to London where Winifred's sister Viva lay dying. Wilfred and Frank had remained firm friends ever since, and now that relationship was harnessed to help those Jews who wanted to leave Germany. The main go-between was one of Frank's secret service agents, Hubert Pollack, who would later serve in Israeli Intelligence and who worked alongside Israel in the Hilfsverein.

Pollack, a school classmate of Wilfred's brother Herbert, had studied law and public finance, and had helped the Berlin Jewish community organisation to set up a system to distribute its charity relief. He was an ardent Zionist, committed to the creation of a permanent Jewish homeland, and set up his own advisory office for Jewish emigrants. Pollack worked closely with Frank, not just on emigration matters but also on intelligence-gathering.

'My work was mainly secret and brought me into contact with various categories of political agents,' he later wrote. 'I was in regular and close contact with Capt Foley and cooperated with him time and again on matters that were not strictly passport control.' Pollack, who routinely carried a Mauser pistol and from his work with Frank already had a network of contacts inside the Gestapo, was the hard man of the operation.

Very often the best way of ensuring Nazi connivance in the departure of a Jew was through bribery, Pollack said.

> I alone paid out more than 8,000 Reichsmarks in bribes to Nazi officials. They were Reichsbank exchange control inspectors; tax officials; police officers; customs inspectors; Gestapo and SS men of all ranks. Individual sums ranged from 20 marks to 350. The normal amount was around 25 marks.
>
> Passports, tax clearance certificates; foreign exchange approval; visas for stateless persons and foreigners; and release from prisons, although not from concentration camps, were all produced as if by magic. I would meet two or three men in civilian clothes or black or blue uniform in a certain wine restaurant in the Potsdamer or Französischen Strasse and handed over the right sum. It always worked.

In the early days of the Third Reich, most of Pollack's collaboration with Frank was devoted to getting Jews out of Germany. 'Pollack was on very good terms with Foley and could refer certain cases to him,' said Arnold Horwell, who worked with Pollack in the Hilfsverein. 'Somehow he managed to obtain visas when the position of obtaining visas was limited. He knew he was risking himself. But he could trust Pollack and Pollack trusted him. Pollack would be very careful and only submit cases where he knew they would not cause problems. It is impossible to say how many owe Frank Foley their lives.'

Together Frank, Hubert Pollack and Wilfred Israel worked their way around the system, in company with Werner Senator, to help Jews who could not otherwise get out. Israel provided the cash, Pollack the contacts within the Gestapo and Frank – by hook or by crook – the necessary visa.

But this was by no means a one-way street. Despite the growing exclusion of Jews from the professions, many of Frank's Jewish contacts still held prominent positions and were able to provide him with useful intelligence on what was going on inside the new regime.

While there remained a widespread belief within Whitehall that Hitler was a man with whom Britain could do business, alarm bells had begun to ring on a number of fronts.

The general attitude in Britain to the arrival of the first few thousand Jewish refugees from Germany was one of sympathy and outrage at the behaviour of the Nazi authorities, perhaps best exemplified by Commander Oliver Locker-Lampson, MP, when he told the House of Commons that 'it is un-English, it is caddish to bully a minority'.

But not everyone was quite so welcoming. The Unionist MP for Tottenham North, Edward Doran, told Parliament that 'hundreds of thousands of Jews are now leaving Germany and scurrying from there to this country. Are we prepared in this country to allow aliens to come in here from every country while we have 3,000,000 unemployed? If you are asking for a von Hitler in this country, we will soon get one.'

While there were certainly some within Whitehall who agreed with Doran's openly anti-Semitic views, the prevailing view was one of sympathy tempered by a determination not to let the trickle become a flood. The Jewish community had undertaken to fund all costs of the refugees, but its estimates of how many might arrive had been extremely optimistic and had already been exceeded.

British consular staff were told that while the government was 'not at all dissatisfied' with the numbers of refugees arriving from Germany, 'we most certainly don't want numbers increased and it is our policy therefore to do nothing to encourage further immigration. You should be careful to make it clear that you have no sort of reason to suppose that there could possibly be any opening for anyone here in the United Kingdom.'

As for Palestine and the Empire, the number of Jewish refugees that could be allowed in was strictly limited. 'There is no reason to suppose that room could be found in Palestine in the near future for any appreciable number of German refugees,' a cabinet sub-committee ruled. 'The number of refugees who might be trans-migrated to the Colonies generally must be treated as negligible.'

There was also concern in some quarters about the German rearmament plans. The recruitment of Jonny X had been a brilliant success against Soviet intelligence and communist attempts to infiltrate and subvert the West. But a shortage of funds for intelligence operations – the Chief complained that his annual budget in the 1930s was less than the cost of operating a destroyer in home waters – and the additional threat from Nazi Germany were intensifying the pressure to relax the 'Third Country Rule' that supposedly prevented MI6 stations from operating against the countries in which they were based. Increasingly, Frank's secret dealings involving Germany were aimed not just at helping the Jews but also at gathering intelligence on his hosts.

The Reverend John B. Kelley, Frank's nephew, who visited the Foleys with his mother Joyce, Kay's sister, in the summer of 1934, remembers men appearing at strange times of the night in the Foleys' large new apartment at Lessingstrasse 56, in the Moabit district of Berlin.

'There would be this knock on the door at 2 o'clock or 3 o'clock in the morning and we would hear Frank go downstairs to talk them. A lot of these people were Jews who were looking to get out of Germany, but some of the late-night visitors may well have been espionage contacts. We never knew about that aspect of his life until some time after the war, we thought Frank was in the diplomatic corps.'

Frank's secret contacts at this time included Paul Rosbaud, a young Austrian physicist who had become scientific adviser to Springer Verlag, one of Germany's largest publishing houses. Rosbaud was a Catholic but he had a Jewish wife and had therefore become involved in helping Jews to get out. It was through this that he met Frank and was recruited to work for MI6.

The two men had much in common. They both despised Hitler and wanted to do everything they could to help the Jews. They also had a shared experience of the horrors of the First World War and had no wish to see a new conflagration.

'My first two days as a prisoner under British guard were the origin of my long-time Anglophilia,' said Rosbaud. 'For the British soldiers, war was over and forgotten. They did not treat us as enemies but as unfortunate losers of the war.'

Although taller than Frank, Rosbaud was a fairly small man with sharp features, the fingers of a concert pianist and a soft, forceful voice, who was rarely seen without his pipe. He had good contacts through his job with some of the country's leading scientists.

Albert Einstein, himself a Jew, was abroad when the Nazis came to power, and had not returned, but Germany remained home to numerous scientific pioneers like Carl Bosch, Otto Hahn, Fritz Strassmann, Lise Meitner, Werner Heisenberg, Max Born and Hans Bethe. The last two, both Jews, were soon to be dismissed. Meitner, who was also Jewish, would eventually follow them abroad. But for now she and the others were allowed to continue their work, despite their adherence to modern 'non-Aryan ideas' such as Einstein's theory of relativity.

Rosbaud appears to have passed very little information direct to Frank in the period between 1933 and 1938, partly because Head Office was not being pressed for scientific material and was therefore not prepared to allocate scarce resources to keeping track of it and partly because of the ban, in theory at least, on MI6 officers working against the countries in which they were stationed.

But Frank realised Rosbaud's potential value, putting him in touch with a number of prominent British scientists whom he 'just happened to know' and who were interested in having 'confidential discussions' with the young physicist. Apart from such contacts, which took place during Rosbaud's routine business trips to London, he was deliberately kept at a distance, held in place for the moment when he would be needed.

Joyce Kelley's extended visit, with her young son John, brought some welcome relief from the increasing pressure put on Frank by the number of Jews seeking ways of getting out of Germany and Head Office's demands for more information on Hitler's intentions. He appears to have treated six-year-old John as the son he now knew he would never have.

'John B arrived safely on Thursday and brought his mother with him,' Frank wrote to his brother-in-law.

> He has since taken charge of this apartment and of most of Berlin. He does not agree with everything he sees, but the orangeade is much to his liking. The word cute seems to be John's favourite and whatever is cute is good.
>
> We are all going to England in July for a spot of leave and shall take Joyce with us if John is agreeable. He is my partner and we try to look after the women between us. It is quite hard work sometimes but when things are very critical, John smiles and then we are all smiles. He has the most fascinating smile I have ever seen. I took John, and John took his mother, to the Zoological Gardens this afternoon. When we set out he took my hand and said to me: 'Come on Uncle Frank, we two men will go together'.

The Reverend John B. Kelley remembers feeling a similar affinity with his uncle. 'He took me shopping,' he recalled.

> He said: 'Come on John. We gentlemen are going out shopping.' He took me to a very new, very modern department store where I saw my first revolving door and my first escalator.
>
> I remember seeing a fascinating cast-iron toy bomber, props

spun, rubber tyres, and I believe a retracting landing gear, with a couple of small bombs under each wing that could be loaded with caps and then dropped by a trigger.

I wanted that plane in the worst way but I guess it was pretty expensive since Frank didn't buy it for me. But he promised to make me one like it when we returned home, which he did. Not out of cast iron but cardboard and, I think, some wood, using the celluloid cover from either Kay's or my mother's face-powder box for the cockpit cover, I remember that very clearly, with sure enough some bombs hanging from the wings that could be dropped.

I was delighted with it and played with it until it wore out. It does show a really creative streak in Frank. He only saw that toy the one time with me, came home and, as far as I recall, duplicated it almost perfectly – certainly well enough to make this little boy very happy.

Of the less pleasant side of Berlin, Kelley has vague memories of standing on the balcony of the Passport Control Office, overlooking the Tiergarten and seeing a group of Brownshirts running riot. He also remembers his mother recounting a meeting with Hitler. 'My mother attended a diplomatic function with Frank and Kay while we were in Berlin. She met Hitler, Göring and von Ribbentrop in the receiving line and told me that "Hitler had the most hypnotic eyes of any man I have ever met".'

After the initial flurry of laws against 'non-Aryans' that followed Hitler's *Machtergreifung*, the persecution of the Jews appeared to die down during late 1933 and most of 1934. Some of those who had fled to neighbouring countries, and even as far as Palestine, returned home, preferring to live in their own country and believing that things were reverting to normal.

'In the autumn of 1933, a lull appeared to have set in in the campaign of anti-semitism,' Frank wrote in a dispatch to London.

Hopes were entertained by the Jews that the revolution so far as it affected the Jewish question might be considered to be completed.

As a consequence of the Frontline Fighters paragraph, many Jews had been able to retain their livelihoods and a feeling of greater security began to develop amongst them. This feeling was further strengthened by a decree issued in January 1934 by the Reich Minister for the Interior to the effect that the tendencies which had become apparent to exclude Jewish elements from German economic life were unjustified.

For the moment, Hitler had other concerns. The German Army, limited to just one hundred thousand men by the Versailles Treaty, had remained highly suspicious of the Nazi Party and resentful of the power of the two-and-a-half-million-strong SA storm troopers. But the army had the support of big business and the right-wing establishment on whose backing Hitler still depended. He also realised that when he attempted to retake the land lost at Versailles, he would need trained soldiers, not the organised thuggery of the Brownshirts.

The SA had become an embarrassment. Their terrorist activities against Hitler's opponents had been a useful way of cowing the population, but the storm troopers had become a law unto themselves. They were largely drawn from among the working class, and their backing for the party was often based on the socialist principles of the Twenty-Five Point Plan which Hitler wanted to drop. In addition, the power of Ernst Röhm, their charismatic leader, was resented by many within Hitler's inner circle who criticised him for his openly promiscuous homo-sexuality and portrayed him as a threat even to the Führer himself.

Röhm, a former army captain who had stood alongside Hitler during the Beer Hall Putsch, was one of his loyalist supporters and one of only a handful of people who could address Hitler using the familiar *Du*. But he had been unsuccessfully pressuring the Führer to allow the SA to take over the army and was rapidly falling from grace.

'Hitler is a swine,' he had unwisely declared during a drunken late-night conversation. 'He is betraying all of us. He is getting matey with the Prussian generals. Adolf knows exactly what I want. I've told him often enough. The generals are a lot of old fogeys. I'm the nucleus of the new army, don't you see that. Hitler puts me off with fine words.'

On 30 June 1933 – the so-called Night of the Long Knives – Hitler acted. The SA leadership was called to a meeting at Bad Wiessee in Bavaria. Eric Kempka, Hitler's chauffeur, recalled what happened as they drove into the town to see Röhm, who was waiting in his hotel.

> Just before Bad Wiessee, Hitler suddenly breaks his silence: 'Kempka,' he says. 'Drive carefully when we come to the Pension Hanselbauer. You must drive up without making any noise. If you see an SA guard in the front of the hotel, don't wait for them to report to me; drive on and stop at the hotel entrance.' Then after a moment of deadly silence: 'Röhm wants to carry out a coup.'
>
> Hitler entered Röhm's bedroom alone with a whip in his hand. Behind him were two detectives with pistols at the ready. He spat out the words: 'Röhm, you are under arrest.' Röhm looked up sleepily from his pillow: 'Heil my Fuehrer,' he said. 'You are under arrest,' bawled Hitler for the second time, turning on his heel and leaving the room.

Up to two hundred people, including Röhm and the vast bulk of the SA leadership, were executed by Himmler's SS, which up until now had been a subordinate part of the SA. Hitler also took the opportunity to dispose of a number of other potential rivals, including Schleicher, the former Chancellor, claiming that they had taken part in the plot against him.

A month later, Hindenburg died. Hitler made himself both President and Chancellor. The last constitutional check on his power had been removed. He was now not only Chancellor but also head of state and commander of the army.

'Any doubts about the loyalty of the army were done away with before the old Field-Marshal's body was hardly cold,' wrote William Shirer, an American newspaper reporter, in his diary.

Every soldier was made to swear an oath of loyalty and 'unconditional obedience to the Führer of the German Reich and the people'. Hitler's power had become absolute.

Now the party's attention could be turned back to the Jews. In December, the Nazi newspaper, the *Frankfurter Volksblatt*, published a list of names and addresses of six thousand Jews living in Frankfurt am Main, describing it as 'an answer to the atrocity and boycott campaign conducted by the Jews abroad'.

The British consul-general, R.T. Smallbones, noted that 'on the face of it the object of this publication would appear to be to aid the true Aryan in avoiding intercourse with the contaminated and to warn him against placing his custom with the national enemy'. But it was clear from an article accompanying the directory that there was more to it.

'If this publication makes the international boycott campaigners realise, in view of this copious list, how many of their racial fellows are affected by their campaign of slander it will have achieved a good part of its purpose,' the newspaper said. Smallbones concluded that the tone of the article as a whole was one of veiled threat. 'It would therefore appear,' he said, 'that the directory has also been compiled with a view to having ready at hand a list and the addresses of potential hostages.'

In the run-up to Christmas, the local Union of Nazi Shopkeepers persuaded the Frankfurt party leadership to impose a city-wide boycott to ensure that good Aryans did not buy their Christmas presents from Jewish businesses.

'Pickets stood outside these shops and only suffered Jews or people who professed to be Jews to enter,' Smallbones recorded. 'Some of the public were loud in their protests against the interference with their Christmas purchases.' On Christmas Eve, a British nurse had been spat on and called a traitor as she left a Jewish shoe shop. 'One man, an Aryan, called at a police station and asked for assistance to buy what he wanted. He was told that the police had received no instructions what to do.'

Within a few weeks, it was clear that this had not been an

isolated incident. 'Since the beginning of 1935, a recrudescence of anti-semitism has become evident,' Frank wrote in a confidential report for London.

> It is becoming increasingly apparent that the Party has not departed from its original intentions and that its ultimate aim remains the disappearance of the Jews from Germany or, failing that, their relegation to a position of powerlessness and inferiority.
>
> Indications of this recrudescence of anti-semitism are apparent in recent legislative measures, in regulations governing admission to the liberal professions, in the boycotting of Jewish concerns and in the increasing virulence of speeches of leading members of the Party.

Professor Oscar Fehr, consultant optometrist to the German royal family, was in charge of the eye department of the Rudolf Virchov Hospital in Berlin. His daughter Inge recalled the growing anti-Semitism among her schoolfriends.

> There was one Jewish girl in our class and we sent her to Coventry. Nobody spoke to her. Whenever she came into the playground, we all went into the opposite corner. My friend's father was high up in the Nazi Party and I was as bad as all the rest.
>
> I was 11 and we were going to collect for the winter relief with the Hitler Youth when it was announced in the school hall that I would not be able to go. 'Why not?' I asked. 'Because your father is a Jew,' they said. 'It's impossible,' I said. I had been taught that a Jew was the lowest form of life, my wonderful father could not be a Jew. Then I found out that my mother was a Jew too so I was classified as a full Jew.
>
> We were having daily lessons in Race Knowledge, learning about the superiority of the German race. We were told that the Germans and Scandinavians had descended from monkeys. Jews had descended from Negroes. Miss Dummer, my form teacher, who was a patient of my father, took me aside after the first lesson and said: 'Please ignore the rubbish I am forced to teach you.'
>
> Everything changed from then on. My father had to leave the hospital – two years earlier, on his 60th birthday, the Lord Mayor had written to him saying: 'We hope Berlin will still have many,

many years of your valuable service.' But in 1934, all Jews had to leave public service and now a letter came telling him that he was forbidden to enter the hospital again.

Frank told London that from now on all applicants for the medical or dental professions had to be Aryan.

> No Jewish dentist, whether a frontline fighter or not, may now be admitted as a panel dentist. No Jewish lawyer, whether a frontline fighter or not, may now be admitted as a professional legal adviser. No apprentice may be entered to the publishing trade unless of Aryan origin. Almost all Jewish artists have been forbidden from exercising their calling.
>
> For the Jewish youth, the future holds out no prospects in Germany and the greater part will be forced to emigrate. The liberal professions are now completely closed to them.

Chapter 7

A Catch-22 Situation

Wolfgang Meyer-Michael was a prominent Jewish artist who before the First World War had his own studio at the Berliner Akademie and was a master-pupil of the leading sculptor Louis Tuaillon. He served in the Imperial German Army from 1914 to 1918 before returning to Berlin and achieving recognition during the 1920s as a popular and successful sculptor and potter.

But Meyer-Michael had read *Mein Kampf* and had realised early on that if the Nazis ever got into power being a Jew in Germany would become intolerable. Asked in 1932 to sculpt Hitler, he declined. When the client who had offered the commission asked why, Meyer-Michael explained that he was a Jew. 'I don't mind,' the man said. 'No, but you will,' Meyer-Michael replied. 'You will.'

Jews dominated the arts in Germany during the 1920s, and the Nazis came to power determined to end this 'unhealthy' influence over Aryan culture. Shortly after the March 1933 elections – when the extreme right gained more than 50 per cent of the vote, consolidating Hitler's position as Chancellor – all members of the Prussian Academy of the Arts received a letter warning them that they would henceforth have to show the correct 'national cultural attitude' and refrain from criticising the new regime or they would be expelled.

The Nazis instigated a virulent campaign against 'non-German culture' leading to the 10 May bonfires when students and members of the SA burned thousands of so-called 'non-Aryan' books in front of the University of Berlin and the State Opera House. By September, all the arts had been brought under the direct control of Josef Goebbels, Hitler's Enlightenment and Propaganda Minister, through the creation of the Reichskulturkammer, or Reich Chamber of Culture. Six months later, Goebbels announced that all non-Aryans were to be banned from membership of the new organisation and the systematic expulsion of Jews from all areas of the arts began.

After the boycott of Jewish businesses on 1 April, 1933, Meyer-Michael had quit his high-profile studio in Berlin. He took his mother, his wife Alice and their two daughters, Susanne and Sabine, and moved to Rheda, near Bielefeld, for what he hoped would be a quieter life in the countryside. Now he received a letter from the president of the Reichskulturkammer forbidding him from working as a sculptor and potter 'in view of the fact that you are non-Aryan and as such do not possess the necessary reliability and suitability for the creation of German cultural objects'. Since his war service had not been at the front, he could not claim exemption as a 'Frontline Fighter'. Not only could he no longer work, the persecution of the Jews was worse in the countryside than in the capital.

Susanne Meyer-Michael recalled how in the end she and her sister had to be taken out of school. 'I was harassed by my fellow pupils. I had a terrible time. Spat at, kicked at, called names and excluded from school activities. One girl actually kicked me down the stairs. I was called Jewish bitch. As a 13-year-old I objected. The children in my age had to join the Hitler Youth. One of my teachers arrived with jackboots and a revolver. That's not a very good atmosphere to learn in.' Her father had considered emigrating. 'But my grandmother was very old and when she was still alive he couldn't leave her alone.'

When his mother died in 1935, Meyer-Michael looked first to England, writing to the Wedgwood pottery company to see if they had a position to offer him. But they had nothing, and without the promise of a job in America or Britain, the family decided to move to Palestine. The number of Jewish immigrants arriving there in the immediate wake of Hitler's appointment as Chancellor had sparked riots among the Arab inhabitants, and the British were sticking to strict limits on the number of visas issued.

They were available to dependents of those already living in Palestine and to those who had definite offers of jobs. But the jobs available there were almost exclusively agricultural or industrial, while most German Jews were members of the professional and business classes or, like Meyer-Michael, employed in cultural occupations. For them the only option was a *Kapitalistenzertifikat* or Capitalist Visa as 'a person of independent means' for which potential immigrants had to be able to show that they had £1,000, around £40,000 at today's values, to help them to start a new life.

But with many people now wanting to emigrate, it was virtually impossible to sell a house or business for anything more than a fraction of the real value. 'Much was given away or sold very cheaply,' Meyer-Michael wrote in his memoirs. 'It was hard to leave everything behind. Apart from a few bronzes and some busts which my mother-in-law took into her flat, I destroyed all the pieces of art with an axe.'

Even the limited amount of money retrieved from the sale of the family's goods was not entirely theirs to keep. If a potential emigrant possessed capital worth more than fifty thousand marks or had earned more than twenty thousand marks in any one year, they also had to pay a *Reichsfluchtssteuer* 'flight tax' of 25 per cent of the last assessed value of their property.

The remainder of their marks were then paid into a *Sonderkonto*, a special blocked account with the Reichsbank which then transferred a thousand pounds to the Templar Bank in Palestine, albeit at a highly punitive rate of exchange. It was not until this money was transferred that they could obtain their visas and, with the amount of foreign currency available to the Reichsbank severely limited, it could take many months for the cash to be released.

The Meyer-Michaels barely had the thousand pounds they needed, and this was in a blocked account with no guarantee that it would ever be transferred to the Templar Bank. 'I just had enough for a £1,000 visa but I only had the promise of its use once I had gone abroad,' Wolfgang Meyer-Michael wrote. This was no use. Frank had been given blocks of two hundred capitalist visas which he could grant without reference to the authorities in Jerusalem, but the potential emigrant had to have immediate access to the equivalent of a thousand pounds before he or she could be issued with a visa.

'When I looked up the British Passport Control Officer in Berlin, he regretted not being able to give me a *Kapitalistenzertifikat*,' Meyer-Michael said.

> It was a Catch-22 situation. I could only get the money once I was in Palestine and the British passport official couldn't give me an entry visa before I had the money in hand.
>
> He was a very charming man, a Captain Foley who was very interested in my plans and quite obviously prepared to help. When he heard that I was a sculptor and potter, he softened, telling me about clay found in Wales, fetching books and maps pertaining to pottery, and keeping me there for about an hour. He wondered if there wasn't some way out, perhaps someone who could advance me £1,000, didn't I have friends or relatives who would help?

Foley then suggested that there could perhaps be another way. Might not someone write a letter 'vouchsafing' the money? 'Mr Foley was very far-sighted,' said Sabine Comberti, the Meyer-Michaels' other daughter. 'He could see the dilemma my father was in. "There must be somebody," he sort of put it to him. "Can't you just get a promise? You don't have to use it." And my father said he would try.'

A cousin had emigrated to Amsterdam when the Nazi persecutions of the Jews began and had established his own bank. 'I looked him up and explained my problem,' recalled Wolfgang Meyer-Michael. 'He was ready to help and we drew up two documents. In one document, he promised to lend me £1,000 when I needed it. In a second, I declared the first one invalid and said I would make no use of it whatsoever.'

He took the banker's note promising the money to Foley.

> The whole thing was a ploy. Mr Foley knew that as well as I, and he also knew that I knew that he knew. But he said enthusiastically that this was marvellous and he would give me the visa immediately. Within half an hour, I had the precious document in my hands. He was really very charming and I promised him that I would send him my first 'decent' piece of pottery.

In a dispatch back to London, Foley complained that Meyer-Michael's problem was not unusual. The Reichsbank was freeing less and less foreign exchange.

> Applications for the release of foreign exchange for emigration purposes at present take up to twelve months and I have at present 700 such cases awaiting settlement. Emigration is equally impossible by way of *Sonderkonto* as approximately 14 million marks are still awaiting clearance.
>
> The position of the Jew in Germany, even if he possesses capital, is therefore a desperate one: he is being ruined economically and at the same time he is unable to emigrate as he cannot obtain the release of even a moderate proportion of his capital sufficient to enable him to do so.

Shortly afterwards, the Meyer-Michaels were, thanks to Foley's intervention, able to emigrate. 'I shall be forever grateful to this truly good man,' wrote Wolfgang Meyer-Michael. 'A man who fulfilled his task with humanity, who feared greatly for the future of the Jews, many of whom simply refused to recognise the severity of the situation and refused to move heaven and earth to leave Germany.'

Meyer-Michael was not alone in believing his fellow Jews to be overly optimistic, if not naïve. William Shirer spent the Easter weekend out of the capital in Bad Saarow. 'The hotel mainly filled with Jews and we are a little surprised to see so many of them still prospering and apparently unafraid,' he wrote. 'I think they are unduly optimistic.' More than 50,000 Jews had already fled Germany. But about 450,000 more had stayed put, many of them genuinely believing that the Nazi persecution was a phase, that things would eventually get better, even return to normal. It was not to be.

Not all Jews were quite so sanguine. In January 1935, the population of the Saarland voted to return to Germany. More than 90 per cent decided that they wanted to be part of Hitler's new Germany. 'They *do* have the Nazi bug badly,' William Shirer wrote in his diary. A substantial proportion of those who voted against unification were Jewish. All five thousand of the region's Jews chose to take Belgian or French citizenship.

The Night of the Long Knives was only the first of a series of measures aimed at winning over the generals. In early 1935, during a period of tension between the Reichswehr and the SS, Hitler warned the party not to intrude on the army's activities, declaring that the Reichswehr was 'the sole bearer of arms'. In March, shortly after the reoccupation of the Saarland, Hitler enacted a law 'for the Recreation of the National Defence Forces', wiping out the military sections of the Versailles Treaty and setting up a Thirty-six-division army, renamed the Wehrmacht and based on conscription.

'Hitler read the law out to a combined meeting of his cabinet and the Army General Staff,' Shirer wrote. 'According to one informant, the cabinet members embraced one another after Hitler's magic voice had died down. Grey-haired General von Blomberg then led all present in three lusty cheers for Hitler. The Junkers who are running the Army will forget a lot – and swallow a lot – now that Hitler has given them what they want.'

But not all the senior officers were happy with what was going on. With increasing concern in London at the pace of German rearmament, Frank recruited a number of senior officials who shared that disquiet. Perhaps the best source was a Luftwaffe colonel working in the the German Air Ministry who volunteered his services in return for cash.

Given the colonel's access to high-grade intelligence from Göring's office and the panic in London over a claim by Hitler that the Luftwaffe had reached parity with the RAF, Head Office agreed to pay him. Budgets had been urgently increased in the wake of Hitler's decision to build up his armed forces, so there was hard cash available for good intelligence.

His information contradicted the more conservative estimates of the RAF, leading Lord Londonderry, the British Secretary of State for Air, to dismiss it – a typical example of the difficulties the service faced in putting across information the source of which could not be disclosed.

'He doubted whether the opinion of the Secret Service in a matter of this kind, which had some technical aspects, was as good as that of the department concerned,' the Cabinet minutes record. 'The Air Ministry interpretation and deduction was more likely to be the correct one.'

Over the next three years, Frank met the Luftwaffe officer every two weeks and the two men became firm friends. The colonel regularly handed over photocopies of top-secret documents with details of both the structure of the rapidly expanding Luftwaffe and its strategy.

Theoretically, the so-called Third Country Rule prevented Frank from mounting such operations against Germany. But in reality, this rule was frequently ignored, and with German rearmament in full swing no one in Head Office was likely to argue with him, as long as he wasn't caught and as long as the ambassador didn't find out. MI6 heads of station often found their activities seriously hampered by the ambassador's preference for a quiet time.

'The powers of the MI6 representatives abroad are severely limited,' Kim Philby wrote in one of his wartime reports to Moscow.

> The station head is under the control of the Minister or Ambassador, and the latter can always limit the activities of the MI6 representatives if he judges them to be politically dangerous. A protest from the ambassador to the FO will always suffice to secure the reprimand of the MI6 representative.
>
> In practice, it is usually found that the ambassador whose natural inclination it is to avoid 'trouble' with the government to which he is accredited, keeps a jealous eye on the activity of MI6 and to a great extent hampers its work. Unless the case for MI6 is overwhelmingly strong, it is obvious that the Foreign Office will support a cautious ambassador rather than a vigorous MI6 representative.

Frank also had close, and in some cases professional, relationships with British newspaper correspondents like Norman Ebbutt of *The Times*, and Ian Colvin of the *News Chronicle*, both of whom had good contacts within the German establishment. Colvin's contacts were so good that during the war he was consulted by the Prime Minister himself.

'He plunged very deeply into German politics,' Churchill wrote, 'and established contacts of a most secret character with some of the important German generals, and also with independent men of character and quality in Germany who saw in the Hitler Movement the approaching ruin of their land.'

Frank would meet them in the Taverne, an Italian restaurant where the British and American journalists congregated each night after filing their copy.

'We have a *Stammtisch* – a table always reserved for us in the corner – and from about ten pm until three or four in the morning it is usually filled,' wrote Shirer.

> Usually Norman Ebbutt presides, sucking at an old pipe the night long, talking and arguing in a weak, high-pitched voice, imparting wisdom, for he has been here a long time, has contacts throughout the government, party, churches, and army, and has a keen intelligence. Of late he has complained to me in private that *The Times* does not print all he sends, that it does not want to hear too much of the bad side of Nazi Germany and apparently has been captured by the pro-Nazis in London.

Throughout the early part of 1935, there was increasing pressure from within the Nazi Party for further official measures against the Jews. 'The number of Jew bastards in Germany is terribly large,' Julius Streicher, Gauleiter of Franconia and editor of the rabidly right-wing *Der Stürmer*, told an audience in Nuremberg. 'We must not believe that we have yet obtained the victory. A hard road lies before us.'

The particular target was Jewish businesses. 'The danger is in our midst since there are still Jews in Germany,' one regional party boss declared, calling for ordinary Germans to do more. 'They are trying to recapture their trade. The fight against this cannot be considered as a matter of legislation.'

Another accused the middle classes, many of whom had bridled at the anti-Jewish measures and continued to buy goods from the mainly Jewish-owned department stores, of 'betrayal of the German economy', and said it was as much their 'duty' as it was that of the authorities to ensure that Jewish shops were put out of business.

'The National-Socialist state has dealt with Jewry more humanely than Jewry would ever have done had the position been reversed,' he claimed. 'Laws were made, which it is true, entailed a repression of Jewish influence but all the laws have not yet been passed which are needed to protect our people against the Jewish danger.'

While such calls for further measures against the Jews could be dismissed as simply poisonous rhetoric from people whose positions were already well known, they provoked an almost immediate, and far more ominous, response from the authorities. Wilhelm Frick, the Interior Minister, announced in April that legislation was being prepared under which citizenship would be refused to 'unworthy persons or enemies of the state'. There would be 'a condition of racial membership of the German people'.

Those ordinary Germans who declined to follow the Nazi Party's lead were left in little doubt that they were making a mistake, as one Englishman formerly resident in Berlin explained in April 1935 to Ramsay MacDonald, the British Prime Minister.

'My German adopted son and I had to come back to England,' Harold Picton wrote.

> He was working in the Social Services but as he was no Nazi his career was ended. The atmosphere of oppression, cruelty and spying became more and more intolerable. Most of our trusted friends have lost their work, others retain it only by doing as if they were Nazi.
>
> One was put in a concentration camp because of adverse musical criticism of a performance at the State Opera House in Berlin. At that time I still had some influence and I managed to get him released. But he is gradually being forced out of employment. Another friend, a Brown Shirt and a convinced Nazi, promised me he would oppose cruelty. His comrades told him his outspokenness on this would bring him into a concentration camp. He is in one now. He was arrested in January and the authorities have up till now refused to give any reason for the arrest.
>
> When a Jewish medical friends of ours was, after long negotiations, restored to the [medical] panel because of distinguished war service, his patients were at the same time told that no true German consults a Jewish doctor. This slipperiness pervades the whole Nazi method. You can never pin them down.

The various calls for further anti-Semitic measures led to more attacks on Jews and Jewish businesses. On 16 and 17 July, anti-Jewish riots broke out in Berlin. Spurred on by a series of inflammatory articles in the Nazi newspapers, around a hundred young men in civilian clothes rampaged down the Kurfürstendamm pulling Jews out of cafés to cries of 'Show us your nose' and beating them up.

The authorities said the violence had occurred when 'sinister elements' intent on bringing the SA into disrepute 'misused a natural anti-Jewish demonstration'. But this was shown to be nonsense by an order issued the next day to the Berlin-Brandenburg SA forbidding them to take part in anti-Jewish demonstrations 'even when out of uniform'.

Frank reported an increase in the Aryanisation of companies and moves to force Jewish concerns out of business. 'In Berlin, under pressure from the Party, numerous concerns had to be sold and transferred to Aryans, whilst leading Jewish directors and employees have been dismissed and many Jewish workmen deprived of their employment,' he wrote.

> To illustrate the difficulties of the smaller Jewish tradesmen I may instance the case of a Kosher butcher whose premises are in my street. During the last two or three months his plate glass window has been smashed at least twelve times during the night. After about the eighth time, the insurance company appealed to the presumably Aryan window-smashers to cease their activities, as they were destroying not Jewish property but German property. The bandits have refused to be enlightened. The police seem to be uninterested. The window-breaking continues.

At the annual Nazi Party rally in Nuremberg in September 1935, Hitler announced two new laws, the first, repeatedly flagged since Frick's speech, made German citizenship open only to 'a national of German or kindred blood'. The second was the Law for the Protection of German Blood and Honour which defined Jews as not being of German blood and banned sexual relations or marriage between Jew and non-Jew. There was now no way back. 'German policy is clearly to eliminate the Jew from German life,' Frank told London. 'And the Nazis do not mind how this is accomplished. Mortality and emigration provide the means.'

87

Chapter 8

'Only a Fool Will Grumble'

One of the first arrests under the new laws was that of Hans Serelman, a Jewish doctor sent to a concentration camp for seven months after giving a blood transfusion to a non-Jew. In order to save the man's life, Dr Serelman had been forced to give him his own blood. Under the new laws, the man was not a patient but a victim. Dr Serelman was not a hero. He was a criminal, guilty of 'race defilement'.

The 'regulation' of the Jewish position continued through-out the rest of 1935, with the dismissal of all those Jewish civil servants who had previously kept their posts as a result of the 'Frontline Fighters' exemption and a series of complex debates over how many 'full Jewish' grandparents one needed to have had to be classified under the regulations as a Jew.

A senior Palestinian official who visited Berlin shortly after the announcement of the Nuremberg Laws concluded that the Jews were 'the direct objects of coldly intelligent evil'. Eric Mills, Commissioner for Migration and Statistics in Palestine, toured Berlin, accompanied by Frank and Werner Senator, and met Jewish leaders and German officials to discuss the problems facing the thousands of Jews who wanted to leave.

'While before I went to Germany, I knew that the Jewish situation was bad,' Mills said.

> I had not realised as I now do that the fate of German Jews is a tragedy which for cold, intelligent planning by those in authority takes rank with that of those who were out of sympathy with the Bolshevist regime in Russia; or the elimination of Armenians from the Turkish Empire.
>
> In the provinces, the conditions of Jews are particularly unpleasant. Outside villages and provincial towns are found notice boards on which it is proudly proclaimed that 'This place is empty of Jews'. In the cases of villages and towns not so 'fortunate' the notice boards display the photographs of the Jewish residents accompanied by biographical details.
>
> Masked men appeared one night in one town and frightened the Jewish inhabitants from their houses so that these fled to the hills for three or four nights, food being brought to some of them by a few Aryan friends. Gaining confidence they returned to their homes. Masked men again appeared, this time with fire-engines, and flooded the houses by means of fire hoses.

Mills found few ordinary Germans prepared to criticise such behaviour. 'Among people of my generation and of older generations there may be feelings of distrust of the regime and unhappiness,' he said.

> If so prudence prevents the exercise of moral courage so that criticism is rare to find. Secrecy and the Secret Police dominate the situation. Only a fool will grumble. The grumbler will certainly be given a period of 'correctional' restraint and when that is over he will not speak of the nature of the 'correction'.
>
> The policy is to eliminate the Jews from Germany by a process of complete impoverishment. Many Jews are homeless and hundreds are facing starvation. The Jew is to be eliminated and the State has no regard for the manner of the elimination. If Jews can emigrate let it be so, but the State will not facilitate emigration; it will hinder emigration by its imposts on capital and foreign exchange manipulation.

The economic difficulties placed in the way of the emigrating Jews were immense. 'The regulations were very, very limited,' one of Frank's former colleagues said. 'There were very few chances of giving anybody a visa for Palestine in those days. It was all trying to keep the numbers down because they knew the Arabs were going to revolt at some time.'

Throughout 1934 and 1935, the amount of foreign currency available in Germany shrank and as a result the Reichsbank was frequently unable to transfer pounds to the Templar Bank and people depositing their £1,000 were given a waiting number. Only when their number came up and the money was transferred were they eligible for a visa.

There was another way of transferring money. Anyone going to Palestine could take advantage of the *Haavara* or Transfer Agreement, a special deal negotiated by the Jewish Agency which allowed them to transfer funds to Palestine by paying the money into the Palestina Treuhand-Stelle, or Paltreu, which used the money to pay German companies in marks for exports to Palestine. This meant they could often take substantially more out of the country than emigrants to other countries.

As the amount of sterling available to the Reichsbank dried up, Jews trying to get to Palestine increasingly used the *Haavara* to transfer across the £1,000 required to qualify for a capitalist visa. The result was that the Paltreu soon found itself in a similar position to that of the Reichsbank, swamped by deposits of marks and without sufficient sterling to back them up. The waiting lists for capitalist visas were growing and growing.

Berthold Kahn, a Jewish lawyer in Zweibrücken, south-west Germany, had served in the German Army during the First World War, winning the Iron Cross. But when the Nazis came to power, the SA mounted guard on his chambers with a sign saying: 'Do not frequent Jewish lawyers'.

He was shoved down the steps of the law courts by SA louts and his largest client, the chemical company IG Farben, for whom he had never lost a case, dispensed with his services. His daughter

Elsbeth came home to find him in despair. 'Papa had broken down completely,' she said. 'His world had collapsed. We had become lepers. He was sitting in an absolute confused state in our living room, staring at his Iron Cross.'

Elsbeth, then just eighteen, had planned to study medicine, but eventually took a job as a medical secretary in Berlin, where she became a Zionist. In the summer of 1935, she applied to go to Palestine on a capitalist certificate and deposited her £1,000 with the Reichsbank.

'I was given a "waiting number" which was very high, over 8,000,' she said.

> This meant I would have to wait for at least four or five years until I could get the visa – if ever. There was of course the danger that the regulations would be changed and I would never be able to transfer the money and get my visa.
>
> Being an ardent Zionist I spent most of my free time studying Hebrew in the Meineckestrasse, the headquarters of the Zionist Organisation. One of the members of the Zionist Executive was Gerhard Walbach, who was in charge of the Exit Visas Department, and he knew Mr Foley very well.
>
> Since I was rather desperate because of the high number I had been given and the impossibility to quickly get out of Nazi Germany, he approached Mr Foley, telling him about my plight. To this day, I remember with deep gratitude when I got the phone call that Mr Foley had granted me a capitalist visa, with the capital on paper only. He most probably saved my life. It was August 15, 1935. Six weeks later I sailed for Haifa, with just ten German marks in my hand.

Elsbeth's sister Hilde emigrated to America in 1938, and a year later her father and mother were issued with a transit visa to France, from where they joined Hilde in New York. On crossing the border, Berthold Kahn threw his Iron Cross in the Rhine.

His elder brother Paul was murdered in 1942 in the Oranienburg concentration camp. His younger brother Hermann, who was married to an Aryan, was left alone until she died in 1943, when he was taken to Auschwitz and gassed. Elsbeth's aunts Clara and Emma were deported to Theresienstadt. Clara died of starvation in 1944. Emma was liberated in 1945.

'I never met Mr Foley personally but I shall for ever and ever be grateful to him,' said Elsbeth. 'In view of the development in the following years, it goes without saying that due to Mr Foley's empathy and human courage I was saved from perishing in a concentration camp.'

Miriam Rabow was just sixteen years old when her family was evicted from their home because they were Jewish.

> For 25 years, we had lived in the East Prussian town of Königsberg in a comfortable five-room apartment in a very good residential neighbourhood. However the landlord was a Nazi and toward the end of 1935 forced my parents to move out. I had to drop out of school before the matriculation; I was expelled from the local sports association, and from our tennis club. These and other signs did not augur well.

Her father Albert, a sixty-six-year-old insurance agent, and her sixty-one-year-old mother Paula, decided that they must now follow their son and elder daughter to Palestine on a capitalist visa. 'The circumstances and atmosphere in those days left little doubt as to the future and they were anxious to get out of Germany as quickly as possible,' Miriam recalled. But the increasing waiting lists for the transfer of funds to Palestine meant that this would take time, and Mr and Mrs Rabow were anxious that their daughter should be removed from danger as soon as possible.

> My mother travelled with me to Berlin. As Capt Foley's readiness to help was well known within the German Jewish community we tried our luck with him. And indeed after some pleading on the part of my mother, I received the visa and was able to leave Germany at the beginning of October. To this day, I remain grateful to Capt Foley who helped me at a time when visas to Palestine were at a premium. He had courage and goodwill in what were very difficult times.

Amazingly, while many Jews were trying desperately to emigrate, others who had succeeded in getting out during the early days of the Third Reich were now trying to come home. They had found it hard to settle abroad. They were Germans. They wanted to live in Germany. But on their return, they found themselves thrown into concentration camps.

'It is estimated that some 150 to 200 have been interned in this manner up to date,' Frank reported. 'Any such returned emigrant who proves by the production of railway tickets or ship's passage that he intends again to emigrate is released and handed his passport at the frontier station of exit.'

One of those who came home was Heinz Romberg, a twenty-five-year-old Berliner. He had emigrated to Spain in October 1934 but had been unable to settle there. 'I returned to Berlin in July 1935 with a return visa valid for three months to find that my parents had emigrated to Palestine with the rest of the family. My wife, whom I married in Berlin in the middle of August 1935, also wanted to go there.'

If Romberg did not leave before his three-month visa expired, he faced arrest like the other returnees. But despite his technical and mechanical training, his attempts to get a certificate showing that he was a qualified technician, and therefore eligible for emigration to Palestine as a Category C emigrant 'having a definite prospect of employment', came to nothing.

Since he did not have any money, he could not qualify for a £1,000 capitalist visa. 'Somehow, I succeeded in seeing Capt Foley who gave us both a capitalist certificate without any money,' Romberg said. 'On the last day of my three months, we both got out to Barcelona and on 1st November 1935 to Marseille arriving in Jaffa on 7 November 1935. I have never forgotten and never will forget Captain Foley.'

The measures against the Jews continued unabated. In early December, Dr Heinrich Sahm, the Lord Mayor of Berlin, was forced to resign after being denounced at a 'court of honour' for 'staining his honour' by buying goods in Jewish shops.

At the end of the year, James G. McDonald, League of Nations High Commissioner for Refugees, stepped down, appealing to the world to to help Germany's Jews and other opponents of the Nazi regime.

'Tens of thousands are anxiously seeking ways to flee abroad,' he said in his resignation letter.

> But except for those prepared to sacrifice the whole or greater part of their savings, the official restrictions on export of capital effectively bar the road to escape. Relentlessly, the Jews and non-Aryans are excluded from all public offices and any part in the cultural and intellectual life of Germany. They are subjected to every kind of humiliation.
>
> It is being made increasingly difficult for Jews and non-Aryans to sustain life. In many parts of the country, there is a systematic attempt at starvation. The number of suicides, the distortion of minds and the breaking down of bodies, the deaths of children through malnutrition are tragic witnesses.

But with appeasement now an established policy in Britain, the Foreign Office dismissed McDonald's letter as 'an unwise document which did a disservice to the real interests of the Jews in Germany'. The degree to which the Foreign Office was prepared to ignore virtually anything Hitler did in the vain hope that it would maintain peace in Europe was about to be demonstrated in full.

In March 1936, Hitler tore up the Locarno Treaty under which Britain, France, Belgium and Italy guaranteed to keep the Rhineland as a demilitarised zone and sent in the Wehrmacht.

'Tonight for the first time since 1870, grey-clad German soldiers and blue-clad French troops face each other across the upper Rhine,' wrote Shirer in his diary. 'The Reichstag, more tense than I have ever felt it (apparently the hand-picked deputies on the main floor had not yet been told what had happened, though they knew something was afoot), began promptly at noon.'

Hitler began with a long harangue on the dangers of Bolshevism and then claimed that the soon-to-be-signed Franco–Soviet Pact had invalidated the Locarno Pact. In the interests of the 'primitive rights' of the German people to the security of their frontier and the safeguarding of their defence, the German government had re-established the absolute and unrestricted sovereignty of the Reich in the demilitarised zone, he said.

> Now the six hundred deputies, personal appointees all of Hitler, little men with big bodies and bulging necks and cropped hair and pouched bellies and brown uniforms and heavy boots, little men of clay in his fine arms, leap to their feet like automatons, their right arms upstretched in the Nazi salute, and scream 'Heils', the first two or three wildly, the next twenty-five in unison. Hitler raises his hand for silence. It comes slowly. Slowly the automatons sit down. Hitler now has them in his claws.
>
> He appears to sense it. He says in a deep, resonant voice: 'Men of the German Reichstag.' The silence is utter. 'In this historic hour, when in the Reich's western provinces, German troops are at this minute marching into their future peace-time garrisons, we all unite in two sacred vows.' He can go no further.
>
> It is news to this hysterical 'parliamentary' mob that German soldiers are already on the move into the Rhineland. All the militarism in their German blood surges to their heads. They spring, yelling and crying, to their feet. Their hands are raised in slavish salute, their faces now contorted with hysteria, their mouths wide open, shouting, shouting, their eyes, burning with fanaticism, glued on the new god, the Messiah.

Hitler vowed not to yield to any forceful response and pledged to make every effort to maintain peace in Europe. He had taken an immense risk. Had the French government sent in troops, it would undoubtedly have forced the Germans to retreat in a humiliating defeat for Hitler. But the French chose instead to appeal weakly to the League of Nations while the British could scarcely hide their indifference. Indeed, in some quarters in London, the reoccupation of the Rhineland was greeted with relief.

'Germany's latest stroke may be said to have cleared the air,' claimed the *Daily Mail*. 'This is a moment when it is most important to beware of the Bolshevik trouble-makers. Their aim, as French critics have pointed out in the debates on the unfortunate pact with the Soviet Union, is to involve the Great Powers of Europe in a suicidal war.'

The 1936 Winter Olympics, followed by the summer Olympics in Berlin, placed the eyes of the world on Germany and took the pressure off the Jews, forestalling a predicted pogrom over the murder by a Jewish protestor of Wilhelm Gustloff, the Nazi Party representative in Switzerland.

Within hours of Gustloff's death, strict orders had been passed down that there were to be no retaliatory actions that might cause damage to the Winter Olympics which were opening that day in Garmisch-Partenkirchen. All over Germany, anti-Jewish signs were taken down and the open violence on the streets subsided. But behind the scenes the pressure on the Jews continued.

'The persecution is as relentless as ever though perhaps more subtle in method,' Frank told London. 'I venture to submit that German Jews should be encouraged to emigrate to Palestine in preference to any other country. I foresee anti-semitism rising in other countries if the inflow of Jews becomes too noticeable to the native population. It is to be hoped the economic situation of Palestine will enable the Government to increase the next quota.'

But this was a vain hope. The increased Jewish emigration to Palestine was now causing problems for the British Mandate authorities. In April 1936, the Arabs declared a general strike, attacking Jewish property and killing twenty-one Jews. As the protests escalated through the summer into an Arab revolt, the British clamped down dramatically on the number of Jews to be allowed into Palestine.

'After the Arab unrest began, the British Government limited the influx of Jews to Palestine more and more severely,' said Benno Cohn, co-chairman of the German Zionist Organisation.

And the more time went on and the greater the power of the Nazis and the fear of them grew, the more severely immigration was restricted.

It was the period of the British policy of appeasement when everything was done in Britain to placate the Nazis and to reduce Arab pressure in Palestine and the whole of the Middle East to a minimum. There were British envoys in posts in Berlin at that time who carried out London's policy to the letter, who were impervious to humanitarian considerations and who more often worked for the greater good of the Nazi regime in friendly cooperation with its ministers.

One man stood out above all others. Captain Foley had to carry out official policy. A happy chance had however brought to the post in Berlin a man who not only fully understood the orders issued to him but also had a heart for the people who often stood in long, anxious queues before him. He took advantage of his powers in so broadminded a way that many who under a stricter interpretation of orders would probably have been refused, were issued with the coveted visas to Palestine. To many who had to deal with him, he appeared almost as a saint.

Despite the constant attention of the Gestapo, Frank and his staff still had no diplomatic immunity and lived in constant risk of being denounced as spies. His position had been made increasingly difficult by Landau, who, having come upon hard times, had published his memoirs. They disclosed that he had been made head of the British Secret Service in Berlin, under cover of the role of Passport Control Officer, and that on leaving he had handed over to a former colleague in the Intelligence Corps – 'Capt Frank Foley'.

Shortly after the book's publication, the German authorities warned the population to be on the lookout for foreign spies. 'A large number of spies are busy in Germany collecting all particulars, especially with regard to the possibilities of economic mobilisations,' the government announced. 'Spies must be energetically brought to book. Great reserve must be shown towards all foreigners encountered in public houses, railway compartments, etc.'

As a result of the spy mania, the British consul in Hanover, Captain W. C. R. Aue, had his official recognition withdrawn, having reported to his superiors 'certain matters of common knowledge in Hanover regarding German re-armament which had come to his attention in a professional capacity'.

Frank remained cool in the face of the Gestapo pressure, which was largely confined to hassling the Jews who flooded the Passport Control Offices in Tiergartenstrasse 17, looking for visas.

'There would be lots of people waiting for Foley to hand out visas so the Gestapo would come round and try to frighten them away,' one former colleague in MI6 said. 'Foley would come out and say: "You gentlemen have come to apply for a visa I suppose. Could you join the queue?" And when they said: "No we haven't," he'd reply: "Well, could you kindly get out because this room's a bit crowded." He was a quite outstanding officer.'

Chapter 9

'Like Vultures Swarming Down'

The enforced Aryanisation of Jewish businesses continued throughout 1937, taking a variety of forms from repeated attacks by young thugs – breaking windows, daubing graffiti on shopfronts and hassling customers – to more pragmatic decisions by large companies to pay off Jewish directors.

There was no shortage of unscrupulous Aryan businessmen prepared to take advantage of the attacks to buy out their Jewish competitors at knock-down prices, and sharp practice was endemic. One Munich businessman refused to serve as a consultant on Aryanisation, telling the authorities that while he was a member of both the party and the SA, and naturally an admirer of Hitler, he was disgusted by the 'brutal and extraordinary' methods employed by those seeking to take over Jewish firms.

'From now on, I refuse to be involved in any way with Aryanisations, although this means losing a handsome fee,' he said.

> As an old, honest and upstanding businessman, I no longer stand by and countenance the way many 'Aryan' businessmen, entrepreneurs and the like are shamelessly attempting to grab up Jewish shops and factories etc. as cheaply as possible and for a ridiculous price. These people are like vultures swarming down,

their eyes bleary, their tongues hanging out with greed to feed upon the Jewish carcass.

From the middle of 1937, a further obstacle was placed in the way of Jewish emigration when the authorities began confiscating passports, or turning them into 'Inland Passports' by stamping them with the words 'not for countries abroad'. But for non-Jews, life in Berlin seemed to go on as normal. Frederick Winterbotham, the head of air intelligence in MI6, made a brief trip to the German capital to visit one of his own private intelligence sources.

'Berlin was gay that summer for boys and girls,' he said.

> Kranzlers restaurant on the Kurfürstendamm was packed out and the pavements in the evenings were crowded. True it was difficult to tell whether or not you were being accosted by a boy or a girl but that was not unusual in Berlin. The Kakadu Bar did great business though now it was more or less given over to foreigners and Charlie preferred the little bars with the more intimate barmaids. There was a spirit of: Let us make merry for tomorrow . . .

Hitler had been careful not to provoke a confrontation with either of the Christian Churches. He reached a concordat with the Catholic Church under which it was to stay out of politics, and united all the Protestant denominations under a pro-Nazi bishop. But there were a number of outspoken critics within the various Churches. The Protestant dissenters gathered themselves together in an alternative Confessional Church. But even this was infiltrated by the Nazis.

Inge Fehr was confirmed as a Lutheran in Berlin's Kaiser-Wilhelms-Gedächtniskirche by Pastor Gerhard Jacobi, one of the leaders of the Confessional Church, in 1937. 'Pastor Jacobi came to see my father shortly afterwards to have new glasses prescribed. He told us that his spectacles were broken in a fist fight with Pastor Hauk with whom he shared the Gedächtniskirche. Pastor Hauk wanted to put Hitler's photograph on the altar and he had tried to stop him.'

One of the leaders of the Confessional Church, and the most prominent of the Protestant critics of Hitler, was Martin Niemöller, a former U-boat commander and a popular First World War hero. In July 1937, the Gestapo broke up a meeting at his house and arrested him. They threw him into Moabit prison where he was visited by the prison chaplain who asked: 'But brother why are you in prison?' Niemöller replied: 'Brother, why are you *not* in prison?'

Niemöller was tried for 'incitement and disparagement' of state leaders and sent to Sachsenhausen concentration camp as a 'personal prisoner of the Führer'. Miraculously, he survived the war and was liberated from Dachau by American troops.

Shortly after his arrest, the Nazis taken the opportunity afforded by the British expulsion of three German journalists to get rid of another prominent critic of the regime, Frank's friend Norman Ebbutt, Berlin correspondent of *The Times*.

'He was expelled for telling the truth and warning the world of what was coming,' Frank told his niece. William Shirer noted in his diary that the Nazis had taken 'the opportunity to get rid of a man they've hated and feared for years because of his exhaustive knowledge of this country and of what was going on behind the scenes'.

Such expulsions soon became a regular feature in the British community, one of Frank's passport clerks recalled. 'There were all sorts of people being expelled. They would have these huge parties where everything had to be sold or given away. They would say: "Oh, do take something", and you saw people going away lumbered down with bits of furniture. They just didn't want to leave it behind but they couldn't possibly take it with them.'

Shirer joined the throng of friends and colleagues who gathered to say goodbye to Ebbutt. 'We gave Norman a great send-off at the Charlottenburger station,' he wrote. 'The platform full of Gestapo agents noting down our names and photographing us. Ebbutt terribly high-strung, but moved by our sincere, if boisterous, demonstration of farewell.'

As 1938 began, the confiscation of passports spread nationwide. The Gestapo issued instructions that 'Jews may only have passports if they leave the country permanently or if German trade will be served by the granting of a passport.' The replacement of Economy Minister Hjalmar Schacht by the Nazi Walter Funk led to an increased drive for Aryanisation of Jewish businesses, which were now excluded from all public contract work.

'Signs are not wanting that Jews are but grist to the Nazi mill which is slowly but surely grinding them to destitution,' one British official wrote. 'The year 1937 was one of great despondency for the Jews: 1938 is charged with grave apprehension.'

In early 1938, General Werner von Blomberg, the German War Minister, married, with Hitler and Göring as witnesses. Shortly afterwards, it was disclosed that his wife had a dubious past and Blomberg was forced to resign.

His obvious successor, the Wehrmacht Supreme Commander General Werner von Fritsch, was smeared with evidence, concocted by the Gestapo, that he was homosexual. Hitler seized on the situation to get rid of a number of generals who, like Fritsch, had been opposed to measures that might lead to war, and made himself Supreme Commander of the Wehrmacht.

In early February 1938, Hitler ordered the Austrian Chancellor, Kurt von Schuschnigg, to appear before him at Berchtesgarten and, with three of the new Wehrmacht High Command sitting in an adjoining room to make sure he got the point, demanded that all Nazis imprisoned in Austria be released, that the party be allowed to act as it liked, and that a leading Austrian Nazi, Arthur Seyss-Inquart, be made Interior Minister.

'The Führer went so far as to threaten that in the case of disorders in Austria, he would "march", being unable to resist any longer the pleas of the "downtrodden German population in Austria",' wrote Eric Gedye, Vienna Correspondent of the *Daily Telegraph*.

Von Schuschnigg acquiesced on all counts. Within days, Austrian Nazis were making preparations to take over Jewish firms in confident expectation that the country was about to become part of Greater Germany.

But after returning to Vienna, the Austrian Chancellor attempted to frustrate Hitler's ambitions for an expanded German state, calling a plebiscite on whether or not Austria should remain independent. If the Austrians were allowed to vote, there was only likely to be one result, and it would signify a devastating rejection of Hitler, with potentially catastrophic consequences for the Nazis in Germany.

On 12 March, German troops crossed the border into Austria, and on the following day the Anschluss was declared. Austria was now Ostmark, a province of the German Reich with no more separate rights than Saxony or Bavaria. The anti-Semitic measures that had taken five years to perfect in Germany hit Austria's 190,000 Jews in the space of a few days.

Self-styled 'Commissars' plundered Jewish shops and homes in the name of 'Aryanisation'. Thousands of Jews, men, women and children, were beaten up in the street. Elderly women and men were forced to scrub the pavements with acid while crowds watched, laughing and jeering. Rabbis were made to dance in their synagogues for the amusement of brown-shirted young Nazis, as their sacred scrolls were destroyed in the streets. Hundreds of Jews were packed on to trains to be transported across the border to Dachau and to the newly opened concentration camp at Buchenwald, near Weimar. Eric Gedye recalled the events that followed the suicide of a young Jewish doctor and his mother.

'From my window,' Gedye wrote,

> I could watch for many days how they would arrest Jewish passers-by – generally doctors, lawyers or merchants, for they preferred their victims to belong to the better educated classes – and force them to scrub, polish and beat carpets in the flat where the tragedy had taken place, while insisting that the doctor's non-Jewish maid should sit at ease in a chair and look on. When I say that one's Jewish friends spoke to one of their intention to commit suicide with no more emotion than they had formerly talked of making an hour's journey by train, I cannot expect to be believed.

Within a month of the Anschluss, more than five hundred Jews had committed suicide.

They swamped the foreign consulates, trying to find a way out. 'The distress and despair amongst the Jews is appalling,' the British consul-general in Vienna told London. 'This Consulate-General is literally besieged every day by hundreds of Jews who have been told to leave the country and who come vainly searching for a visa to go anywhere. Unless pressure from international quarters can be brought to bear upon the Reich Government to force them to intervene in Austria, it is impossible to predict the horrors which may come about.'

The Vienna head of station, Thomas Kendrick, and his deputy now found themselves facing the same problems that had confronted Frank for the past five years.

'They were queuing up all night,' the deputy recalled.

> They used to fill the courtyard by about nine o'clock in the morning and I used to stand on the steps and give them a lecture on what chance they had of getting away. 'Your only chance of getting to Palestine now is either if you've got relatives or a capitalist visa. But you might be able to get to Grenada. You might be able to get to Jamaica. India will only take you if you are a qualified dentist,' and so on.
>
> Then during the day they were coming in one after the other. I had a whole lot of women who were examiners working for me spread through the office. But the stories were so terrible. That they had been separated from their children. That they had seen loved ones go off in a Nazi convoy with the Gestapo and so on and it just went on all day and at the end of it it made one desperately unhappy that you could do nothing. The American vice-consul who was a pal of mine said: 'I've got to the point where if any woman leaves my office not in tears, I feel I haven't done my job.' It was a dreadful, dreadful time.

Those queuing for visas were not exempt from the Nazi harassment, the consul-general noted. 'On Monday morning, the SA and SS brought several motor cars on to the street where the

Consulate-General is situated, collected Jews from neighbouring offices and shops and forced them to wash the motor cars in the pouring rain,' he noted. 'At that time, there were great numbers of Jews in the Consulate-General applying for immigration certificates to various parts of the British empire and as they left the building they too were seized and forced to wash the cars.'

The German process of Aryanisation was subtlety itself compared to its Austrian equivalent. A few days after the Anschluss, Franz Rothenberg, the Jewish chairman of Kreditanstalt, the country's largest bank, was taken for a drive by a group of storm troopers who killed him by throwing him out of the car at speed. Isidor Pollack, director-general of the chemical company Pulverfabrik, died from injuries sustained during an SA search of his home.

The Deutsche Bank took over Kreditanstalt while the German chemical giant I G Farben 'Aryanised' Pulverfabrik. I G Farben had started the Nazi rule with a large number of Jewish directors. It was to end it by supplying Zyklon B to Auschwitz.

With no requirement for visas to Britain, a flood of Austrian refugees appeared at Croydon Airport and at the seaports, provoking near-panic within the Home Office. Sir Samuel Hoare, the then Home Secretary, told the Cabinet that 'a curious story had reached him from MI5 suggesting the Germans were anxious to inundate this country with Jews with a view to creating a Jewish problem in this country'. The Cabinet set up a sub-committee to look into the Austrian refugee problem, 'adopting as humane an attitude as possible and at the same time avoiding the creation of a Jewish problem in this country'.

After taking advice from a variety of quarters, including Jewish relief organisations and both MI5 and MI6, the committee recommended the reintroduction of visas between Britain and Germany on the grounds that it would be 'impossible to admit indiscriminately all persons claiming to be refugees, and if would-be immigrants were to arrive in large numbers without any preliminary examination, great difficulty would be created at the ports and unnecessary hardship might be inflicted on applicants whom it might be found necessary to reject'.

Passport Control Officers were urged to ensure that no potential refugees came to Britain on a visitor's visa.

> Such persons, particularly those who appear to be of Jewish or partly Jewish origin, or have non-Aryan affiliations, should be discreetly questioned as to their family circumstances, and how their business or employment has been affected by recent events; and if it is suspected that emigration is intended, the applicant should be invited to say so frankly. If he persists that a visit only is intended, he should be warned that if he overstays the period allowed, steps will be taken to compel him to return to Germany or Austria.

Under pressure from unions and professional organisations, the entry requirements for Britain were even stricter than those for Palestine. If Frank were to follow the rules to the letter, he would not be able to issue visas to an apparently all-embracing list of people.

The Foreign Office issued a guide as to who might be regarded as unsuitable: 'Small shopkeepers, retail traders, artisans, and persons likely to seek employment. Agents and middlemen, whose livelihood depends on commission and, therefore, on trade activity. Minor musicians and commercial artists of all kinds. The rank and file of professional men – lawyers, doctors, dentists.'

As the use of such descriptions as 'minor' and 'rank and file' implied, exceptions could be made for the great and good, who it could be argued would be 'an asset to the United Kingdom', although a more cynical view might be that their exclusion would have been more likely to lead to damaging publicity and questions in the House of Commons. Otherwise, virtually anyone in the Jewish community who did not have a substantial private income was excluded.

With the forced Aryanisation of business, the difficulty of obtaining anything like the real value of investments, the *Reichsfluchtsteuer*, and the limitations on the exchange of marks for foreign currency, very few people who did not have relatives already in Britain to support them would now qualify for a British visa.

Shortly before the regulations came in, Foley managed to get Hilde Rosbaud, the Jewish wife of his promising scientific source Paul Rosbaud, to London, where friends had already found her a small flat.

Among those who were not allowed to emigrate to Britain, Palestine or the colonies were the infirm, anyone with a criminal record, those who could not support themselves and 'people with unacceptable politics' – a euphemism for communists. One day, Israel and Pollack sent Frank a young Jewish woman, barely more than a girl, carrying a young baby. She had just spent two years in Wandbeck prison for being a communist. Her boyfriend, the father of her child, had already made his way to Southern Rhodesia and she wanted to join him.

The woman had an exit permit from the Gestapo to leave. But as well as being a communist, she had no money and no passport. The Southern Rhodesian consulate would have turned her down flat. Fortunately she went first to the Hilfsverein – to Israel and Pollack. 'It was clear that to all intents and purposes a prison sentence for admitting being a communist excluded any successful visa application,' Pollack said. 'The girl and her child were on a straight road to a concentration camp.'

They decided to send her to Frank, who as British Passport Control Officer was entitled to issue visas to anywhere in the Empire, including Southern Rhodesia. When she reached the end of the long queue at the tiny office in Tiergartenstrasse 17, the examiner told her that with her record, her politics and her lack of money, she had no chance of getting a visa. But since she was trying to join the father of her child, he took the details of the case into Frank's office to seek his advice.

'How old is she?' Frank asked. Told that she was only nineteen, he replied: 'She was in prison for two years. That means she must have been just 17 when she was a communist. It seems to me that at that age anyone is likely to commit a youthful folly without being aware of the consequences. Tell her to come and see me tomorrow. I want to see her, then I will decide.' When the girl went back the next day, Frank issued her with a visa. She sailed for Southern Rhodesia from Bremerhaven just twelve hours before her Gestapo exit permit expired.

'Immigration rules were very strict in those days of economic depression in order to prevent the entry of additional manpower looking for employment,' Pollack said.

> But in the conflict between official duty and human duty Captain Foley decided unreservedly for the fulfilling of his human duty.
>
> He never chose the easy way out. He never tried to make himself popular with the ambassador or the Home Office by giving a strict and narrow interpretation of the rules. He did not mind incurring the displeasure of top officials in the British Foreign Office and Home Office. On the contrary, he was not above sophistic interpretation if he could help Jews to emigrate.

On the day after the young Jewish communist girl sailed for Rhodesia, the Gestapo rang Pollack. He was responsible for the woman. Where was she? 'On board a Dutch steamer somewhere between Bremerhaven and Rotterdam,' Pollack told them. 'But if you want to know exactly where she is ask the customs officials at Bremerhaven. They would obviously know far better than I.'

'I know already,' the Gestapo official replied. 'I have all the details in front of me. I just wanted to be sure that everything was the way it should be with you, that you were nervous. Heil Hitler.' It might have been official policy to force them to leave, but nothing was to be made easy for the Jews.

Chapter 10

Jews and Dogs Not Wanted

Another young Jewish woman who arrived in Frank's office in the summer of 1938 was Adele Wertheimer. Her husband Leopold, a textile merchant, had been thrown into jail in Nuremberg after a Nazi business rival took him to court, claiming that as a Jew he was illegally taking business away from him.

The charge was so obviously trumped up that the court ordered a one-year sentence, the minimum it could award. Their son Simon, just seven at the time, recalled being bullied by the other children at his school in Neumarkt, Bavaria, and seeing signs on shops and *Gasthaüse* saying: 'Jews and dogs not wanted.'

'I remember I fell into a well,' he said. 'My mother saved me. I was backing away from children who were shouting at me, Jew or whatever, and I was throwing stones at them and as I backed away I fell into a big well.'

As the persecution grew, the family were forced to move out of their large house and their maid was no longer allowed to work for them. Since his grandmother and aunt lived in Nuremberg, he and his mother moved in with them so she could visit his father more easily and Simon could go to a Jewish school.

By now, Jews released from prison were frequently being collected and taken straight to prison camps. All their friends and relatives told Adele Wertheimer she should have the family's emigration papers ready before her husband came out. She made numerous frantic attempts to get a visa. She went to the British consuls in Munich and Frankfurt, to the Jewish Agency, which could also issue visas to Palestine, to the Zionist Organisation and to the Hilfsverein.

'She went here, there and everywhere but everywhere she was turned down,' said Simon Wertheimer.

> Then she was told that the last hope, the last possible chance was Capt Foley. So in desperation she and her sister went to Berlin to see him. I don't know how long it took her to get an interview but it was all done in a day.
>
> She said he was very kind and interested, not officious at all. He took the time to calm her down and he listened very attentively. He explained to her the immigration restrictions and the long waiting list but in the end he told her to come back in a couple of hours. When she returned the *Zertifikaten* for my parents and myself were waiting for her. He said he was giving it for the child.

A few weeks after Leopold Wertheimer got out of prison, the family left for Palestine. Simon Wertheimer's aunt had fallen in love and was engaged to be married, so she stayed behind. By the time she decided things were so bad she must leave it was too late. She would die in Treblinka, just one of the estimated 840,000 who went to the gas chambers in that camp alone.

'My mother talked about Capt Foley a lot,' Simon Wertheimer said. 'She wrote to him in Berlin telling him how we were and he wrote back to her, saying he was glad that I was making good progress at school. She always said he saved our lives. She held him up as an example I had to live up to. She would say: "We are here because of him".'

As if in reaction to the anti-Semitic excesses taking place in Austria, the campaign against Germany's Jews accelerated at a far more rapid pace than had been evident in the previous two years.

Sir Nevile Henderson, the new ambassador in Berlin, told the Foreign Office that 'a new and intensified campaign against the Jews' had been put in place. 'It has been variously ascribed to the influx of Jews from Vienna who have been talking freely of "escaping to Berlin", to anxiety not to be outdone by Austrian National-Socialists who have been setting a hot pace, and to the reputed success of the latter's endeavours in driving very large numbers of Jews to emigration.'

Göring, in his role as Commissioner for the Four-Year Plan, ordered that all Jews possessing more than 5,000 marks, about £250 at the then exchange rate, were to declare it so that it could be 'used in accordance with the requirements of German business and industry'. Failure to comply with the new regulation was punishable by a maximum sentence of ten years' imprisonment.

The Times reported that Jewish funds appropriated under Göring's order were expected to be funnelled into the Reichswerke Hermann Göring AG, which need capital to develop a foundry. Welcoming the move, with what can only be taken to be unintended irony, the Nazi newspaper *Der Angriff* noted: 'We can assume with complete certainty that a large proportion of this wealth was earned by improper methods. This regulation will be greeted by all Germans as a true expression of popular right and as an act of liberation.'

Even this was not enough for *SA-Mann*, the Brownshirts' journal, which called for emigrating Jews to be stripped of all their possessions and the remainder reduced to starvation in the ghetto. 'Only when the Jew is isolated, when he can do business with no one but Jews, when no ear will be exposed to his cackle, then alone will the domestic Jewish problem be solved,' it said. Shortly afterwards, the 25 per cent *Reichsfluchtssteuer* 'flight tax' was imposed on all wealthy Jews, regardless of whether or not they intended to emigrate.

A boycott of 'non-Aryan' businesses in Wiesbaden and a court ruling that employers were entitled to dismiss instantly anyone caught buying goods from Jewish shops produced devastating consequences. 'One shopkeeper whose establishment was pick-eted has I learn committed suicide and it is reported that four shopkeepers at Wiesbaden similarly placed have also committed suicide,' wrote one of Frank's colleagues.

On a tour of Berlin's East End, Frank himself found that large numbers of Jewish shops were being 'painted with the word "Jew", with offensive expressions or even with a representation of a Jew hanging from a gallows'.

The task of those defacing the shops, many of whom were members of the Hitler Youth, had been made easier by an order the previous day to all Jewish shopkeepers that they should write their names on their shops in white paint. The painters were being followed by large groups of people cheering them on. Many of the shops had been looted and seven had been totally gutted by fire.

Meanwhile, the list of occupations from which Jews were excluded was expanded to include stockbrokers, estate agents, travel agents, sales representatives or 'brokers of any kind'.

The health authorities announced that from the end of September the permits allowing Jewish doctors to practise would cease to be valid. From November, the remaining Jewish lawyers were to be excluded from the Bar. Jewish doctors and lawyers would only be able to work for Jews, one British consular official noted, adding: 'It is becoming more and more difficult for the Jews remaining in Germany to earn a living.'

The most worrying aspect of the new campaign was that while previously the actions against the Jews had been led by the SA, now they were being orchestrated by the police, Henderson said.

> Very large numbers of arrests are reported from all over Germany, the majority on flimsy excuses, and the victims seem mainly to have been transported direct to concentration camps.
>
> The figure of several thousand cases has been mentioned to me. A series of raids has been carried out on cafés and other resorts in the Kurfürstendamm area of Berlin which are known to be frequented by Jews and large numbers have been hauled off to police headquarters.

> There the catch is examined and if any previous conviction, even against the traffic regulations, can be proved the individual concerned is immediately sent to a concentration camp to emerge, if he is lucky, in a few months' time on a promise to emigrate immediately. Other Jews have simply disappeared after leaving home in the morning and have not been heard of since.

Shortly before the round-ups began, Goebbels, in his role as Gauleiter of Berlin, had told Count Wolf Heinrich Helldorf, the city's chief of police, that he wanted proposals for new ways of segregating and harassing the Jews. 'Against all sentimentality,' he recorded in his diary after addressing three hundred of the city's police officers. 'The motto is not law but harassment. The Jews must get out of Berlin. The Police will help.'

The fate of those arrested by the police was described by Wilfred Israel in a letter to a leading British Jew. 'They are suffering the tortures of hell in one of the new concentration camps, the so-called quarries of death,' he wrote. 'Discipline is enforced by lashing old and young to tree trunks and beating them. The only way to escape this torture is to run into wire entanglements loaded with high-tension electricity. Deaths are frequent for this and other reasons.'

Prior to the Anschluss, the Jews were a minority inside the concentration camps, but in its wake, increasing numbers were incarcerated. Frank reported 'systematic house-to-house searches for, and arrests of, Jews so that they could be arrested and detained in concentration camps,' adding: 'It is no exaggeration to say that Jews have been hunted like rats in their homes, and for fear of arrest many sleep at a different address overnight.'

It was not just the Jews who were now in danger. If Frank had any doubts as to his own position, they were dispelled in August 1938 when Captain Thomas Kendrick, the Passport Control Officer and MI6 head of station in Vienna, was arrested by the German authorities as he and his wife left on holiday.

Kendrick was driven back to Vienna and held in the Hotel Metropole, the Gestapo headquarters, 'because proofs are to hand that he engaged in espionage'. One former MI6 officer who knew Kendrick said: 'They shut him up for two days. I don't think they tortured him but they gave him a bad time. They showed him just how much they knew which was really terrifying.' Fearing for the safety of Frank and his MI6 staff, Hugh 'Quex' Sinclair, the then Chief of the Secret Service, recalled them to London.

Since the Anschluss, there had been repeated reports from MI6 agents and military contacts that Hitler also intended to march into the Sudetenland, where the majority of the population was of German origin. The General Staff had been ordered to prepare a plan of invasion in April, but it was not until 12 September that German troops were moved to the border.

In an atmosphere of crisis that threatened to drag both Britain and France into a war for which neither side was prepared, Sinclair was asked by Chamberlain to advise him on his next move. MI6 had repeatedly warned of the dangers of allowing German rearmament to go on unhindered. But now Sinclair backed his Prime Minister's preference for appeasement, if only to give time to build up Britain's own defences.

'It seems undesirable to give Hitler any pretext for saying Germany is being encircled or that hostile combinations are being built up against her,' Sinclair wrote. Britain should aim to achieve a peaceful separation of the Sudetenland from Czechoslovakia 'and make the Czechs realise they stand alone if they refuse such a solution'.

A similar approach should be adopted to Germany's other territorial gains, Sinclair suggested.

> International steps of some sort should be taken, without undue delay, to see what really legitimate grievances Germany has and what surgical operations are necessary to rectify them.
>
> It may be argued that this would be giving in to Germany, strengthening Hitler's position and encouraging him to go to extremes. Better however that realities be faced and that wrongs if they do exist be righted than leave it to Hitler to do the righting in his own way and time. Particularly, if concurrently we and

the French unremittingly build up our own strength and lessen
Germany's potentialities for making trouble. Our only chance of
preserving peace is to be ready for war on any scale.

Chamberlain was certainly in no need of such encouragement. A
few months earlier he had declared: 'In war, whichever side may
call itself the victor, there are no winners, but all are losers.'

After a period of shuttling between Germany and London in
a vain attempt to wring any sort of concession out of Hitler, he
gave further vent to his feelings in a radio broadcast: 'How horrible,
fantastic, incredible it is that we should be digging trenches and
trying on gas masks here because of a quarrel in a far-away country
of which we know nothing.'

A few days later, at the Munich Conference, Chamberlain was
party to the craven meetings that, presumably on Sinclair's advice,
conceded far more to Hitler than even he was demanding.

'The Munich conference was in every way a sad affair,' wrote
Ivone Kirkpatrick, Frank's former First World War colleague, who
was now a First Secretary in the Berlin embassy.

> I can remember no redeeming features.
> The French were resolved to reach agreement at any cost.
> They were a harried lot of men who showed no shame at being
> parties to the dismemberment of their ally. In fact nerves were
> so on edge that from time to time they gave the impression
> that Czechoslovakia was to be blamed for having brought all this
> trouble on us. In this atmosphere, Hitler had little difficulty in
> getting his way.

Chamberlain and his French counterpart, Edouard Daladier,
advised the Czechoslovakian President Eduard Benes to accept
Hitler's demands. The British Prime Minister then flew back to
Croydon, clutching the agreement which he claimed meant 'peace
for our time . . . peace with honour'.

The reduction in tension caused by the Munich Agreement
allowed Frank and his staff to return to Berlin, to a difficult
combination of intelligence-gathering and helping the Jews in

a situation where there was increasing reluctance in some quarters to see them given shelter.

The right-wing *Daily Express* claimed that there was an 'underground railway' smuggling Jews into Britain. Perhaps more representative of the general feeling was the view of the left-wing *Daily Herald* that while the refugees were clearly innocent victims 'charity begins at home and we shall never keep the standards that have been won for us, if the influx of aliens goes on unchecked'.

A London magistrate sent three refugees to prison for landing in the country without permission, declaring that it was becoming an outrage the way in which stateless Jews were 'pouring in from every port of this country'. As far as he was concerned, he intended to enforce the law to the fullest extent.

One of Frank's agents within Berlin's Jewish community was Willi Preis, a prominent furrier whose contacts within the German fur trade allowed him to pick up a good deal of information on what the Nazi leaders were doing, particularly – given their tendency to shower expensive gifts like fur coats on their mistresses – within their private lives.

Shortly after Frank arrived back in Berlin, Preis was arrested and taken to the Gestapo headquarters on the Alexanderplatz. He managed to contact his wife Lotte and told her to get in touch with Frank Foley at the British Passport Control Office in the Tiergartenstrasse.

'My mother proceeded to the British consulate and found both the entrances and staircases crammed with people asking for various services and assistance,' said Preis's son Ohniel. 'My mother took out of her bag a visiting card of my father's and was able to attract the attention of one of Mr Foley's secretaries who was able to lead my mother into the offices where Mr Foley was contacted.'

Frank hurried over to the Alexanderplatz with a visa for Willi and Lotte Preis and their two children Ohniel and his sixteen-year-old sister Eli. 'My father was released and brought to the airport for a flight to Holland the same night.'

Another of the tragic cases waiting for Frank on his return was that of the daughter of a young Nazi. Martyl Karweik was a

Hamburg when Foley was working there as a teacher before the First World
War

Members of the Inns of Court Officer Training Corps camped out in
'Kitchener's Field' at Berkhamsted (*Imperial War Museum*)

The permanent staff of the Inns of Court Officer Training Corps outside the officers' mess in Berkhamsted (*Imperial War Museum*)

Members of the Inns of Court Officer Training Corps on parade at Berkhamsted (*Imperial War Museum*)

Foley's parents
Isabella and
Andrew Wood
Foley

Kay (facing camera)
with her sister Jane,
around the time of her
engagement to Foley
(*William Lee Kelley*)

1911		Marriage solemnized at	The Parish Church			in the	Parish	
		of S. Saviour's Dartmouth				in the County of	Devon.	
No.	When Married.	Name and Surname.	Age.	Condition.	Rank or Profession	Residence at the time of Marriage	Father's Name and Surname.	Rank or Profession of Fa...
571	June 24	Francis Edward Foley	36	Bachelor	Captain & Passport Control Officer.	St. George's Berlin	Andrew Wood Foley	Civil Engineer
	1911	Katharine Eva Lee	24	Spinster	—	Dartmouth	William John Lee	Horse Proprietor.

Married in the Parish Church according to the Rites and Ceremonies of the Established Church by — or after Banns by

This Marriage was solemnized between us, { Francis Edward Foley / Katharine Eva Lee } in the Presence of us, { Wm. J. Lee / Eva Lee. }

J. Fred V. Lee
Rector of Crawford Micia.

The Foleys' wedding certificate

Foley pictured on the balcony of couple's Wilhelmsdorf flat shortly after his marriage to Kay

Kay Foley and her sister Jane attending a German Foreign Ministry dinner at which they were received by Hitler (*The Rev. John B. Kelley*)

Wilfred Israel (front of picture) with his mother Amy and brother Herbert

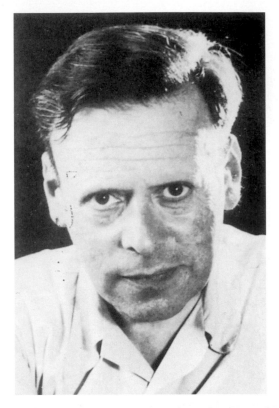

Hubert Pollack, one of Foley's main agents both in helping the Jews and on espionage matters

Frank and Ursula on holiday in England, July 1933 (*William Lee Kelley*)

Josef Goebbels,
Hitler's Propaganda
Minister

Reichsmarschall
Hermann Göring,
Hitler's chosen
successor

Rudolf Hess, Hitler's deputy, with the Führer before his flight to England

Wolfgang Meyer-Michael, a prominent Jewish artist granted a 'capitalist visa' for Palestine on the basis of a promise of funds which both he and Foley knew to be false

Mischling — half-Jewish, half-Aryan. Her father, anxious to further his party career, had divorced Martyl's mother and disowned his daughter. But fortunately, she and her mother lived near a leading German scientist who had influence with those who could get them out.

Hans Ferdinand Meyer had been born in Pforzheim on 23 October 1895. He joined the Imperial German Army during the First World War but was disabled on his first day at the front. Discharged from the army, he went to college, studying electronics under the Nobel Prize-winner Philipp Lenard before becoming a leading expert in the field, working as head of research and development for the German company Siemens.

Mayer, who opposed the Nazis' policies towards the Jews, had close contacts with Cobden Turner, a representative of the British General Electric Company, and told him Martyl Karweik's sad story.

'The mother had received an order of expulsion, but was not allowed to take Martyl with her because she was half-Aryan,' Mayer said. 'The father did not want to take Martyl because she was half-Jewish. This meant eventually confinement to a forced-labour camp, a place of no return.'

Turner was visibly affected by this case. Not long afterwards he went to see Foley, who gave him a passport for Martyl, allowing her to return with Turner to England, where she lived as a member of his family until after the war, when she joined her mother in New York.

Frank had clearly bent the rules in giving Martyl a passport as if she were the daughter of Turner. He wanted to know all the details of the case before doing so, and told the British engineer to ask Mayer if he was willing to tell the British about any of the top-secret government projects Siemens were working on.

Mayer was grateful that the British had assisted Martyl to escape the concentration camps. Although he told Turner that things had not yet reached a level where he was prepared to pass such details to the British, he would keep in touch. Frank's cavalier attitude to the rules would pay huge dividends once the war had begun.

Chapter 11

The Night of Broken Glass

At the same time as Martyl was having so much trouble getting out of Germany, the SS was forcing Zindel Grynszpann across the border into Poland. The Nazis' efforts to persuade 'non-Aryans' to leave had been hampered by the reluctance of the Polish authorities to allow Polish Jews living in Germany to return home. In October 1938, the government in Warsaw announced that the passports of all Poles still living abroad at the end of that month would be cancelled. The Nazis' response was swift. Himmler ordered all male Polish Jews to be taken across the border and dumped on Polish territory.

Grynszpann's eldest son Herschel was a student in Paris. But Zindel and his younger son Mordechai were dragged out of their Hanover home and put on a train with thousands of other Polish Jews. They were taken to a station close to the Polish border before being made to walk the last mile and a half on foot. 'The SS men were whipping us, those who faltered were beaten,' Zindel Grynszpann said. 'Blood flowed down the road. They treated us in a most barbaric fashion. This was the first time I had ever seen the savagery of the Germans. They shouted at us: "Run! Run!" I myself received a blow and I fell in a ditch. My son helped me, and he said: "Run, run, papa — otherwise you'll die!"'

There were twelve thousand Polish Jews in all, Grynzspann said. They were taken to the small village of Zbaszyn.

> The rain was driving hard, people were fainting. Some suffered heart attacks. Our suffering was great. We had had no food. There was no room for us and we were taken to a military camp and put in stables full of horse dung. Lorries came with bread. They threw loaves over the heads of the people. Those who caught ate. Those who didn't catch, didn't eat. More lorries with food arrived until all the people had food. Then I managed to write a letter to Herschel in Paris.

The seventeen-year-old was outraged by what his father told him. 'My heart bleeds when I think of our tragedy and that of the 12,000 Jews,' he wrote in a letter to his uncle. 'I have to protest in a way that the whole world hears.' On Monday, 7 November 1938, Herschel Grynszpann bought a pistol and went to the German embassy where he insisted he had urgent papers for the ambassador. He was taken up to see Ernst von Rath, the ambassador's private secretary. As soon as they were alone, Grynszpann fired five shots. Only two hit their mark. The first, fatal shot hit the German diplomat in the chest. The second hit him in the loin.

For the next two days, until von Rath died, the German newspapers were full of the latest news from Paris, with hysterically virulent editorials calling for 'a final settlement of the Jewish problem'. *Der Angriff*, the newspaper closest to Goebbels, published lists of streets in Berlin where Jews lived. 'We will no longer look on while Jews batten on us in Germany and outside the Reich shoot down Germans in so cowardly a fashion,' it said. SA storm troopers responded with a series of what would turn out to be relatively minor attacks on Jewish property.

Von Rath died on Wednesday, 9 February, the anniversary of Hitler's 1923 attempted putsch and a sacred day in the Nazi calendar. Hitler and Goebbels, in Munich for a meeting of the veterans of the putsch, discussed the response. The Reichsführer ordered that the nationwide series of 'spontaneous' demonstrations against the Jews sparked off by the shooting should be allowed to continue, Goebbels recorded in his diaries. 'The police should be withdrawn. For once the Jews should get the feel of popular anger.' The message to the SA storm troopers was clear.

Across the Reich, it became open season on the Jews and their property. Synagogues were set on fire or blown up with dynamite, Jewish shops were wrecked and Jews themselves beaten up on the street. Among the estimated 100 killed was the caretaker of a synagogue in Berlin's Prinzregentenstrasse who was trapped inside the building with his young family as it burned to the ground.

Inge Fehr was a student at the Goldschmidt Schule, an English Jewish school in the Grünewald district of the city.

> Our headmistress told us a pogrom was in progress. We had to evacuate because members of the Hitler Youth carrying stones were gathering at the front and they were setting other buildings alight. We were all to leave quickly by the back door and not to return to school until further notice.
>
> On my way home, I followed the smoke and arrived at the synogogue in the Fasanenstrasse which had been set alight. Crowds were watching from the opposite pavement. I then passed through the Tauentzienstrasse where I saw crowds smashing Jewish shop windows and jeering as the owners tried to salvage their goods. When I got to our house I saw that our chauffeur, who had worked for us for 12 years, had painted 'Fehr Jude' in red paint on the pavement outside.

Frank drove around the city doing what he could to help. Ohniel Preis recalled that during his childhood in Palestine his parents repeatedly mentioned 'the name of this brave official who travelled at the time of the Kristallnacht through the blazing city, reported everything he saw to the British authorities and helped many Jewish Berlin citizens'. Kay accompanied Frank on his tour of the city. 'I wore inconspicuous clothes to mingle among the crowds and I saw the Nazis defiling a synagogue and smashing the windows of Jewish shops,' she said. The extent to which the city's population became swept up in the atrocities was horrific.

'Mob law ruled in Berlin throughout this afternoon and evening as hordes of hooligans indulged in an orgy of destruction,' the *Daily Telegraph*'s correspondent Hugh Carleton Greene reported.

> On the Kurfürstendamm, the interior of every Jewish shop was systematically demolished by youths armed with hammers, brooms and lengths of lead piping. In Dobrin, a fashionable Jewish café, the mob smashed the counter and the table and chairs and then stamped cream cakes and confectionery into the floor. Weisz Czarda, a restaurant owned by a Hungarian Jew, was invaded by another horde which cast chairs and tables out on to the street.

Israel's, the department store owned by Wilfred Israel's family and one of the biggest in Europe, was among the Jewish premises destroyed in the onslaught. Ebbutt's successor as the *Times* correspondent, James Holburn, noted the leading role played by members of the Hitler Youth, directed by sinister young men who had lists of buildings and people to be attacked and were 'evidently acting according to a systematic plan'. Frequently, SA thugs simply broke into the homes of Jews and either shot them or beat them to death. The Justice Ministry ruled that no one was to be prosecuted for the murder of a Jew as long as it was not committed for 'selfish reasons'. Many of the intended victims did not wait for the knock on the door, they simply committed suicide.

'I have seen several anti-Jewish outbreaks in Germany during the last five years but never anything as nauseating as this,' Carleton Greene said.

> Racial hatred and hysteria seemed to have taken hold of otherwise decent people. I saw fashionably dressed women clapping their hands and screaming with glee while respectable middle-class mothers held up their babies to see the 'fun'. Women who remonstrated with children who were running away with toys looted from a wrecked Jewish shop were spat on and attacked by the mob.
> There were remarkably few policemen on the streets. Those who were there, when their attention was drawn to the outrages

which were proceeding before their eyes, shrugged their shoulders and refused to take any action. Several hundred Jewish shopkeepers were, however, put under 'protective custody' for attempting to shield their property. A state of hopeless panic reigns tonight throughout Jewish circles. Hundreds of Jews have gone into hiding and many businessmen and financial experts of international repute have not dared to sleep in their own homes.

Goebbels gleefully recorded the orgy of destruction in his diaries. 'From all over the Reich information is flowing in: 50, then 70 synagogues are burning. The Führer has ordered that 20–30,000 Jews should be arrested. In Berlin five, then 15 synagogues burn down. Now popular anger rages. It should be given free rein.' He issued a public statement describing the attacks as 'the justified and understandable indignation of the German people at the cowardly Jewish assassination of a German diplomat'.

The synagogue in the small town of Wittlich, on the Mosel, suffered the same fate as those in the bigger cities. 'The intricate lead crystal window above the door crashed into the street and pieces of furniture came flying through doors and windows,' one eye-witness wrote. 'A shouting SA man climbed to the roof, waving rolls of the Torah. "Wipe your asses with it, Jews," he screamed while he hurled them like bands of confetti on Karnival.'

Wim van Leer, a young Dutch Jew who had been sent to Germany by the Quakers to help get refugees out, was in Leipzig when the attacks there began. 'It must have been about seven o'clock,' he said.

It was drizzling, and there was hardly a person in the street. In the distance, uniformed men were smashing plate-glass windows. There was much shouting and clanging of approaching fire-brigade trucks. Far away, more clanging and, against the low overcast sky, a glow of distant fires.

A truck loaded with SA pulled up across the road a few houses down and some 20 young louts jumped down. One carried a clipboard and directed the men to shops and houses in various directions. Some of the storm troopers rang bells on the opposite side of the road, waited for a reaction, and if this was not forthcoming, smashed the glass windows in the door and bolted up the stairs. In the street, storm troopers with long steel pikes began smashing shop windows to the loud hooray of their mates. From the houses across the street I could hear screams and yelling, and presently men in heavy coats were being frog-marched down, their clinging wives being peeled off at the door. They were loaded onto the trucks.

For most the destination was the nearest concentration camp. While before Kristallnacht – the Night of Broken Glass, as the Nazis sneeringly dubbed the pogrom – the Jews represented a minority of the inmates of the camps, thereafter they provided the bulk of those there. The Gestapo were told that 'as many Jews, especially rich ones, are to be arrested as can be accommodated in the existing jails. For the time being only healthy men, not too old, should be arrested. Upon their arrest, the appropriate concentration camps should be contacted immediately in order to confine them to these camps as fast as possible.'

Hitler's orders were followed to the letter. More than thirty thousand Jews were rounded up and taken into 'protective custody'. The police appeared to have quotas, Benno Cohn said. When they failed to find the people listed on their clipboards, they arrested others indiscriminately off the street. Finding the offices of the Zionist Organisation wrecked by a mob, Cohn went into hiding, from where he attempted to co-ordinate rescue activities. The authorities were prepared to release only those who could get visas to emigrate.

Foley now embarked on a dangerous path, hiding a number of Jews in his home at Lessingstrasse 56, including Leo Baeck, chairman of the Association of German Rabbis. 'They would ring up and ask for help and Frank would slip down to the door late at night and let them in,' said Kay Foley. 'They knew that if they stayed in their own houses at night they ran the risk of being dragged away by the Gestapo.' Given the concern in London that

Frank might be arrested as a spy at any minute, it was a brave thing to do. But in view of what was happening to the Jews, both he and Kay believed it to be the right thing to do.

'I do not know what the Nazis would have done if they had discovered we were hiding Jews,' Mrs Foley said.

> One night we were already hiding four men when a fifth arrived and pleaded to be let in. I told him that there was not so much as an armchair left, but he merely said: 'Please may I sit on the floor?' There was one young Jew whom we sheltered many times. He had always left by breakfast. But he never failed to leave something on my plate as a token of his gratitude, sometimes a little box of chocolates, sometimes a rose. Some eventually got away. But others were not so lucky. Often we heard how wives were called to Gestapo headquarters to collect their husbands' belongings. When they got there, they were handed an envelope containing ashes.

At considerable risk to himself, Frank allowed Baeck to use his home to brief selected foreign journalists, including Colvin, Sefton Delmer and Carleton Greene, on what was happening to the Jews.

'After Kristallnacht, things became impossible for anyone who was Jewish,' recalled Inge Fehr. 'My father had a telephone call advising him to take an immediate holiday. Officially, he went to Breslau for a consultation. In fact, he went first to Dresden to friends, and then to Munich to half-Aryan relatives. He and my mother agreed a code on the telephone in case the Gestapo were looking for him.'

Among the Jews rounded up in the pogrom was Ernst Ruppel, who owned two factories, producing metalware and machine tools. He was taken from his home in Gotha, in Thuringen, to the nearby Buchenwald concentration camp. The next day, his manager, a non-Jew who had been rewarded for his work with a few shares in the company, arrived at the camp and had the Ruppel factories signed over to him at pistol point. 'My parents lost pretty well everything,' the Ruppels' younger son Ernest said.

Ernst Kramer was one of those taken to Buchenwald with Ernst Ruppel senior that day. There were around ten thousand prisoners there, most of them Jews, held in wooden huts with wooden benches lined up as beds. 'The whole day long, men were dragged out of the ranks at random and beaten before our eyes, hung up with their hands handcuffed behind their backs, or strapped on to the dreaded "horse" and beaten with rubber truncheons,' Kramer said. 'During the course of that first night, many went mad. Some were driven against the electrified wire fence and, during the night, two were also drowned in the latrine. But officially they all died a "natural" death.'

The prisoners received nothing to eat or drink until the evening of the third day when they were given a piece of bread and sausage. They were not allowed water to wash. The state of the food they were given was appalling, and many of the prisoners suffered from diarrhoea. Anyone who attempted to go out of the huts at night was either shot or beaten to death 'for trying to escape'. Several hundred died in the first few weeks of incarceration while a further 165 simply went mad.

'My mother Anne-Marie was non-Jewish,' said the young Ernest Ruppel.

> She approached the SS commander in Weimar, an SS-Brigadeführer Hennicke, and pleaded with him to let her husband go free. She knew, typical German, that he had a tremendous routine and he always had his morning coffee in a certain café. So she bribed the waiter to ask him to come out and she told him: 'My husband's in Buchenwald.' 'Oh yes, I know,' he replied. 'Well how do I get him out?' she asked. He was in a good mood that day, he said well if you buy a boat ticket to leave Germany on such and such a day we'll release him for that day.

In desperation, Anne-Marie Ruppel rang Ruppel's British agent, Frank Law, and asked who she should talk to at the British embassy to get visas for herself, her husband, his mother and their two young sons: eight-year-old Robert and five-year-old

Ernest. By coincidence, Foley's sister-in-law Rita was married to a solicitor who lived near Law, and they had met each other when the Foleys were home on leave. It seems likely that if the Ruppels had not known someone acquainted with Foley they might never have got out. The queues in front of the Berlin Passport Control Office were now so long that it was very difficult to be seen without sitting outside Tiergartenstrasse 17 from the early hours of the morning. To get a visa at such short notice was virtually impossible.

'Desperate Jews continue to flock to the British passport control offices in Berlin and elsewhere in Germany in the hope of gaining admission to Great Britain, Palestine or one of the Crown Colonies,' wrote James Holburn, a week after Kristallnacht.

> A visit to the Passport Control Office here this morning showed that families were often represented only by their womenfolk, many of them in tears, while the men of the family waited in a concentration camp until some evidence of likelihood of emigration could be shown to the Secret Police.
>
> While harassed officials dealt firmly but as kindly as possible with such fortunate applicants as had come early enough to reach the inner offices – about 85 persons were seen this morning – a far larger crowd waited on the stairs outside or in the courtyard beneath in the hope of admittance. The doors were closed and guarded much to the annoyance of Germans seeking visas, some of whom complained angrily of being forced to wait among Jews and demanded preferential treatment, though without success.

But Mrs Ruppel did get preferential treatment. Her family's connection with Foley through Law meant she had a note saying she was to see the Passport Control Officer himself, her son recalled. 'She was called to the front and there was this chap absolutely beavering away and trying to get people visas and we got our visa. Foley was a chap who hid his light under a bushel. But all the time he was working away, helping people get out of Germany and it wasn't that easy. He was a great man. He was instrumental in getting a lot of Jews out of Germany.'

A very relieved Anne-Marie Ruppel went to Buchenwald to get her husband out. Before leaving he was forced to sign a written undertaking that he would not talk about his treatment or about anything he had seen or heard there. The trauma of having been incarcerated in a concentration camp, even for two weeks, was horrendous. It was not until they were on board the Dutch aircraft flying them out of Germany that Ernst Ruppel senior was able to relax, falling into a fitful sleep. 'My father said he kept thinking he was going to be rearrested. But he felt absolutely safe the minute he walked on board that KLM plane. The stewardess knew from the way he looked where he'd been and at one point she woke him up. "I just wanted to tell you," she said. "We've crossed the German border".'

Ruppel had been one of the lucky ones. Within three months of Kristallnacht, 244 of those rounded up with him and taken to Buchenwald had been murdered. While he had spent only two weeks in the camp, it had seemed much longer, he said in an interview after the war. 'I have heard others describe Capt Foley as a saint,' he added. 'I would not quarrel with that. Nothing you could say about him would be too good. I owe him my life.'

Chapter 12

'An Active Little Man'

W ith no sign of the queues abating, Foley sent 'strongly worded' cables to Eric Mills, the Palestine Commissioner for Migration, pleading for additional blank visa certificates, and to London demanding urgent reinforcements to help cope with the increased workload.

'Anybody who approached the consulate building in the Tiergartenstrasse at that time saw long queues of women waiting to be admitted,' recalled Benno Cohn, co-chairman of the Zionist Organisation.

> The Consulate's premises had virtually been transformed into a place of refuge for the Jews who sought protection from persecution.
>
> Thirty-two thousand men were held in concentration camps in those weeks and their wives besieged Capt Foley in order to effect the liberation of their husbands from the camps. At that time it was a question of life and death for many thousands. In those days, he revealed himself in all his humanity. Day and night he was at the disposal of those who sought help. He issued visas of all kinds on a large scale and thereby assisted in the liberation of many thousands from the concentration camps.
>
> What were the motives that stirred him to act like this? We who worked closely with him in those days often asked ourselves

this question. Before all else, Foley was humane. In those dark days in Germany, to encounter a human being was no common occurrence. He told us that he was acting as a Christian and that he wanted to show us how little the Christians who were then in power in Germany had to do with real Christianity. He detested the Nazis and looked on their political system – as he once told me – as the rule of Satan upon earth. He loathed their base doings and regarded himself as duty bound to assist the victims of their misdeeds.

Foley acted however also as a good Englishman. He saw all the crimes of the regime at closest quarters and therefore realised better than ministers in London that there could never be any real peace with these people. His links with the leaders of the Jewish organisations were however useful too for his own country. Foley fulfilled other important functions in the service of his country and obtained continual and invaluable information from us about the Nazis' newest crimes and intentions. Through his endeavours, the British authorities received an accurate picture of what was currently going on in Germany.

Frank appropriated three of the embassy night porters, former soldiers, to control the crowds besieging the embassy. 'They organised the visitors in four lines which stretched from the street through the forecourt and up the stairs into the reception hall,' Pollack said. 'They understood no German, were very polite – but also assertive – wore uniforms, with lots of First World War medal ribbons, and were Goys [gentiles]. As a result, there was exemplary order regardless of the dreadful November and December weather and the very great nervousness of the visitors. For those who had no time to queue up, Capt Foley wrote out passes in his own hand.'

One of those dispatched to Berlin to assist him was Margaret Reid, a twenty-six-year-old doctor's daughter who, on coming down from Girton College, Cambridge, had joined MI6 as a clerk. She arrived on Monday, 12 December 1938, a few weeks after Kristallnacht. That evening she wrote to her mother recording the day's exciting events.

'I cannot tell you much about my work as we are under the Official Secrets Act and not supposed to gossip,' she said.

But today I spent entirely on filing – work that ought to have been seen to days before. The staff is about double its normal size and they are closing the office for two days a week in an effort to keep pace with the rush. There was a queue waiting when we got there at nine this morning and I believe some of them had been there since 4 am. When we had elbowed our way through, the porter tried to turn us away until I explained three times that we were here to work, when he laughed and took us to Captain Foley – our chief.

The reinforcements were followed by a package from Eric Mills containing the blank visa certificates for Palestine Foley had requested, plus a further thousand special 'Youth Aliya' certificates that allowed young Jews to go to Palestine without their parents. Foley's response was a four-word cable saying simply: 'God bless you. Foley'. At the Passport Control Department, based behind MI6 'head office' in Broadway Buildings, the officials handling those applications too contentious for Foley to push through became used to receiving a 'God bless you' message from Berlin following a positive decision.

Despite the German authorities' efforts to get Jews to emigrate, numerous bureaucratic measures stood in their way. Quite apart from the financial restraints facing them, each applicant had to be in possession of an exit permit issued by the Gestapo before they could be given a visa. In order to obtain one of these, the applicant needed to show that he had paid all the various fines and taxes imposed on the fleeing Jews. 'All these requisites were hard to come by when one was confined to the barbed wire compound in Buchenwald,' noted one aid worker. In addition, young candidates were also supposed to have clearance from the Hitler Youth, showing that they had served their allotted period – 'no easy matter for Jews not permitted to join in the first place'.

To make matters worse the exit permits had strict time limits attached, and if the visa arrived after the permit ran out, the whole process had to be started again. The frustrations and worry this produced frequently led to suicides among those caught in the time trap. So whenever applications were held up in London, Foley would send a stream of reminders pestering them to send back a visa. 'Letter after letter. Pressing, persuading, pleading,' his wife said.

> Jews trying to find a way out of Germany queued in their hundreds outside the British consulate, clinging to the hope that they would get a passport or a visa. Day after day we saw them standing along the corridors, down the steps and across the large courtyard, waiting their turn to fill in the forms that might lead to freedom.
>
> In the end, that queue grew to be a mile long. Some were hysterical. Many wept. All were desperate. With them came a flood of cables and letters from other parts of the country, all pleading for visas and begging for help. For them, Frank's yes or no really meant the difference between a new life and the concentration camps. But there were many difficulties. How could so many people be interviewed before their turn came for that dreaded knock on the door?

The commissionaires holding the crowds back allowed just twelve people at a time into the office's small reception hall. There they were met by a Messenger, who checked their exit permit and helped them to fill in the application card. He then asked them to sit in the waiting room while he took their application card and, if they had one, their passport to the Registry Clerk, who compared the applicant with a card index and blacklist of known undesirables and subversives who could not be allowed into the Empire.

Their applications were then passed to an Examiner who interviewed them to determine why they wanted to go to whatever country they were seeking a visa for and, where the case was routine, issued or refused it. Overseeing all this was Foley, who took any difficult cases with remarkable patience. 'He worked from 7am to 10pm without a break,' Mrs Foley said. 'He would handle as many applications himself as he could manage and he would walk among his staff of examiners to see where he could assist them, or give advice and words of comfort to those who waited.'

In her work as a Registry Clerk, Margaret Reid rarely had to consult Foley. But as a member of the MI6 support staff, she had other work to do for him once the Passport Control Office had been closed for the night. For Foley still had to carry out what remained his real role – collecting intelligence on the increasing German preparations for war. 'He is an active little man, wears a brown Harris Tweed jacket and appears to work 14 hours a day and remain good-tempered,' she told her mother.

> He is not at all terrifying to work for and we are just managing to get each day's letters opened and numbered now that the staff is about doubled.
>
> I sit all day at the card index with two other new girls and a man who came over from London a few weeks ago and the phone goes non-stop from nine am. I thought it would be weeks before I was qualified to answer it. But after two days I found myself sitting helplessly before it and no-one to help me. So I had to struggle with it and now I no longer care two hoots and take trunk calls from Breslau and London and answer questions about Palestine and Rhodesia and Trinidad. I probably don't know the answers to any of them but nothing final can be said by phone anyway and the people are mostly just fussing and have to be told to wait until we write to them.
>
> There are of course pathetic tales of woe and people who ring from the aerodrome just before their plane leaves in a final attempt to get a visa to get out of the country. The big businessmen seem to have been preparing, some of them for a long time, and have the necessary capital in foreign banks, but more pathetic are the uneducated letters from wives whose husbands are in concentration camps (some of them have died there or are in hospital as a result of infection caught there and undernourishment). It is a panic-stricken land and many former adherents of the regime are now apparently violently anti.

Before coming to Berlin, Margaret had asked Paula Weber, a

young German friend working in London, for advice on where she might stay cheaply. 'Well, have my room,' said Weber. 'It's empty, I'm in London. My parents will be delighted.'

Paula Weber's father August was a banker and former Staatspartei representative in the Reichstag who since 1933 had been imprisoned seven times. Although he was not Jewish, his wife Maria was and he had been a vociferous opponent of the Nazis.

'He came from the North-West of Germany which was not very pro-Hitler,' said Paula.

> He was an MP in his own right, a banker and an agriculturist. He had read *Mein Kampf*, the first edition, and he got up in the Reichstag and said: 'I've put on the table of the house documents that will show that members of the Nazi party have criminal convictions.' Goebbels got up with his whole party and said: 'We won't forget', and they didn't.
>
> The day after the Kristallnacht, one of my German colleagues rang me to say your mother is alive, she is all right. Get your skates on and get her out. So I went into the City of London and one of the many rich Jews gave me a guarantee for my mother so she could come out.
>
> Then it came to burning time for my father. He was warned by the Gestapo that he had better make tracks out because they wouldn't let him go another time. This Gestapo man appeared in my father's flat to give him a warning. I rang the British embassy and asked for Margaret, not knowing where she worked only knowing she was in the embassy.
>
> I said: 'Look, Margaret, my father must leave quickly. But he won't be allowed to leave by the Nazis if he gets an immigration permit to England.' So I asked her if it would be possible to get a one-week holiday visa that could be transferred into a permanent visa once he was in England. It needed to be transferable because the British immigration authorities had strict orders not to let anyone stay as a refugee if they came in on a visitor's visa.
>
> If you came as a refugee and you had lots of money you could come in but in the case of my father there was just my earnings and I was just a secretary. Foley arranged for my father that once he got onto English soil he could transfer his visiting permit to an

immigration permit and that saved his life. There is no doubt that without Foley, my father would have been killed. Foley had a very strong conscience. He was a very simple humble person with great foresight and a real understanding of what was happening. He was fully aware of what swine the Nazis were.

The problems faced by the desperate Jews were compounded by an announcement from the German government that 20 per cent of every Jew's property was to be confiscated as part of a 1,000 million mark fine to pay for the damage done on Kristallnacht. 'The Führer wants to take very sharp measures against the Jews,' Goebbels recorded in his diaries. 'They must themselves put their businesses in order again. The insurance companies will not pay them a thing. Then the Führer wants a gradual expropriation of Jewish businesses. I give appropriate secret orders.'

A series of other measures was swiftly instigated, aimed at increasing the despair felt among the Jewish community and forcing them out, the most devastating being a ban on all Jewish business activity. All Jewish firms, shares and land were to be sold by 1 January 1939. Jews were forbidden to buy property or to buy, pawn or sell gold, platinum, silver, diamonds, pearls, jewellery and works of art worth more than one thousand marks.

Jewish children were to be banned from German schools and universities. Jews were excluded from the social security system. Their newspapers and cultural organisations were closed down. All Jews had their driving licences withdrawn. The list of professions from which they were excluded was expanded to include pharmacy and midwifery. They were banned from using dining and sleeping carriages on trains and from swimming pools.

By early December, Berlin's police chief had banned Jews from wide areas of the city, including all government offices and virtually any recreational area. 'We could no longer go to any place of entertainment like cinemas, theatres, the circus, concerts or the zoo,' recalled Inge Fehr. The cabarets on the Ku'damm, fairs, museums, sports stadiums, even skating rinks, were out of bounds to the Jews. 'We are no longer allowed in

German hospitals and schools,' she recorded in her diaries. 'Jews are not allowed on the main roads in Berlin. We are forbidden even to sit on public benches, only on yellow benches marked *Judenbank*.'

The main aim, Göring made clear, was to force the Jews to leave. 'At the head of all our considerations and measures there is the idea of transferring the Jews as rapidly and as effectively as possible to foreign countries,' he said, adding: 'I should not like to be a Jew in Germany.'

Appealing to the Foreign Office to take more measures to help the Jews, Sir George Ogilvie-Forbes, British Chargé d'Affaires, noted that most Jewish men were now on the run. 'Position of Jewish Community is becoming more desperate,' Ogilvie-Forbes said. 'There have already been many suicides. Brutalities continue in concentration camps and further repressive measures are antici-pated. Even General Göring informs me that policy was for speedy elimination of the Jews.'

Wim van Leer had been briefed by the Quakers to make contact discreetly with Captain Foley, who had been warned that the young Jew was trying to help people get out and might need his help. Van Leer found the MI6 head of station 'an extraordinary person' with a genuine compassion for the people thronging around the consulate building.

'The winter of 1938 was a harsh one and elderly men and women waited from six in the morning, queuing up in the snow and biting wind,' he said.

> Captain Foley saw to it that a uniformed commissionaire trundled a tea-urn on a trolley along the line of frozen misery, and all this despite the clientele, neurotic with frustration and cold. Others pleaded, offered bribes, threatened, flattered, wept, and threw fits.
>
> Capt Foley always maintained his composure. As an ex-Army man, he knew that it was fear that motivated the heavy-coated bundles of despair outside his front door, wriggling to escape the closing claw. As a deeply devout Christian in deed as well as in

spirit, he would not allow himself to be upset by the traumatised herd stampeding across his desk.

The assistance Foley offered van Leer did not extend just to the issuing of visas. He taught the young man many of the tricks he had learned in his twenty years of Secret Service activity, even passing on details of the MI6 escape lines, including his own personal escape route through Emden and Termunten which he had used to get out of Germany at the start of the First World War.

'I learned a lot from him,' van Leer wrote.

> Where to get genuine fake passports, mainly from South American banana republics; the names of small, helpful print shops willing to produce one-off forms; rubber stamp makers on whose discretion one could rely, and a number of escape routes and procedures, as well as reliable addresses for succour and guidance in the vicinity of certain German frontier crossing points into Belgium, Holland and Switzerland. Most addresses were those of minor dignitaries of the church.

Despite the increased workload caused by the numbers of Jews trying to leave the country, Frank continued to gather vital intelligence for Head Office, but there was a major setback when Henderson discovered that MI6 was running a prime source inside the Charlottenburg headquarters of the Luftwaffe High Command. At the insistence of the Foreign Office, Frank was ordered to drop his air force colonel.

'During the war, we broached the subject of the difficulties being placed before us in Madrid by the British ambassador there,' recalled one of Frank's wartime colleagues in MI6. 'Foley said: "That's nothing. In Berlin I had an agent who was a very friendly colonel in the Luftwaffe HQ. He passed me reports twice a month – all top-level stuff. But at the end of 1938, I was instructed by the Foreign Office to drop this chap. Just imagine. The best source we had in Germany and in a strategic position." It was obviously part of the "Olive Branch" mentality at the time. It also embarrassed Foley like hell because they'd become close friends.'

Meanwhile, another of Frank's contacts was about to bear fruit in a spectacular fashion. Shortly before Christmas, Berlin had been the scene of one of the most important experiments in the history of science. For some time, Otto Hahn and Fritz Strassmann had been at work in a laboratory at the Kaiser Wilhelm Institute of Chemistry in the city's Dahlem suburb, bombarding uranium atoms with slow-speed neutrons. On the evening of 22 December 1938, Hahn telephoned his old friend Paul Rosbaud to tell him excitedly that they had found that the neutron bombardment created new elements of much lower atomic weight.

As chemists, Hahn and Strassmann knew their discovery was an important development in physics, but they were not yet aware of how important. Their key adviser during the experiments was the Jewish physicist Lise Meitner, who had been described by Einstein as 'Germany's Marie Curie'. A few months earlier, Rosbaud and Hahn had helped Meitner escape from Germany. She had gone to Sweden from where she remained in contact with Hahn, and it was to her that he had sent the results of the research for evaluation. 'Perhaps, you can come up with some kind of fantastic explanation,' Hahn said.

Meitner took a walk through the snow-covered woods around the Baltic resort of Kungalv with her nephew Otto Frisch, himself a prominent physicist, and discussed the Dahlem experiment with him. As they rested for a while on a tree trunk, the full significance of what had happened dawned on them. Hahn and Strassmann had split the atom, releasing enormous amounts of energy and opening the way for the atomic bomb which Frisch and another émigré German, Rudolf Peierls, had already predicted in work carried out at the University of Birmingham.

Rosbaud rang Fritz Sueffert, the editor of *Naturwissenschaften*, one of the Springer scientific journals, and persuaded him to pull an article from the next edition to make way for the results of the Hahn–Strassmann experiment, ensuring that the news that the atom had been split went around the world before the German government had even realised its significance. A few months later, the Nazis ordered German nuclear physicists to start work on an atomic bomb. A strict ban was imposed on any public discussion of the experiments. But Rosbaud, with his close relationship to Hahn, remained inside the loop, and was able to pass news of the progress made by the German scientists on to his friends in Britain.

Frank's intelligence-gathering activities and his attempts to get Jews out of Germany had already merged in the recruitment of Jewish sources like Pollack and Rosbaud, and in his assistance to aid workers like van Leer. Now his close links with the Zionists brought him into contact with a newly formed organisation specifically designed to use secret-service activity to help Jews to escape from the Nazis – Mossad leAliyah Bet.

Chapter 13

All the Fault of England

Mossad, as it swiftly became known, was formed in late 1938, but not as the intelligence organisation it is now. Its first role was to get those Jews who could not obtain visas from the Mandate authorities out of central Europe and into Palestine by any means possible. To the Zionists, the right of Jews to emigrate to Israel was absolute. There could be no illegal *aliyah*, as the Jews called immigration into Palestine. There was either Class A immigration, i.e. with permission, or Class B, without. Hence the name Mossad LeAliyah Bet, Institute for Immigration B.

Illegal shiploads of Jews had sailed for Palestine since 1934, when young members of the Hehalutz, a Polish Zionist youth organisation, bought the *Velos*, a Greek ship, and took several hundred unauthorised refugees to Palestine. A series of similar trips followed. But illegal immigration was opposed by both the Jewish Agency and the Zionist leadership until a combination of the increasing persecution of German Jews epitomised by Kristallnacht and the steady reduction in the numbers being allowed into Palestine persuaded the majority that there was no choice.

David Ben Gurion, who would become the first Prime Minister of Israel, told a meeting of the Jewish Agency on 11 November

1938, two days after Kristallnacht, that what was needed now was 'neither a selective aliyah nor a broad-based aliyah, but a mass aliyah of hundreds and thousands. Without a mass aliyah, Zionism is liable to fail and we are liable to lose this country.'

Mossad LeAliyah Bet was set up by the Jewish Trade Union Federation, Histadrut, and the underground Jewish defence organisation, the Hagana. Overall control was exercised from Tel Aviv by Shaul Avigur, the organisation's head. But operations were co-ordinated from the 'Apparat' in Paris mainly by veterans of the Hehalutz operations drafted into the newly formed institute. Agents were sent out to the capitals of all the major countries from which Jewish refugees were fleeing. There they selected potential refugees, organised them into groups and raised the cash to pay for the trips. Funding was largely supplied by the Zionist Organisation, and only richer refugees paid anything more than a small contribution towards the cost of their passage.

They had to make close contact with the appropriate authorities throughout central Europe in order to obtain permission for the Jews to leave. In Berlin and Vienna, this clearly meant they had to keep in close touch with the Gestapo. It quickly became clear that the Nazis were prepared to back illegal immigration in order to get rid of Jews while at the same time causing problems for the British in Palestine.

The Nazi support for illegal immigration was based on an organisation set up in Vienna by the expert on Zionism within the Sicherheitsdienst, the Nazi Party's own internal security service. His name was Adolf Eichmann. So successful was his Central Bureau for Jewish Emigration that Reinhard Heydrich, head of the Sicherheitsdienst, had a similar office set up in Berlin.

Heydrich, under orders from Göring to use emigration in order to solve 'the Jewish problem', told his officials that Germany should continue to promote emigration 'by all available means'. The Jews were in the best position to raise funds to pay for this and while in theory illegal emigration was something that should be opposed it was undeniable that groups were making their way to Palestine.

'Germany should also, at least unofficially, take advantage of this opportunity.'

Once permission had been granted for them to leave, the immigrants were moved down to either the Adriatic or the Black Sea, where they were put on chartered freighters and taken to Palestine to be landed illegally on the beaches. The first Mossad-organised group of Jewish refugees, a total of 280 people, left Berlin in March 1939, ostensibly for Zionist training farms in Yugoslavia. They travelled under Gestapo escort in a train organised by the Nazi authorities to Vienna, where more refugees were collected. The group then crossed into Yugoslavia and set sail from the Adriatic port of Susak, successfully getting through the British patrols and landing safely in Palestine.

Frank's work with Jewish leaders like Benno Cohn inevitably brought him into contact with the Mossad representatives in Berlin, Pino Ginzberg and Max Zimmels, who were based at the Meineckestrasse headquarters of Cohn's German Zionist Organisation, and the MI6 head of station appears to have been trusted with some of the details of their operations.

As the government official charged with ensuring that all immigration to British-controlled territories was strictly within the rules, he should have reported any attempts at smuggling Jews into Palestine. But according to Pollack:

> When Aliyah Bet was started in 1938, Foley was well aware of it and owing to his not-so-official duties he usually knew when a transport left a Black Sea or a Yugoslav port. I was in contact with Capt Foley right up until July 1939 and he told me that despite being a British intelligence officer and despite having known about some of the operations of Mossad LeAliyah Bet, he did not inform the Palestine Police. The Palestine authorities never got the slightest hint from him.

Since part of the role of the Mossad agents was to collect intelligence that would ensure the safe passage of the illegal immigrants, it seems likely that Frank's willingness to stay quiet about the Aliyah

Bet operations was based not just on humanity but on a sharing of intelligence between the two sides.

Nevertheless, Arnold Horwitz, who worked with Pollack in the Hilfsverein, said there was no doubt that Frank's commitment to helping the Jews was pursued without any thought to the possible consequences to himself. 'He certainly risked his career in order to save people,' Horwitz said. 'The truth is that many people who were saved by Frank Foley are unaware that he issued the papers that allowed them to escape from the Holocaust.'

The British Passport Control Office in Vienna had developed a well-organised system for dealing with the endless queues of people applying for visas. The staff was doubled to cope with the deluge, with an extra passport examiner and two secretaries transferred from Sofia and Copenhagen, but could only handle between 150 and 175 people a day. Sometimes there were as many as 600 people waiting to be seen. Everyone who was not dealt with was given a numbered and dated ticket entitling them to be seen in future as a priority case. But this led to the *Schieber*, the black marketeers, placing their own people in the queues purely to obtain tickets which could then be sold to the unfortunate Jews.

'Once I had been out at some coffee party or something and arrived back at the consulate-general late at night,' recalled the deputy PCO in Vienna. 'For some reason I wanted to check something in my office. I got out of the taxi, pulled out my wallet and two cards fell out into the mud. I was bending down to pick them up and the porter who was there said: "No mein Herr you mustn't do that. They will sell them for a 100 Schillings each tomorrow morning."'

As in most Passport Control Offices, some of the staff were MI6 officers working under cover, while others were ordinary consular staff who had no idea that their offices served any secret purpose. For the members of MI6 based in Vienna, the pressures of the demand for visas was exacerbated by the increasing need for more intelligence from inside Germany. Marjorie Weller had been transferred from Sofia to help.

We had these queues outside and I used to say, I had this pile of passports here and a pile of secret ink letters there and I was doing both you see.

It was terribly sad. Pregnant women would lay about in the consulate in the hope that they'd have the babies on British territory. I remember one occasion when a couple went away and committed suicide. There was just nothing I could do for them. They asked questions about it in the Commons about these horrible men and women in Vienna who were stopping these unfortunate Jewish women coming over here.

Given the number of people desperate for visas and the size of the queues, it was perhaps inevitable that there should be accusations of unfair treatment by those who were unsuccessful, and the Vienna office was the subject of a number of complaints, most notably in an article in the British journal *The Spectator*, which accused it of being 'an excellent contributor, however unintentionally, to the persecution of the Jews'.

But the consul-general defended the passport control staff. 'It is admitted that some people have to be firmly dealt with as if discipline were relaxed it would be quite impossible to handle the large crowds which flock to the offices,' he said. 'The ushers are pushed about and occasionally even struck and often insulted. The wildest accusations are made daily against Kendrick, myself and all of the staff. It is not possible for anybody who is not directly concerned with the work to form an idea of the difficulties involved. Kendrick tells me that his staff are so overwrought that they will burst into tears at the slightest provocation.'

After Kendrick's expulsion, his deputy took over as Passport Control Officer. He and his staff 'stretched the rules' wherever they could, but it was inevitable that those refused would be angry. 'The people who came into our offices all had stories to tell of sons, daughters, husbands who had been picked up by the Brownshirts and bundled into trucks, and then nothing,' he said.

No news, no official notification of any kind, no courtroom trial. They had disappeared into a black hole and there was no knowing whether they were alive or dead. But the Jews knew how brutal and sadistic the Brownshirts could be. There had been enough examples in the streets for everybody to see. They feared the worst, but they could not be sure.

And there were we, governmental officials with power to give them access to places all over the world – and we refused them, all too often, even the chance of a visa to get to some far-away place, out of reach of those trucks. Anywhere but that black hole of uncertainty. No wonder they were resentful. We heard more than once: 'It's all your fault. *England hat Schuld daran* (England is to blame for it all).' They couldn't believe that our world empire was unable to stop the Nazis in their tracks. One said bitterly: 'You ought to have a notice on the door: Abandon hope all ye who enter here.' After a day of seeing those tearful, desperate faces, that was what got us down.

The only time he ever cried in his life was during his period in charge of the Vienna office, he said.

It had been building up, these streams of people coming to my office and talking to them, and in so many cases telling them: 'You have no hope of getting a visa to Palestine and I can't see how you can get anywhere else with a British visa.'

You would see them going away, very often in tears, some of them trying to bribe you with money. It happened so often they thought they could fix you and then they would go away desperately unhappy, saying: '*England ist an alles schuld*. It's all the fault of England,' as if we should have stopped the Nazis coming to power in the first place. We had only been married a short time and one day I came home and we sat out to have a drink on the terrace and I just burst into tears. My wife couldn't understand it to start with but it was that. I wept for about an hour I think. I had never cried in my life until that one time and I haven't cried since. It gets under your skin you see. In the end it just builds up.

Both the Berlin and Vienna offices were desperate for reinforcements. One of those sent out was Ann Forbes-Robertson, who arrived in Berlin in January straight out of school.

I really was most terribly young. I got the job because I had been to a German school in Switzerland for five years and I really did speak German like a German. I was asked if I would go to Vienna – I said yes – and then at the last moment they asked would I mind going to Berlin? I was only 17. I was astonished they took me on.

When I got out there, dear Frank Foley met me and he said: 'My goodness look what they're sending us now.' He wasn't terribly tall. I think he was white-haired. He would have done perfectly as a jolly Father Christmas type. He wasn't fat. But at the same time he was just sort of a good shape. Just enormously friendly. He was the most charming man.

I remember when I arrived. It was rather a fine mock 18th century building. Nice big grounds around it. Gates to go in. Courtyard at the front. It was reminiscent of Regent's Park going round places like that. You went up steps. We went upstairs to our office and I was put on typing. I was hopeless at it but Frank was very kind. Because the beauty of Frank was that he was a very nice man. He had no side to him. He was just very friendly and very pleasant and very encouraging.

He put me on to interviewing people once they had been given their visa. I shared the job with a fellow called Kenneth Paxton who was just out of university. He'd taken a degree in Greek mythology or something – very suitable – and between us we did the passports. It was 13s 6d for the visa and RM8.30 in German marks. Every evening we had to balance the books and there was this huge clientele, non-stop people coming in.

One of the Jewish aid workers most closely associated with Frank's work to get the Jews out of Germany was Georg Landauer, Director of the Central Bureau for the Settlement of German Jews in Palestine, who described the worsening situation in Berlin in early 1939 in a letter to a colleague in Jerusalem.

Only the employees of the Jewish organisations and some people who rent rooms or cater meals are still earning something. In Berlin, a Jew can get a coffee only in the waiting room of the Zoo Station and a meal in a Chinese or some other foreign restaurant.

As the Jews' leases are constantly being rescinded in buildings inhabited by 'mixed population' they increasingly move in with each other and brood over their fate. Many of them have not yet recovered from the 10th of November and are still fleeing from place to place in Germany or hiding in their apartments.

Travel agencies, mainly in Paris, get in touch with consulates that can be bribed – this is mainly true of Central and South American republics – and purchase visas to foreign countries for high prices and enormous commissions. It has often happened that, having suddenly granted several hundred visas, consuls pocketed the money and were then dismissed by their governments. After that, the chances of Jews to enter the countries concerned disappear for a long time. Early in the morning, Jews appear at travel agencies and stand in long lines waiting to ask what visas one can obtain today.'

The only place in the world the Jews could now go without visas was the International Settlement in Shanghai. Having paid for their passage, few had any money on which to live once they arrived there. But in the wake of Kristallnacht many decided that this was better than waiting to see what the Nazis had in store for them. 'A favourite way to obtain release from detention was to buy a one-way steamship ticket to Shanghai which, as a bonus, gave permission to take up residence,' wrote Wim van Leer. 'Many Jews, in desperation, took this route. Some blew out their brains on arrival.'

The British consul general in Shanghai implored the Foreign Office to do something to stop the seemingly unstoppable flood of refugees, most of whom were destitute. The Jewish community in Shanghai was helping with charitable relief but 'the entire financial burden of local refugee problem is resting on the shoulders of four or five Jews who are genuinely alarmed,' he said. 'I venture once again to stress the very serious situation that is developing here and to request that every effort may be made to persuade London organisation to remit adequate funds immediately failing which local Jewish community has declared it will be quite impossible for them to continue to succour refugees here already.'

With thousands of Jewish refugees pouring into Shanghai, the Foreign Office sent telegrams to the Passport Control Offices and consulates in Germany, urging them to do everything they could to dissuade the Jews from going there. Frank's official response, attached to a report from Henderson, was a censored version of his original thoughts on the matter, but was nonetheless blunt.

> We in this office have warned Jews and Jewish organisations here of the danger of proceeding to Shanghai. They refuse to listen to us and say that Shanghai under any conditions is infinitely better than a concentration camp in Germany. One can perhaps understand their point of view. It is useless to talk to the German Government whose declared object is to destroy these people body and soul. It makes no difference to them whether destruction takes place in Germany or in Shanghai.
>
> It might be considered humane on our part not to interfere officially to prevent Jews choosing their own graveyards. The people who sail for Shanghai have usually been warned to leave Germany within a few weeks or enter or return to a concentration camp. They know the horrors of a concentration camp. They would rather die as free men in Shanghai than as slaves in Dachau.

It was not long before the Gestapo realised that this was another way of getting rid of Jews and began chartering special ships to take refugees to Shanghai. One was about to sail from Danzig, Frank wrote, in an emotionally charged report for the Foreign Office. 'She will carry 700 refugees from East Prussia. They will be forcibly embarked.' Each of the refugees was to pay a thousand marks towards the cost of his or her passage.

> If he/she is not able to raise that sum, the Hilfsverein has, under Gestapo orders, to contribute up to a maximum of RM1,000 per head.
>
> Perhaps the Chancery will forgive me for stating my opinion that both on grounds of humanity and of wider British interests, it is an infinite pity these unfortunate people are not allowed to emigrate to Palestine. We in this office are the daily witnesses of

the sufferings of old and broken people under orders to leave this country. They beseech us to allow them to join their children in Palestine. I have referred hundreds of cases to Palestine. If I am not sent hundreds of certificates in the near future, I fear they too will be dumped in Shanghai.

Chapter 14

Looking for a Final Solution

At the end of January 1939, on the sixteenth anniversary of his appointment as Chancellor, Hitler addressed the Reichstag, scathingly attacking the British, American and French government for their criticism of Germany's treatment of the Jews.

Under the Weimar Republic, the Jews had dominated German society, particularly its culture, he said. If Britain, America and France believed that 'such highly cultured people' were being so harshly treated, why were they so reluctant to allow them into their own countries? he asked sarcastically. Why weren't they grateful for this 'magnificent' gift that Germany was offering them?

He then gave an ominous warning of things to come.

> I believe that this problem will be solved – and the sooner the better. Europe cannot find peace before the Jewish question is out of the way.
>
> If the international Jewish financiers inside and outside Europe again succeed in precipitating the nations into a world war, the result will not be the Bolshevisation of the earth and with it a Jewish victory but the annihilation of the Jewish race in Europe.

With increasing numbers of Jews falling through the regulations, the British government allowed the London-based Council for

German Jewry to open up an old military base, Kitchener Camp, at Richborough, Kent, as a transit camp to house refugees who intended to go on to another country.

This gave Frank far more scope to persuade the Home Office to allow people into Britain, many of whom, he must have known, would never actually re-emigrate. Working with Pollack, Frank gave the Hilfsverein a virtually free choice of whom it wanted to get out of Germany.

'I don't know to what extent Capt Foley had any influence over the details of the "Refugee Scheme", but I do know he spoke in favour of it,' Pollack said.

> After the British Home Office began confirming permits for Richborough Camp by telegraph, I had dozens of these telegrams in my hand and marvelled at the wisdom of a foreign service whose main principle in questions of issuing visas was: 'The full responsibility rests with the man on the spot,' but which gives the man on the spot the dictatorial power necessary to fulfil this responsibility.
>
> When the permits came, the British passport control officer cooperated with us in an effective and trusting way of shortening the process of deciding how the visas should be distributed. In an unusual concession which showed quite how much trust Capt Foley had in us, the applicant was not required to appear in person.
>
> I should add that this trust was not undeserved. As a result of our vigilance, there were no Jewish criminals or Gestapo informers among the people who went to England. They were good people that we sent to Richborough. When the war began, many of our people put on uniforms, others found their place in work service.

As Pollack implied, many of these people never left, joining the British armed forces or working in the factories and on the land. The British decision to open the transit camp prompted the Americans to make it clear that no one was guaranteed a place in the United States. A number of refugees had been allowed into Britain under the misapprehension that registration numbers they had been given represented a promise of a place in America. But shortly after the new scheme came into place, the American consul general in Berlin called on Frank to inform him that this was not the case.

Frank began to brief him on the new British scheme. 'My remarks were superfluous as he had received full details from the American Consul in London.' US officials who had provided lists of 'quota numbers' had exceeded their authority. The registration numbers which candidates held had no more significance than that their application had been duly indexed under that number, the American consul said, adding that the US government 'did not look with favour on the procedure which the British Home Office had adopted'.

The Home Office was thrown into confusion by the American pronouncement. 'If it became generally known that a large proportion of the refugees to whom we have given temporary asylum would not be able to proceed to the United States of America eventually, there would be strong opposition on the part of a section of the public to any further admissions,' one official wrote.

'If action taken by the American immigration authorities were to result in excluding a large number of refugees who have already applied for visas, we should be compelled to re-examine our position.' Sir Samuel Hoare, the British Home Secretary, expressed repeated concern that this 'stagnant pool of refugees' might cause 'an awkward political situation'.

Meanwhile, Frank continued to issue the refugees recommended by the Hilfsverein with Home Office letters guaranteeing them temporary asylum in Britain pending their re-emigration, said Pollack. 'The last group, 300 men, left Germany two days after my own departure, on 30 August 1939, and reached England safely before the outbreak of war. All of these people and tens of thousands of other Jews and non-Jews can thank Capt Foley and his staff for their salvation. But unfortunately only a few of them are aware of this.'

With war drawing ever closer, Frank had not only to help the never-ending queue of would-be emigrants, he also had to provide an increasing amount of intelligence from inside Germany as well as set up the systems by which he could keep control of his agents there.

Like many of the civil servants drafted in to help to cope with the rush of refugees, Ann Forbes-Robertson had no idea of the real job behind the cover of passport control.

> There were some people in the office who one was always rather suspicious about and of course there were so many people roaming round the office that one thought: 'Oh, cloak and dagger here,' but I never actually pinned MI6 onto them.
>
> There was a man called Insall who was Foley's number two; a fellow called Leslie Mitchell, who was so secretive, and David McEwen. He was always kowtowing with people in the embassy. I think he thought the consulate was a bit below him. But there were so many people roaming about in and out of the office. Another fellow who was frequently there was Ian Colvin of the *News Chronicle*.
>
> Nobody knew exactly what went on in Frank's office. I would think that was about 75 per cent of the business there, and Frank was the front man. He was the most normal pleasant man. He purposely had this role of being rather a feckless, awfully nice chap, but not really somebody you could take seriously. You would never have dreamt.

David McEwen was in fact a particularly useful member of the station. The son of an RAF air vice-marshal, he had extensive contacts among homosexual members of the Nazi Party, and in particular the leadership of the Hitler Youth. During the war, he was posted to Stockholm, where he was frequently visited by his influential German homosexual friends.

The multiple demands of the increasing need for intelligence, the contingency plans for war and the non-stop flow of Jews through the office inevitably got Frank down. 'The strain of the work and the pitiful stories he heard began to tell on Frank to the point where he felt he could go on no longer,' Kay Foley said. 'He said little about what he was doing even to me: he said nothing at all to others.'

The atmosphere in Berlin was so oppressive that she had frequently gone home to England to get away from it, Kay said in an interview with the local newspaper in Stourbridge in which she was described only as 'Mrs X'. 'I felt that a few months was the longest time I could stay there at a stretch, and I invariably came home two or three times a year. One became so depressed and oppressed that one simply had to get out of the country.'

She and Frank had many friends among their German neighbours.

> They hate this business as much as we do, but none of them has the guts to stand against it, but all submit like sheep. Few are Nazis at heart and there is much dissatisfaction with conditions.
>
> There is a shortage of most foods. We were lucky because we used to get parcels from London, containing such things as butter, tea, coffee, flour, marmalade and bacon.

If there was anything she could not use, she would pass it on to her neighbours. 'Judging from their gratitude, it would appear that they value half a pound of butter more than half a pound of gold.'

Frank was only rarely able to join her on her trips to England. The British Passport Control Office in the Tiergarten had become known throughout the Greater Reich as a place of sanctuary where Captain Foley was prepared to do everything he could to help. 'He was a very kind, religious man who felt it was the job of every good human being to save people,' said Arieh Handler, who worked for Youth Aliyah, the organisation that helped to get young people to Palestine. 'Despite the British policy of giving visas only to a few selected Jews, it was known that he would do everything he could.'

As more and more people heard about what Frank was doing, the numbers outside his offices grew and grew, and he and his staff became swamped with work. 'There were so many people it really was incredibly busy,' said Ann Forbes-Robertson.

> We had a commissionaire at the door of course and I reckon on a good day there were between 250 and 300 standing there waiting to come in. The commissionaire kept them downstairs so there was always a controllable number, I should think about 12 in the waiting room. They weren't just German Jews. There were quite a few Austrians, quite a few Hungarians. It was a non-stop stream. Frequently they were desperate. It was very sad.

Richard Lachs had been a company administrator until the firm he worked for in Cologne was Aryanised. After Kristallnacht he went into hiding to escape the round-ups of Jews for the concentration camps. 'We left the house so that if anybody did come to the house there was no one there,' said his son Werner. 'We went to the house of his ex-boss who had already been sent to a concentration camp so nobody was looking for anybody there.'

The Lachs family had been issued with an affidavit allowing them entry into the United States in 1938, but because of quota restrictions had been unable to take it up, said Werner Lachs.

> We then made an application for temporary visas to come to England where I had an uncle. However he himself being a recent immigrant could not obtain the necessary guarantee.
>
> My aunt Erna Lachs was one of 50 German Jewish dentists who in 1936 were permitted by royal proclamation to come to this country and set up practice immediately. My Uncle Fred Lachs was a medical doctor and couldn't therefore practise. His wife was keeping him and her mother. So they could not themselves give a guarantee nor could they find anyone to do it.

The family made an application anyway in the hope that somehow they would get a guarantee, Lachs said.

> The application might take months. But we knew we couldn't get visas until this guarantee which we were hoping to get but didn't.

Then suddenly the visa came out of the blue. I remember it so very vividly, it was one of those things that you do remember as a child, I was only 12 at the time.

It was a Sunday morning, a friend was there, and the post produced a letter from the British Passport Control Office in Berlin, requesting that my parents should send their passports to receive their visa. We just jumped up and down for joy. An immediate inquiry about myself and my sister was answered positively – yes, send their passports as well.

Like many of those helped by Frank, they assumed he had simply made a mistake.

He was not supposed to give visas out without a guarantee and there were some other people with the same name coming to England at the same time. But the other people didn't have any children and Foley was also offering visas to the children so it couldn't have been for them.

We duly left Germany in July 1939 and on reporting to the Jewish Refugee Committee in London, were 'invited' to go back because we had no guarantee. Naturally that brought a dusty reply from my father. The committee didn't have much money and it wasn't allowed to draw on public funds so they didn't want to support us. They said without support we couldn't stay. But they knew perfectly well that we wouldn't go.

We proceeded to Manchester to a life of near poverty, but as time went on we established ourselves here, fully integrated in British life. When I think back as to what could have been I am eternally grateful to this country and I am sure that much of that gratitude is due to Frank Foley. I am 99 percent certain that but for Mr Foley, I and my family might well have become another statistic of the Holocaust.

The experience of Jewish doctors like Fred Lachs, who found that even if they managed to get a visa to come to Britain they could not practise was the rule rather than the exception. Between 1933 and 1936, around two hundred Jewish doctors were allowed to establish themselves in practice in Britain, albeit only after obtaining a British qualification. But under pressure from the

British Medical Association, the Home Office put a temporary block on immigrants being allowed to practise in Britain. When it attempted to relax it in the wake of the Anschluss by allowing five hundred in, the BMA protested and the figure was cut to just fifty.

Sir Samuel Hoare, the then Home Secretary, recalled in his memoirs that he 'would gladly have admitted the Austrian medical schools *en bloc*' but was shocked by the attitude of the BMA which assured him that 'British medicine had nothing to gain from new blood and much to lose from foreign dilution'.

It is difficult for a more modern generation to appreciate the extent of the latent anti-Semitism current at the time, even among many of those who were trying to help the Jews. In a private letter written in 1939, Neville Chamberlain, the British Prime Minister, lamented the cruel treatment being meted out to the Jews in Germany. 'No doubt Jews aren't a lovable people,' he wrote. 'I don't care about them myself. But that is not sufficient to explain a pogrom.'

One of the few German Jewish doctors who was allowed to go to Britain to practise was Inge Fehr's father Oscar. As an eye specialist of international repute, he was exempt from the quotas. 'England gave us permission to emigrate but my father would have to retake his medical examinations before being allowed to practise,' she said. It took them more than six months to get their passports back.

'Two days later, we went to the British Consulate where Captain Foley gave us visas. He told us that my father was the only doctor he knew who had received permission to work in England and that he was one of only a few who had been given a permit for permanent residence in England.' Before catching the ferry from Bremerhaven, they stopped off in Hamburg to see Inge's Aunt Sarah and Uncle Jacob. It was the last time she would see them. Jacob and Sarah Rosenbacher-Levy gassed themselves in 1941, the night before they were due to be deported to the Theresienstadt concentration camp.

In among the Jewish refugees trying to get out were a number of German spies. Frank's close relationship with the Jewish refugee organisations meant that he was usually tipped off about them. But even when he was not his vast experience ensured that he was rarely, if ever, fooled.

'He was one of the few Englishmen in Germany who was never taken in by Nazi trickery and thus one of the few British officials in Berlin whose mission was a success,' Pollack wrote.

One morning when I entered the waiting room of the British Passport Control Office there was a tall, well-dressed, intelligent-looking German who presented his passport and application for a visa to Captain Foley. He spoke fluent English without the least trace of a German accent. Captain Foley looked at the man closely and looked at the passport. Then he took a red pencil, put a line through the application, wrote refused on it and said in German: 'Sorry, I am unable to grant you a visa.'

The German, still in English, began to bluster and showed a letter from a well-known English firm, adding that he understood that the British Home Office had granted a permit on his behalf. Capt Foley replied: 'Yes, I have received the permit. It entitles me to grant you a visa, but it does not bind me to do so.' He declined in all civility to give any reason why he would not issue a visa. But as the door of his room closed behind the German, he commented in an undertone: 'We do not want spies in England.'

When I came to his office another time to ask his help for a pitiable object of Nazi justice, a lively spaniel greeted me. The little dog wagged his tail cheerfully at me until Capt Foley observed: 'Look, he is a good Aryan dog. Jonny, show the gentleman that you are an Aryan. Say Heil Hitler', and he held up a lump of sugar. The dog quickly stood on his hind legs, lifted up the right forefoot and barked in good imitation of the average *Parteigenosse* (party comrade). Then Capt Foley turned to the matter in hand and 48 hours later a young Jew left Sachsenhausen concentration camp for a British colony.

Chapter 15

Into the Camps

Throughout 1939, as conditions for the Jews became increasingly hopeless, Frank's office was inundated with people trying to get out. With the Nazis determined to remove the Jews from Germany, either by forced emigration or worse, the only hope for those incarcerated in the concentration camps was a visa that proved they could leave.

'Frank managed to get some Jews not only out of Germany but out of the camps as well,' said Kay Foley. 'These were cases where they had applied for a visa and then been interned before it arrived. Frank would do all he could to get the visa through then persuade the Gestapo to let the man out of the camp to get out of the country.'

Where there was no relative in Germany to present the visa to the camp authorities, Foley would go into the camps himself to save Jews from their executioners.

Gunter Powitzer had been arrested at the beginning of 1937 for 'race defilement', after getting his non-Jewish girlfriend Friedl pregnant. Powitzer was twenty-four and lived in Würzburgestrasse, in the Reinickendorf district of north Berlin. He owned a car hire firm, but in the past year his profits had dropped dramatically as a result of the Nazi boycott of Jewish businesses. Friedl Detter, his girlfriend, was a twenty-three-year-old receptionist at the Hotel Dom in Berlin.

But the brother of Friedl's stepfather was an ardent Nazi Party official. Offended by the fact that a member of his family was consorting with a Jew, he denounced Powitzer to the Gestapo and one night, when the young Jew went to Friedl's house to pick her up, they were waiting for him. Powitzer was held at Moabit prison for three months before being given an eighteen-month prison sentence. By the time Friedl gave birth to young Walter, the child's father had already been moved to Brandenburg prison.

Powitzer's brother Willi, a radio engineer, had got out early on following an incident in which a live broadcast by the Führer was cut off in full flow. He was now deputy chief engineer for the Palestine Broadcasting Service. 'He apparently moved heaven and earth to get us out,' said Walter. 'He used his contacts with the British mandatory authorities and the word eventually got to Berlin, to Frank Foley.' But by now Gunter Powitzer had finished his prison sentence. The day of release was the most dangerous time for Jewish 'criminals', who were likely to be moved immediately to a concentration camp. Powitzer was taken first to police headquarters in the Alexanderplatz and then on to the Sachsenhausen camp, north of Berlin.

It had already acquired a gruesome reputation. A month earlier, the Berlin police had bussed a group of sixty-two Jews to the camp and handed them over to the SS, who forced them to run the gauntlet of two lines of guards wielding spades, clubs and whips. 'Unable to bear their cries, the police turned their backs,' one witness said. The beatings went on for half an hour, at the end of which '12 of the 62 were dead, their skulls smashed. The others were all unconscious. The eyes of some had been knocked out, their faces flattened and shapeless.'

One of the camp guards would stand resting an axe on his shoulder as he called out the names of the condemned before they were led away. He was known to the prisoners as 'the man with the violin'. Gunter Powitzer knew his name must soon appear on his list but continued working in the camp's brick factory, hoping for a miracle. One day, he was tipped off not to go to work, to plead illness. When he said he was not well, he was sent to the camp kitchen where a guard forced him to run around with a sack of heavy potatoes on his back. Returning late at night to the hut, bruised and tired, he found it empty. When he asked where everyone was, he was told simply: 'They tried out a new machine-gun today.'

A few days later, he heard he had a visitor. 'I was working in the factory when an SS officer came and took me for a shower,' Gunter said.

> Then we went to the clinic where they began treating my whip wounds. 'What happened?' I asked. 'Shut up,' the SS man shouted and threw a grey greatcoat over me. 'Shut up and put it on! You've got a guest.' I was very thin, and when I put the coat on it covered all the wounds on my legs and neck. 'Who knows I'm here?' I wondered. "Who can it be?'
> Dressed for the first time in a month in civilian clothes, bandaged, cleaned up and shaved, I was led by the SS man into the camp office. There sat a small man wearing glasses, who told me in English: 'My name is Foley. I am from the British Consulate in Berlin.'

Powitzer asked if he could have an interpreter. 'Yes of course,' the SS officer said politely for the benefit of the British visitor before going to fetch one. Once they were alone, Powitzer turned to Foley and said: 'I understand English, sir.' Foley smiled and said: 'Tomorrow you'll be free and there are papers at the consulate for you to travel to Palestine.' 'What about the child?' Powitzer asked. 'Don't worry, he is also registered on the papers,' said Foley. 'Your brother in Palestine has taken care of everything.' The next day, someone was waiting at the camp gates to pick Powitzer up and take him to collect his young son. A few days later, they were on their way to Palestine.

Although for some time it had been clear to most people, even

Chamberlain himself, that appeasement would not work, it was finally brought home on 15 March, 1939, when Hitler sent his troops into Bohemia and Moravia, the only parts of the Czech lands left unoccupied. Hitler had originally given the order to invade Czechoslovakia in May 1938. The invasion, planned for October of that year, had only been forestalled by Munich. Now he had acquired Austrian and Czech armaments sufficient to arm more than forty more divisions and immensely strengthened his strategic position in the south. Göring said quite openly that the transfer of Czech arms factories to Germany would be a major advantage 'in the event of an attack on Poland'.

Two days after the invasion of Czechoslovakia, Chamberlain announced that if there were any further attacks by Germany on small states, Britain would 'resist to the utmost of its power'. Few people now doubted that the invasion of Poland would come, and with it a major European war.

Yet despite the gathering storm clouds, Berlin's nightlife remained as lively as it had been in the Golden Twenties. 'There was always something going on really,' said Ann Forbes-Robertson.

> The nightclubs were a very social affair. Great fun. You would see Frank every evening at one or other nightclub with his wife. They were all mostly in the Kurfürstendamm. But it seemed every house was a nightclub. You didn't pay to go in. There were so many of them, they were delighted to welcome you.
>
> Some of them were like in the film *Cabaret*. Some of them laid on quite an elaborate entertainment. I remember there was the Journalists' Club where it was always rather daring, rather naughty anti-state jokes, where you always felt: 'We're going to be raided'. There were also of course the ones that did a little more than others. You know, telephones on the table. You rang up the girls that you wanted but I wasn't really into quite that sort of field of course.

However frivolous the atmosphere in the Ku'damm, for most people the harsh reality was that Germany was a police state. 'It was a funny sort of life,' Forbes-Robertson said.

It was really quite spooky in Germany in those days. People disappearing overnight, all these military processions and the SS rampaging around the streets.

You saw the old professors out on the street being pushed and shoved. One of the girls in the office was quite dark and wore makeup, not a lot, just nicely made up. But she was stopped in the street and shouted at and called a Jewess. She was quite frightened but fortunately somebody was near at hand and they bore her out. But they were really quite aggressive.

The Germans you met never stopped asking you questions and one knew that they were trying to get information of some sort. Goodness knows what for. I suppose they all had to justify themselves. They were all terribly frightened and I've always maintained that there was no way the Germans wanted to know about the concentration camps.

If you could report your neighbour for just not going to a military procession and that was enough to get him whisked off, usually in the middle of the night and disappeared. It could be for an hour, it could be for a week, it could be forever. Well who wants to risk that. So you kept your nose very clean. You just didn't want to know anything however suspicious you might be.

In a further vain attempt to reach some sort of a compromise between the fears of the Arabs that the Jews were intent on driving them out and the demand for ever more places for Jewish refugees, the British government published a White Paper allowing for a total of 75,000 Jewish immigrants to Palestine over the next five years, of whom 25,000 were to represent 'a contribution towards the solution of the Jewish refugee problem'. Thereafter no Jewish immigration would be allowed without Arab consent. In an attempt to bring an end to Aliyah Bet, the number of illegal immigrants was to be deducted from the annual 15,000 quota.

The White Paper was totally unacceptable to both sides and entirely counterproductive. The radical Zionists were now able to argue with some justification that illegal immigration was the only way forward both for the creation of a Jewish homeland and more urgently in order to remove Jews from the dangers they faced if they remained in Germany.

By July, the illegal immigration lines to the Black Sea and the Adriatic were moving an average of more than one hundred Jewish refugees a day into Palestine. The British government announced that as a result of the 'disastrous effect of illegal immigration to Palestine' it was suspending the quota for six months from the beginning of October 1939. The decision gave added urgency to the process of getting Jews out.

Dr David Arian, a former civil servant with the Berlin police, had been one of the first Jews to lose his job. He had successfully applied to Frank for a visa to Palestine and moved to Tel Aviv where he worked for a bank. His father Max and mother Amalie had remained in their home town of Beuthen, but at the beginning of 1938 Max died, shortly after hearing that he had lost his licence as a government lottery collector.

Dr Arian spent the next six months trying to get his mother out of Germany. Eventually Frank allotted her one of the few precious visas he could issue 'for persons living in circumstances of exceptional hardship'. Dr Arian thanked him effusively. 'Having brought my mother home from the boat, I feel like writing to you these few lines,' he said.

> Destiny has placed you in a position where you daily come in touch with sorrow and despair, and where a man like you always feels the restrictions of power to help those who suffer. However, I know that whenever you find a possibility to assist the oppressed you do all you can to help them and by doing so you find happiness and satisfaction. My thanks which I hereby express for the help given to my mother is surely but a small portion of your own heart's satisfaction.
>
> It may also please you to hear that wherever your name is mentioned 'From Dan to Beer Sheva' you are talked of with the greatest respect and devotion and that you and a few other persons effect as a counterweight where the evils of the everyday's politics suppress and destroy the faith in honesty and humanity.

In his reply to Dr Arian, Frank candidly expressed his own opinion of the restrictions on emigration to Palestine. 'You must have been very happy to have your mother with you again,' he said.

> I was particularly pleased when her certificate arrived. She was the envy of all the unfortunate people who were in the office. We wish we had the power of former days so that we could come to the help of thousands instead of a few hundreds.
>
> Conditions are getting worse and worse here for the Jews. I dread to think of the misery and suffering they – especially the older people – will have to face next winter. Their funds are running low, and they do not know where they will find accommodation. The quota is a calamity, especially in these days of rabid persecution and permanent cold pogrom. The courage and fortitude of the Jews are beyond praise. They have our profound admiration.

Bat-sheeva Arian, Dr Arian's widow, recalled that her mother-in-law, who died in 1971 at the age of ninety-three, would frequently talk about Frank, describing him as a man who was admired by everyone who met him. 'She always called him "my Angel",' Mrs Arian said. 'We lived in an atmosphere where Captain Foley was regarded as a saint.'

In early August, Frank returned to London to discuss the best ways of continuing contacts with his agents in the event of war. A few days later, he travelled to Denmark, Sweden and Norway – from where it had been decided he was to control operations inside Germany as Chief Passport Control Officer (Scandinavia). He used the visit to work out the best ways of keeping in contact with his agents in Germany.

On 22 August, Russia and Germany signed the so-called Molotov–Ribbentrop Pact, giving Stalin a large slice of eastern Poland in return for his acquiescence to the Wehrmacht's occupation of the rest of that country. On the following day, Colonel Hans Oster, deputy head of the Abwehr and one of a small group of army officers opposed to Hitler, confirmed to the

Dutch military attaché in Berlin that the invasion of Poland was imminent. The attaché informed his British counterpart and the evacuation of the embassy began.

Frank arranged for Pollack and a number of Wilfred Israel's friends and colleagues to get out. The most vital secret documents were sent out by diplomatic bag, the remainder were burned, and the agents were contacted and told the procedures for getting in touch with Frank, who was to be based in Oslo. Messages to Rosbaud, for example, were to be broadcast in code on the German service of the BBC, preceded by the words: '*Das Haus steht am Hügel*' (The house stands on the hill).

On the morning of 25 August 1939, Hans Borchardt, an official at the Jewish Agency who dealt with emigration to Palestine, England and Scandinavia, received a telephone call from the Gestapo who told him they did not want to see him again. He now knew he had to get out or face being taken to a concentration camp. Shortly afterwards, Frank telephoned him.

'I was informed by Capt Foley that I should collect 80 permits for Great Britain from the British consulate building in the Tiergartenstrasse by not later than 4 o'clock that afternoon,' Borchardt said. 'In this way, 80 young people were saved shortly before the outbreak of war. I am profoundly grateful to Capt Foley for this. I left Berlin before midnight on the same day with a permit to Great Britain signed by Foley.'

After bidding farewell to Borchardt, Frank locked up the Passport Control Office for the last time. Back at Lessingstrasse, Kay had packed their clothes, all they could take with them. 'As we left our lovely home, I slipped a little object I treasured, a little icon, in my pocket,' she said. 'I knew we should not come back. We never saw any of our lovely things again.'

She then joined Ann Forbes-Robertson, Margaret Reid and the rest of the female staff on the train to the Hook of Holland, from where they took the ferry to Harwich. In a letter to her mother written from the boat-train, Margaret Reid expressed her regret at leaving the Berlin Passport Control Office behind. 'They were a good crowd there and though I was worked off my feet I enjoyed the feeling of being of use and trusted.'

Meanwhile, Frank drove north to Copenhagen to make further arrangements for his new posting, and then returned to London for a couple of days' briefing. But even after his departure from Berlin, his efforts to help Jews get out of Germany were continuing. During the first week of the war, Youth Aliyah certificates deposited in Frank's office, and signed by him, were being used by the American embassy to dispatch hundreds of children to Scandinavia and, through Trieste, to Palestine.

Quite how many Jews Frank had saved from the impending Holocaust is impossible to tell. But Pollack, who was one of those best placed to know, said that between 1933 and 1939 tens of thousands more people received visas than should have done under a strict interpretation of the rules.

'I know possibly better than any other Jew alive how great our debt of gratitude is towards that honest and courageous man,' Pollack said.

> People who do not know Capt Foley, or knew him only briefly, might think I am exaggerating or that, for whatever reason, I am according him unjustified honours. Not at all. The number of Jews saved from Germany would have been tens of thousands less, yes, tens of thousands less, if an officious bureaucrat had sat in Foley's place. There is no word of Jewish gratitude towards this man which could be exaggerated.

Chapter 16

The Oslo Report

Kay set up the family home in Stourbridge, where the Foleys rented a house so she could be near her sister Rita. 'Frank and Kay came to live in a small semi-detached house in Eveson Rd, Norton, a few doors above us,' said Irene Berlyn. The house was rented, because all their money had been tied up in Germany. 'When they escaped from the embassy in Germany they had to leave all their belongings behind. They'd had a good life and a wonderful house and they came here with absolutely nothing.'

Their next-door neighbours in Eveson Road were Ken and Beryl Price. 'Kay arrived just two days before the war in a great big Opel which didn't have a British registration,' Beryl said. 'It was in the garage in Eveson Rd and the police were making inquiries and thinking she might be suspicious. I suppose they thought she was a German spy.'

Meanwhile, Frank set off for Copenhagen *en route* for Oslo with Margaret Reid, who was to be his secretary. He had been singularly unimpressed with the organisation of the Oslo office, which like a number of MI6 stations at that time was poorly run and highly insecure, and had insisted that if the agents in Germany were to be run from there everything would have to change. 'My job will be more responsible as I shall have to reorganise the office on Berlin lines and be Captain Foley's private secretary,' Margaret Reid told her mother.

> I must say I think I am one of the favoured ones.
>
> I was to have met my chief on the train at Liverpool St but he missed it! There was a first-class traffic jam. I was not perturbed about Mr F missing his train. I guessed what had happened but was pleased to get a radiogram from him saying 'Flying Copenhagen tomorrow'. The train journey to Copenhagen was tedious as it was a breakdown makeshift train but we had good company in the carriage.

Frank was already in Copenhagen by the time the train arrived.

> The chief and the man in Copenhagen met me at the station, having waited nearly an hour for me, and took me off to the Astoria where I had a lovely room with a bathroom. Then they took me out to see night life in Copenhagen. *The Times* correspondent from Berlin joined us and another man who was on the Berlin staff for a short time. We finished up with bacon and eggs at 3.30 am.

Later that morning, Frank took Margaret out to see the city's sights.

> We had lunch in Copenhagen with about six journalists sitting on the street outside the Angleterre. They had lost flats and cars and property in Berlin but they were all very cheerful and enjoying Danish food. The Russian wife of one of them had smuggled four cats out of Germany and into Denmark (which is forbidden) and couldn't leave the hotel as they were in her room. The two of us spent a delightful afternoon in Kronberg at Hamlet's castle – he is most charming company and draws one out.

Early next morning, Frank and Margaret took the ferry to Malmö and made their way north by train through Sweden to Norway. German troops were already preparing to cross the border into Poland, and a few days after they arrived in Oslo, Britain and Germany were at war.

Frank began reorganising the MI6 station in Oslo. He wanted it moved out of the legation building, out of sight of the minister, Sir Cecil Dormer, who had made it clear he was not keen on secret service activities that might upset relations with the neutral Norwegians. He vetoed the delivery to the MI6 station of one of the new wireless transmitters which the service was gradually introducing. Frank had it smuggled in anyway.

This was a tricky time for Frank. The role of Passport Control Officer Scandinavia had no bureaucratic justification since there were already PCOs in Oslo, Stockholm and Helsinki. Foley was simply there because it was a convenient place from which to run the MI6 agents in Germany.

These were largely Germans or people from countries not at war with Germany, like Norway and Sweden, who would therefore have continued access to the country. They included a network of merchant seamen who were members of the International Transport Federation and had been recruited, with the assistance of Naval Intelligence, before the war, and railwaymen inside Germany, many of whom had also been trade unionists. These agents were able to provide a wide range of intelligence from conditions inside the Third Reich to details of weapons production.

Foley also recruited a number of Norwegian diplomats to act as couriers. They brought out information produced by dissident scientists like Rosbaud, who could occasionally go to Oslo themselves on business to make contact with Foley.

But initially, it was difficult. It would take some time before the agents inside Germany would begin producing useful intelligence, and after the frenetic pace of the last six years in Germany, Frank found it hard to adjust to the slower rhythm.

'My poor chief is a bundle of nervous energy and is very unhappy with not enough to do,' Margaret Reid wrote to her mother. 'I fetched him out this afternoon to do some correspondence and then he took me to tea in a café and we went for a walk along the harbour.'

They were having trouble sorting the office out, Reid said.

> The lady who has been here for 11 years when the office was
> a one-man show is proving very kind in looking for rooms and
> shopping etc. But she has to be handled very tactfully in the
> office. My chief wants all her old methods scrapped but it must
> be done most circumspectly and she is very slow on the uptake
> and is convinced that everything is in a terrible muddle.

To make matters worse, Commander J. B. Newill, the previous
head of station in Oslo, was unhappy at having a new man, albeit
someone of Frank's undoubted experience, being put in above
him and then demanding that everything be changed. 'There
was a certain jealousy between Newill and Foley,' Margaret Reid
recalled.

> Frank suffered, as all small men do, from an inferiority complex
> about himself and his work. He was not always Persona Grata in
> Norway. We came into a situation where there was already an
> officer in charge.
>   Newill was the 'man on the spot' talking Norwegian, and PCO
> Norway in a slummy little office in Drammensveien with a
> Norwegian office boy and Miss Wiley, an elderly woman secretary
> under him. We arrived from Berlin, upset the office, dismissed the
> office boy, took new quarters in the big office block looking over
> the harbour and introduced all sorts of security measures.

But things would soon improve. One of Frank's contacts from the
work with the Jews was about to come up trumps.

Shortly before the war, Hans Ferdinand Mayer had warned
Cobden Turner about 'new and formidable secret weapons' which
Siemens were involved in developing and which might be used to
attack Britain. Mayer refused to provide any further details, but
promised that, if it came to war, he would do so.

Mayer was almost certainly unaware that the British official who
provided Martyl Karweik, the young half-Jewish girl abandoned
by her Nazi father, with a passport was a member of MI6. But

he clearly knew that Cobden Turner had some kind of access to British intelligence officials and that any secret information passed to him would find its way to the right place.

On the outbreak of war, Mayer sought to get in touch with him to give him more details of the German secret weapons. 'I considered Mr Cobden Turner to be the right person, who had the ability and the connections to channel this information to the proper authorities in England,' Mayer said.

In the jargon of the spy, Cobden Turner was a 'cut-out' between Frank and Mayer, a go-between allowing contact between the intelligence officer and his source without either of them ever meeting and falling under suspicion. Shortly before the outbreak of the war, Turner, acting on Frank's instructions, had told Mayer that if he had any information he should pass it to the British legation in Oslo. Frank would be waiting for it.

'By good fortune, I had the possibility to arrange a business trip to Oslo, Norway, on October 29–November 4, 1939,' Mayer later recalled. 'Here, on an old typewriter, borrowed from a hotel porter, I wrote the so-called Oslo Report, which incidentally consisted of two different letters, written on Wednesday, November 1, and Thursday, November 2. These letters were mailed to the British embassy in Oslo. The address was easily found in the Oslo telephone directory.'

Mayer had been concerned at the idea of passing the information on to someone he did not know and considered posting them direct to Cobden Turner in England, but in the end wrote a separate letter to him suggesting that it might be easier in future for them to meet in Denmark. 'For obvious reasons, I signed this letter not with my name but with Martyl.'

In fact, Frank had moved the MI6 station out of the legation building by the time the letters arrived, and they were given to the naval attaché, Admiral Hector Boyes. One of the Norwegians who had close contacts with both Frank Foley and Margaret Reid confirmed that the letters were intended for Frank. 'Regarding the Oslo Report of November 1939,' said General Leif Rolstad, who was the Norwegian liaison officer attached to Frank during the evacuation of Norway, 'I understood that these papers seemingly were intended for Mr Foley, but were by mischance handed to the only British forces attaché on the spot, Rear-Admiral Boyes, who presumably did not know what it was all about and did not inform Foley.'

Boyes would later recall being given the letters and being unsure of their provenance. 'At that period, one was inundated with various anonymous correspondence which it was necessary to sift,' Boyes said. 'On translating the German correspondence, there appeared to be matters of interest though one had a certain mistrust, the letters having been posted in Norway.' Boyes sent the papers back to the Admiralty in London, from where they were passed to the headquarters of MI6 at Broadway Buildings.

There was some delay in their being dealt with, at least in part because the service had just suffered two major setbacks in the space of two days. Under pressure from the Foreign Office to make contact with German opposition groups prepared to form an alternative government, MI6 had been drawn into an elaborate sting set up by the Nazi intelligence service, the Sicherheitsdienst. Two MI6 officers based in Holland were lured to Venlo, on the border with Germany, for a meeting with alleged members of the opposition to Hitler, and then bundled across the frontier by a Sicherheitsdienst snatch squad. Not only was it a major propaganda coup for the Germans, it blew a number of the remaining networks in occupied Europe.

In the middle of the Venlo débâcle, Admiral Hugh Sinclair, the head of MI6, died of cancer and was replaced by Stewart Menzies, one of Frank's former Intelligence Corps colleagues. Eventually, however, the Oslo Report found its way on to the desk of R.V. Jones, the principal scientific adviser to MI6.

'It was the most amazing statement I have ever seen,' Jones said.

It included information that the Germans had under development two kinds of radar, one of which was already in use. It also told us of important experimental stations, that rocket and glider bombs were being developed, and other things too.

It was so comprehensive that many people thought it was a plant, because no one man could possible have that amount of information, particularly in Germany. But as time went on and one item after another in the Oslo Report came out, one obviously had to trust it and in the few dull moments of the war, it became my custom to look up the report to see what should be coming next.

The letters contained details of a new long-range bomber; the first German aircraft carrier; two new types of torpedo; and a remote-controlled glider carrying a large explosive charge – the weapon that was to be developed into the predecessor of the V-1 flying bomb which, the report said, was being developed at Peenemünde, in north-eastern Germany. But like much of the information supplied by MI6 it was disregarded by the armed forces because it did not fit in with their own prejudices. This was surprising, given that the package contained an actual electronic proximity fuse developed by Siemens that was far better than anything the British had at the time. It was not until four years later that major air raids were launched against Peenemünde.

A few weeks later, Frank received some devastating news. Sheila St Clair, his principal secretary for fifteen years both in Berlin and Oslo, was diagnosed as having terminal cancer. 'It was a terrible day when the chief came back from lunch and told me,' Margaret Reid told her mother. 'I found him nearly in tears in his room and had to write a confidential letter to the London Director to inform him and to ask them to get her into a hospital at once.'

By coincidence, Paula Weber, the friend whose bedroom Margaret had stayed in while in Berlin, was now in Oslo and anxious to get a visa for Britain to join her family.

> I went to the British embassy with a German passport – what else was I to do? – and said: 'I want a visa for England'. My passport was taken out of the reception room and back came a little man,

because Frank wasn't very tall, holding my passport. He looked at me and said: 'Who last slept in your bed.' Now the answer was Margaret, his secretary, my friend and I said: 'Margaret'. So then he knew who I was.

He didn't just give me a visa, he asked me to stay because one of his staff had cancer and had to be accompanied to London to a nursing home. He asked me would I mind doing that and I said certainly not. It was two days after the Germans had shot down one of the planes from Norway to Holland and we flew all the way to Holland at 1,000 feet and there we changed planes. We had blacked out windows and I have to this day no idea where we landed. It must have been somewhere in Kent. There was a Foreign Office car to fetch us there and I took her to the nursing home and I went to visit her afterwards.

As an increasing number of reports began to come in from the agents in Germany, Frank acquired the assistance of a deputy, his former colleague from Berlin, Leslie H. Mitchell, a tall, thin young man, with a slight forward stoop and an anxious expression of short-sightedness, who got on well with both his boss and Margaret Reid.

One of the agents who had resurfaced was Rosbaud, who managed to get to Oslo in December. He passed some technical papers to Frank, using a scientific colleague, Odd Hassel, as a cut-out. 'He asked Hassel to deliver a book of some scientific papers to the English embassy,' another scientist and former member of Norwegian Intelligence said. 'My impression was that there was nothing special about these papers but simply that Rosbaud did not want to be seen entering the English embassy. As Rosbaud had said that he had little time because of some meeting, Hassel had consented to do the errand for him. I therefore believe that Hassel had no idea of the real value of the material he was delivering at the embassy.'

Around the same time, the railwaymen and merchant seamen of the ITF networks started to report an ominous build-up of activity in Germany's northern ports. An expeditionary force was being assembled and trained. Merchant ships were being modified to carry troops and vehicles. But the intelligence departments of the Admiralty, the Air Ministry and the War Office were disinclined to believe MI6 agent reports. Over the next few months, a number of other reports indicating an impending invasion of Norway were ignored, including intercepts deciphered by the code-breakers at Bletchley Park placing a German spy ship, the *Theseus*, in Norwegian waters.

As part of the preparations for Operation Weserübung, the planned German invasion of Norway, the Abwehr had placed a team of intelligence officers in the German embassy in Oslo with orders to observe 'the activities of enemy nationals in Norway'; evaluate the strength, disposition and operational objectives of the Norwegian armed forces; and examine the harbour installations in Oslo, Kristiansand, Stavanger, Bergen, Trondheim and Narvik 'with a view to landing troops'.

By March, there had been a plethora of reports indicating that an invasion was imminent, all of which were ignored by the various government departments. The Admiralty believed the increase in German naval movements to be part of an attempt by German warships to break out into the Atlantic. The Air Ministry was convinced that the increased Luftwaffe activity was connected to plans for a major assault on Britain. The War Office did not believe the Germans would want to march into Scandinavia with less than twenty-five divisions – there were only six available – while the Foreign Office was more concerned that Britain's own plans to mine Norwegian waters, and thereby obstruct German supplies of Swedish iron ore from the northern port of Narvik, might imperil relations with Oslo.

'In the days immediately preceding the Germans' move numerous clues as to their intentions were received by Whitehall departments,' said Edward Thomas, a wartime intelligence officer. 'Its failure to coordinate this wealth of evidence and to interpret it correctly is a disgrace to British intelligence.'

This was not the fault of the officers at 'the sharp end', like Frank and Leslie Mitchell, of course. The problem lay in London, with the various intelligence departments that were supposed to be analysing the reports coming in from agents, from the missions overseas and from Bletchley Park.

'Of course, we had full reports days ahead,' Frank said. 'We had all the movements of shipping as they occurred. But they did not know what to make of them in London.'

This was a direct result of the lack of any proper intelligence co-ordination. The Joint Intelligence Committee, which was supposed to perform this task, was still in its infancy. Individual departments saw only those reports that specifically concerned them. So the Admiralty, for example, while fully briefed on the build-up of German naval vessels in the area, was only partially aware of a similar increase in Luftwaffe activity.

'In those days, there was no effective machinery for bringing all the evidence together and thinking what it might mean,' said Edward Thomas. 'Had there been it is scarcely credible that it would not have dented the prevailing view in Whitehall that the Germans would never dare send an expedition across the sea in the face of British naval power.'

By early April, so many reports of German intentions to occupy both Denmark and Norway were coming in that anybody seeing them all could not have failed to predict correctly what was happening. Still the British tinkered with their own plans to lay mines in Norwegian waters and land a fairly limited amount of troops in the event of similar action by the Germans.

On 7 April, the Admiralty effectively negated its own report on the latest pointers towards a German invasion with the words: 'All these reports are of doubtful value and may well be only a further move in the war of words.' A day later, the War Office concluded that the available intelligence did not point definitively to a German attack.

That night, one of Frank's contacts flew into Oslo from Copenhagen with confirmation that the German invasion force was already on its way. As his aircraft crossed the Skagerrak, the straits dividing Norway from Denmark, the waters had been full of

German ships heading north. Frank sent an urgent signal to London, and he and Mitchell began activating the emergency procedures. There were already contingency plans for the agents in Germany to be run from Stockholm in the event of an invasion. But Norwegian agents would need to be briefed to operate as stay-behind networks, reporting on the activities of the German occupation forces.

Two of the few recruited in what little time they had were twenty-one-year-old Oluf Reed Olsen and his friend Kaare Moe. Reed Olsen cannot now remember the identity of the man who recruited him. He only knows that 'a British captain who was then working for the British intelligence system' asked them to carry out a number of small intelligence-gathering tasks.

'Our first jobs were small ones, photographing and sketching German airfields, and mapping them; the same for German defence works and military positions and installations; also finding out about German troop movements, what kind of troops were concerned, to what units the German troops who passed through Oslo belonged, where they came from and where they were going.'

They also carried out minor acts of sabotage and stole a new piece of direction-finding equipment from a Heinkel aircraft parked at Oslo's Fornebu airfield, before sailing a small boat to Britain where they were trained to go back into Norway.

Frank telephoned Margaret Reid at three o'clock in the morning to tell her she should come to the office at once and be ready to go. 'I can hear my "OK" – slightly shrill and hysterical – as I put the phone down,' she wrote in her diary. 'The taxi exchange refused to send me a car, but fortunately I hailed one in the main road and reached the office in time. FF and the Commander were tearing files out of their drawers in the open safes. We took the loose cash and packed the files into waste paper baskets.'

Accompanied by Leslie Mitchell, who had just turned up, they made their way by taxi to the British legation.

> We saw a great bonfire before we reached the grounds. The men there were already at work. We struggled up the muddy slope

with our precious waste-paper baskets and were soon frantically rending code books and files to feed the flames. The fire brigade, unconscious of what was afoot, appeared on the scene shortly and wanted to put the fire out. We laughed and told them to bring some petrol for the blaze.

Chapter 17

The Foley Mission

Around seven o'clock, the embassy staff were organised into various carloads and headed north, through Lillestrom and along Lake Mjosa, to Hamar. Frank's orders from Head Office were to get King Haakon and the Norwegian gold reserves safely back to Britain. It was vital that neither should fall into German hands. The King was needed to give any government-in-exile credibility.

After making sure that Margaret was in one of the cars bound for Hamar, Frank sent Newill and Mitchell to Stockholm to get more wireless equipment, and then went off on a small mission of his own, said Hubert Pollack. 'He arranged – under the most difficult circumstances – for the flight to Sweden of a number of Jews who otherwise would have been trapped by the swiftly advancing Germans.'

Frank then made his own way north through Hamar and on to Hosbjor, a few miles further along the lake, where the legation staff were esconced in a hotel overlooking the water. Meanwhile, the Norwegian government was meeting in emergency session in Hamar, still undecided as to whether or not to accept the German occupation and negotiate terms.

Sir Cecil Dormer, having been in touch with the Foreign Office via the same MI6 wireless transmitter that he had previously refused to allow inside the legation, had informed Dr Halvdan Koht, the Norwegian Foreign Minister, that the British government had 'decided forthwith to extend full aid to Norway and will fight now in full association with them'. British troops were already on their way, although it would take some time for them to get there.

At nine o'clock that evening, Hosbjor was evacuated in the face of the advancing German troops. Both the government and the various foreign missions set off for Elverum, about twenty miles to the west, towards the safety of Sweden.

'H M Minister ordered his staff to leave the hotel within 30 minutes for Elverum,' Frank wrote in a report to the head of MI6. 'During the day, a good many people had collected at the Hosbjor Hotel. A shortage of transport ensued as some cars had been hired.' Margaret and Frank were left stranded with nine other members of the legation staff.

'I had secured a seat for her in the car of a diplomat, but she refused to accept it on the grounds that it was her duty to stay with me,' Frank said. 'She gave her place to another lady. Miss Reid's action was as brave as it was fortunate. She remained to do work which no one else could do.'

Margaret had not seen her action as brave, nor could she yet predict how vital it would be. 'I shall never cease to be grateful for the somewhat selfish piece of strategy by which I managed to remain behind at that point,' she later wrote. 'I confess that I had wanted to stay where my chief was, but I had till then not dared to question orders which were given to me. I suppose the situation was not very bright but somehow I could not believe in this unseen menace – the advancing hordes of Germans who were cutting off our retreat to Sweden.'

By the time they managed to secure two taxis it was too late to go to Elverum – the Germans were almost certainly already in Hamar. So they made their way north towards the coast up a long gorge known as the Gudbrandsdal. They stopped briefly at Lillehammer, but having learned that the Norwegian government had now resolved to resist the German invasion and had ordered a general mobilisation, they then decided that it was better to make use of what transport was still available and so pressed on through the night.

'How we blessed the splendid American cars that serve as taxis in Norway,' Margaret wrote in her diary. 'They were well heated and roomy and one could comfortably sleep in them. I remember my head jolting on the comfortable greatcoat shoulder next to me.'

They stopped halfway up the Gudbrandsdal at a hotel in Otta. Next morning Frank and the legation's press secretary, Rowland Kenney, went off to ask the town's mayor for assistance in procuring transport, Margaret wrote. 'Shortly after 10 o'clock, the two chiefs arrived back in great agitation, having heard that the Germans were advancing along the railway line and were only four kilometres away.'

In fact, the Germans were much further back down the gorge. But Frank and his party were not to know this. They managed to commandeer a bus to take them on past Dombass to the port of Andalsnes, from where they hoped to make their way back to Britain.

By the time they reached Dombass, the Gudbrandsdal had turned into a valley flanked by rolling hills. Here and there were farmhouses with cows searching for grass in amongst the snow. Ahead of them were the Dovrefjell mountains, their snow-capped peaks visible above the clouds, and beyond these lay the port of Andalsnes.

'The only train was not due to go for several hours,' wrote Margaret. 'So we decided to proceed by bus. We were then very glad of the sandwiches our landlady at Otta had packed for us. We gave some to the driver and – fortified with a swig of whisky, which the girls gave me in the Ladies lavatory – I felt warmed and fit for anything that might lie ahead.'

As the bus climbed up the mountainside, the snow began to fall first in small flurries and then suddenly in a raging snowstorm that completely blotted out anything more than a few yards ahead.

Gradually, the storm died away and they found themselves in what appeared to be a completely white wilderness.

A passing lorry driver warned them that there were German bombers over Andalsnes but added to a cheer that there were also three British warships out in the fjord. Occasional carloads of refugees made their way in the opposite direction, and two or three times they saw small groups of reservists gathering with rifles to join the army in its defence of Norway.

As the bus began its downward descent into Andalsnes, the mood among Frank's small party became more cheerful. They sang traditional British Tommies' songs – 'A Long Way To Tipperary' and 'Roll Out The Barrel' – and snatches of Gilbert and Sullivan.

Frank showed Margaret the MI6 emergency codebook – an 1865 edition of John Ruskin's *Sesame and Lilies*. Head Office had an identical copy, allowing for a rudimentary code to be constructed, he told her. But the radio had gone to Stockholm with Newill, and it had been so long since Frank had been shown how to use the code, he could no longer remember what to do. 'I don't know how to use it,' he said. 'I might as well throw it away.'

'Oh, don't do that on any account,' said Margaret. 'I think I know how to work it.' She had never actually used the code but a visiting member of the Copenhagen station had shown her how to operate it once. 'I was trying yesterday to remember how it went,' she said.

They reached Andalsnes in the early evening of Wednesday, 10 April, to discover that the rumour about British warships in the harbour was false. But there were at least enough rooms for them in the Hotel Bellevue, providing hot water for a bath and a comfortable bed for the night.

The next day Margaret found the second-in-command of the local infantry battalion, who took Frank to see his commander. 'The officers did not know whether we British were friends or enemies,' Frank said in his report to Menzies. 'The colonel telephoned to Norwegian headquarters and, on being assured that we were friends, he put the Vigra broadcasting station at our disposal.'

For two days, there had been no contact between Britain and Norway; now at last they could get in touch with London. Margaret's room was set up as an ad hoc secure signals office, and Frank drafted the first message to MI6 headquarters for her to encode.

> TO LONDON. FOLLOWING FROM FOLEY. I HAVE C-IN-C'S PERMISSION
> TO USE W/T. MESSAGES FOLLOW. LISTEN TO ME. 24 HOURS SERVICE.
> MESSAGE ENDS.

The message was broadcast every hour by the Vigra station until it was picked up at Wick in northern Scotland and passed on first to Rugby and then to London. That night there was an air-raid warning in Andalsnes. But the aircraft appeared to have been on a reconnaissance flight and no bombs were dropped. 'I slept tranquilly that night,' Margaret Reid said. 'The last tranquil night for many weeks to come.'

Early next morning they received a reply from Broadway Buildings in London.

> YOUR TELEGRAM RECEIVED AND UNDERSTOOD. WIRELESS OPERATORS
> AND CYPHERS BEING DESPATCHED BY FAST WARSHIP. MESSAGE ENDS.
> P.S. HEARTY CONGRATULATIONS. ENGLAND EXPECTS AND IS NEVER
> LET DOWN. BLACK CATS AND HORSESHOES.

'We were thrilled at this news and hurried to waken the girls to tell them,' Margaret wrote. 'More messages arrived before we had had breakfast and we were soon busy in my room again answering their queries and sending such scraps of information as we had. There was a pause while FF was in conference with the Colonel and we repaired to the sunny balcony off the girls' bedroom and basked there and sang all manner of hearty and sentimental songs.'

That evening there was an urgent telephone call from Major-General Otto Ruge, the Norwegian commander-in-chief, calling Frank to his headquarters on a small farm known as Klokkergarden at Oyer, a few miles north of Lillehammer and some way back down the Gudbrandsdal. 'FF replied that he would come at once on the night train and bring a lady secretary with him for coding,' Margaret wrote. 'He was greatly excited at the news and I had to chase him around the hotel to get him to settle various problems.'

Frank and Margaret travelled down to Oyer by train through the night, Margaret wrote. 'In view of the ordeal in front of us, we put out the carriage lights, took off our boots and tried to sleep.'

At 3.30 a.m. the following morning, having arrived at the Klokkergarden farm, they went into a council of war with General Ruge.

'I have sent for you Mr Foley,' the general said,

> because I heard you were in contact with England and because I myself am without any means of communication with the outside world. I must thank you for your immediate response to my appeal.
>
> I must tell you simply that we cannot hold on unless England comes to our aid at once with all the forces and material she can spare. The Germans have seized at one swoop our stores and ammunition at Oslo, Bergen and Trondheim. The country is now mobilising but when the men are called up there is neither uniform for them to wear nor weapons for them to fight with. Unless we can obtain help from England today or tomorrow we shall be forced to lay down our arms before we have struck a blow in the defence of our country.

Frank explained that he had come, in the absence of the British minister, as a representative of the British government, and assured the Norwegian commander that he would do everything in his power to help him. Margaret also took part in the discussions. 'I think this is one of the few occasions, if not the only one, on which an English girl has attended a Council of War as an actual member,' Frank wrote later. 'It was a council of momentous importance as it kept Norway in the war. It was agreed that an urgent appeal should be telegraphed to the British Prime Minister.'

Foley and Ruge drafted out a series of appeals to Chamberlain and Margaret encoded them. They were then taken to Lillehammer where postal telegraph operators sent them to Vigra. Each was preceded by the words PRIORITY ABSOLUTE. CLEAR THE LINE. The first was a direct appeal from Ruge to Chamberlain.

> WE BEGAN THIS WAR IN THE BELIEF THAT THE BRITISH GOVERNMENT WOULD ACT AT ONCE. WE WERE SURPRISED BEFORE WE HAD TIME TO MOBILISE AND LOST ALL OUR AIRCRAFT, SUPPLIES AND STORES. WE ARE PREPARED TO RECEIVE TROOPS AT ONCE AND TO ACT IMMEDIATELY FROM OUR SIDE. MY KING, CROWN PRINCE AND GOVERNMENT ARE BEING HUNTED BY GERMAN BOMBERS AND WERE BOMBED LAST NIGHT. THE PEOPLE ARE ALL FOR FIGHTING BUT THEY CANNOT FIGHT WITHOUT ASSISTANCE.

A succession of pleas for assistance followed:

> WE MUST HAVE ACTIVE MILITARY ASSISTANCE INSTANTLY AND IMMEDIATELY. THAT IS TODAY AND TOMORROW. IF WE GET THAT THE SITUATION WILL BE REESTABLISHED IN A SHORT TIME. IF WE DO NOT GET IT NORWAY WILL BE GERMAN WITHIN A WEEK.

> IT IS IMPORTANT YOU SHOULD REALISE THAT NORWAY HAS LOST HER ARSENALS AND SUPPLIES IN TOWNS CAPTURED BY GERMANS. THEY ARE FIGHTING ALMOST WITH THEIR BARE FISTS.

Finally, there was a personal message for C from Foley:

> C-IN-C NORWAY WHO IS A VERY LEVEL-HEADED MAN SAYS THAT UNLESS TRONDHEIM IS RECAPTURED AT ONCE BY A RUTHLESS ATTACK THERE WILL BE A FIRST-CLASS DISASTER FROM WHICH THE ALLIES WILL FIND IT HARD TO RECOVER. C-IN-C MEANS EVERY WORD OF HIS TELEGRAM TO THE PM.

Shortly afterwards, the responses began to come back, including a personal assurance from Chamberlain that British troops were on their way. 'We are coming as fast as possible and in great strength,' the British Prime Minister said. 'We are inspired by your message and feel sure that you have only to hold on until we arrive for both our countries to emerge victorious.'

Frank took the message to Ruge. They made a stark contrast, the short, grey-haired British spy in his tweed suit, peering owlishly through his round glasses, and the tall, spare general in crumpled combat fatigues. Ruge's gratitude for the British assurance was immediately evident. He shook Frank's hand vigorously. 'Mr Foley,' he said. 'I thank you. Your name will go down in history.'

Two of the other British secretaries were drafted in to help Margaret while Ruge attached a number of Norwegian troops to what was to become known as 'the Foley Mission'. The Norwegians seemed to regard the British members of the mission with some awe, Margaret said. 'It was amusing to find that they called Frank *Schjefen*, the Chief, which was an office nickname for him. He was also called wuff, the way little dogs bark.'

Leif Rolstad, then a captain, was in charge of Frank's Norwegians, and his reports make clear his admiration for the MI6 officer. 'Foley is continuing his work all day – and has been at it all night – with unfailing energy,' he said.

> Apart from the General, I think I have never experienced any man of such intense energy and speed of work. Always as clear and concise as before, however little he sleeps. He works his people to the bone, but encourages them to do their utmost.
>
> Foley is a fairly short, thickset gentleman in his fifties, slightly bulldog face and always wears a smart dark suit. He has great thoughts of his own prowess, and is a little vain on this point, but has the best of intentions and is otherwise a splendid and most kind fellow. I like him very much indeed. He was a staff captain in World War I and has very sound military judgement. He is using 110 per cent of his energy to help us!

When news came through that an advance party of British troops, the first elements in a ten-thousand-strong Anglo-French intervention force, had landed north of Narvik on 14 April, Frank took it up to General Ruge. 'General,' he said. 'You asked for help today or tomorrow. We could not come today, but we came on the next day.'

The general was unimpressed. Narvik was six hundred miles to the north, too far away to be of any immediate assistance to him. He remained concerned that the British were not serious in their offer of help. That night, Frank and his party were joined by the British military attaché in Helsinki, Lt-Col. E.J.C. King-Salter, and his French counterpart, Commandant Bertrand Vigne, who had been sent to make contact with the Norwegian commander-in-chief.

'I was very relieved to find that a Major Foley, a secretary at the British Legation, assisted by his secretary Miss Reid and later by two other ladies, had joined Norwegian GHQ a day or two previously and with a special code of his own was in touch with London,' wrote King-Salter in his official report. 'For some days this was the only channel of communication and, the code being a very laborious one, there was a limit to the messages that could be received and sent. Major Foley and his staff were working continuously day and night. He had in addition, entirely on his own, been fulfilling admirably the functions of an Allied Mission!'

Frank again reinforced the Norwegian appeals with his own personal messages to C.

I HAVE HAD A CONVERSATION WITH THE COMMANDER-IN-CHIEF WHO TAKES AN OPTIMISTIC VIEW OF THE SITUATION PROVIDED HE CAN GET ASSISTANCE AT ONCE, I.E. TODAY OR TOMORROW. HE IS OF THE OPINION THAT IF THE BRITISH DO NOT HELP HIM NOW THE WAR WILL BE ENDED IN A VERY FEW DAYS.

THE NORWEGIAN GOVERNMENT WENT TO WAR ON THE PROMISE OF DORMER THAT BRITAIN WOULD ACT AT ONCE. THE FORMER COMMANDER-IN-CHIEF RESIGNED TWO DAYS AGO BECAUSE HE DID NOT BELIEVE THE BRITISH WOULD ACT QUICKLY ENOUGH. THE PRESENT COMMANDER-IN-CHIEF, WHO TRUSTED THE BRITISH WORD, MUST NOT BE LET DOWN. HE COMMENDED ME TO TELL YOU AGAIN HE FEARS HE WILL NOT BE ABLE TO HOLD OUT MUCH LONGER. PLEASE TAKE HIS WORD MOST EARNESTLY. YOU CANNOT CONCEIVE PITIABLE CONDITIONS MATERIAL THIS ARMY BUT MEN FINE TYPES.

On 16 April, the telegraph lines were cut and contact with London was temporarily lost. But that morning, Newill and Mitchell arrived with the wireless transmitter and ciphers from the embassy in Stockholm. Frank persuaded the Norwegians to give them a large Pontiac car to use as a mobile base for the wireless in order to make it more difficult for the Germans to track the position of the transmitter down.

Two days later, the British 148th Territorial Brigade, under the command of Brigadier Harold de Reimer Morgan, landed at Andalsnes with orders to secure Dombass, to make contact with the Norwegians and then to march on Trondheim. It was met by King-Salter, who persuaded Morgan that to head for Trondheim with the poorly trained territorial troops he had at his disposal would be suicidal, and it was better to obey the rest of his orders and link up with the Norwegians.

Colonel Dudley Clarke, one of Morgan's officers, described their meeting with General Ruge. 'He was an erect, spare figure with keen blue eyes,' Clarke wrote. 'He made it clear that he was staking everything on help from Britain. Any doubts we may have had before of Norway's determination to fight on disappeared for good, leaving behind some shame that we should ever have voiced them at all.'

Morgan agreed to put his troops at Ruge's disposal in a defensive line north of Lillehammer. The Norwegian commander wanted to use the area around Trondheim as a base from which the Allies could then break out to recapture the rest of Norway.

The Norwegian government and the foreign diplomatic community, including Sir Cecil Dormer, had now arrived in the area, and Frank was beginning to feel slightly displaced, despite the fact that all messages from the Norwegian and British military forces were being sent over the MI6 wireless transmitter.

'With the commander-in-chief he held an undisputed position of trust and honour,' Margaret wrote in her diary. 'No conference was complete without him. There was no question of his being superseded in the esteem of the commander-in-chief. But as he had no official position at GHQ, he felt rather as though the men who had arrived later would gradually leave him with no title.'

But the hastily formed coalition of British and Norwegian soldiers was no match for the Germans. The British were poorly trained territorials, ill-equipped for fighting in alpine conditions and with vastly inferior firepower to the Wehrmacht troops.

In his report to London, Dormer described watching a train-load of Sherwood Foresters and Leicesters passing through Otta station on their way to the front. 'A few days later, we heard that five out of 50 officers and 400 out of 1200 or 1300 men were all that survived. The Germans had artillery and air supremacy and the troops they used were accustomed to mountains and forests whereas our troops had no guns to retaliate with and were fighting in strange surroundings.'

With the Germans relentlessly advancing, the next two weeks would be a steady retreat towards the coast during which 'the Foley Mission' came under repeated fire but remained the only link with the outside world for the Allied forces in Norway. It was also used to pass intelligence in both directions.

The campaign had allowed the code-breakers at the Government Code and Cipher School in Bletchley Park to make dramatic progress in their attempts to crack the German Enigma ciphers. Both the Wehrmacht and the Luftwaffe ciphers in use in Norway were broken shortly after the first Allied troops went ashore.

No one had been prepared for the amount of intelligence this would yield. Unprecedented details of German troop strengths, movements and intentions were being broadcast on the German radio networks. But no arrangements had been put in place to get that information to the people who needed it – the British troops on the ground in Norway.

At this stage, only thirty people outside of Bletchley Park even knew of its existence. Passing Ultra, as the 'Special Intelligence' material was to become known, over normal radio channels would have jeopardised the secrecy of the whole of the Bletchley Park operation. The only way any of the intelligence could be passed to the commanders in the field was via the MI6 radio channel to Foley, albeit disguised as 'information from our own forces'.

At Frank's request, every member of his party was now given military rank to protect them. He, Newill and Mitchell, and possibly Reid too, were listed in German records as members of MI6 and were liable to be shot as spies if they were captured. Frank and Newill were recommissioned in the field as captains. Mitchell was given the rank of lieutenant and Margaret was made a sergeant in the women's Auxiliary Territorial Service.

They were evacuated from the port of Molde by the Royal Navy in the early hours of Wednesday, 1 May 1940. Frank managed to ensure that the Norwegian gold reserves were brought safely back to Britain. But King Haakon refused to leave, sailing on HMS *Glasgow* for Tromso in northern Norway. He was to remain there until June when he was finally persuaded to come to London as a symbol of Norwegian resistance to the Nazis.

Margaret Reid received the Norwegian Krigsmedalje and the MBE, the latter only after a concerted campaign by Frank, who wrote to Sir Stewart Menzies, the head of MI6, spelling out her role in the affair and her 'extreme devotion to duty'. Frank was mentioned in dispatches and was awarded the Knight's Cross of St Olav by King Haakon in August 1943 for his part in the defence of Norway.

'On the entry of the Germans into Oslo, Major Foley arranged to join up with the commander-in-chief of the Norwegian forces who were offering opposition to the Germans,' the citation read. 'He was responsible for handling all communications between the British government and Gen Ruge. He spared no effort to assist the Norwegian forces in their fight against the Germans and was repeatedly very dangerously exposed to enemy fire.'

Chapter 18

The Shetland Bus

The success of 'the Foley Mission' in operating a secure wireless link to London was now seen at Head Office as a way of solving the problem of getting the intelligence coming out of Britain's code-breakers at Bletchley Park to the commanders in the field.

MI6 officers would be put in charge of small units of trained cipher clerks and wireless operators to be attached to overseas commands 'with the double purpose of providing an immediate link for the information and having an officer on the spot charged with seeing that all the necessary precautions were carried out for his security'.

At first sight, Frank – whose understanding of ciphers was so poor that until Margaret Reid dissuaded him he was considering throwing the codebook away and giving up on the radio – must have been a strange choice as the man in charge of the first of these units. But he was fluent in both French and German, and he was the only MI6 officer with any experience in operating a secure radio link in the field.

When Bletchley began breaking the Luftwaffe Enigma ciphers in May 1940, he was sent to France with a mobile MI6 special intelligence unit to interpret and disseminate the flood of operational intelligence that the code-breakers were producing.

With the bulk of the British Expeditionary Force about to be evacuated from Dunkirk, and the remaining Allied troops already in full retreat, no one seems to have been under any illusions over how much effect his mission might have on the fighting. Margaret Reid wrote to tell her mother that she was moving into Frank's Chelsea flat while he was away. 'Captain Foley is being sent this week on a continental trip,' she said. 'It should not last more than three weeks.'

Unfortunately, the lack of confidence was justified. The military had such a poor regard for MI6 that disguising the intercepted material as agents' reports merely ensured that the commanders did not believe it. But perhaps more importantly, with the Allied troops already in full retreat, even when they did accept that the intelligence Frank's unit was producing was accurate, they were in no position to make proper use of it. He and his men retreated through France with the British troops to Bordeaux from where they were to be evacuated back to Britain.

The city was crowded with refugees: French, Belgians, Britons and Poles, among them a large contingent of Jews, fleeing the impending holocaust. The British consulate was besieged with people seeking visas for Britain, a sight that must have brought back unpleasant memories for Frank. A Royal Navy warship, HMS *Arethusa*, was in the mouth of the Gironde ready to take off the British diplomats and military, who included Commander Ian Fleming, later the creator of James Bond but then a Naval Intelligence officer.

The *Arethusa* could not take civilians. There were, however, a number of merchant ships standing by in the estuary, including two P&O liners. Foley and Fleming helped to organise the evacuation, persuading the master of a car ferry to carry the refugees out to the waiting ships with a bundle of cash that Fleming had rescued from the safe of the MI6 station in Paris. Escorted by two British destroyers, the convoy crossed the Channel to Falmouth overnight, and by the next morning Frank was taking a train for London.

His mission had not contributed much to holding up the

Germans but the principle of using mobile MI6 wireless links to interpret and pass on the intelligence produced by the code-breakers had been shown to be workable, if only the problem of getting the commanders in the field to believe it could be overcome. In all future campaigns, MI6 Special Liaison Units, as they subsequently became known, were sent into battle to pass on the results of the code-breakers' work to the commanders.

Following the fall of France, the intelligence collection or 'Operations' department of MI6 was reorganised into G Sections, covering different areas of the world that were either neutral or unoccupied by the Germans, and A Sections for the occupied or hostile areas of Europe. These so-called 'production' sections were put under the control of the Assistant Chief of the Secret Service, Lt-Col. Claude Dansey, an ageing former soldier and businessman.

Dansey had been passed over for the post of 'C' on Sinclair's death, and as a result was both deeply cynical and cantankerous, particularly in his dealings with Vivian, who was now the Vice-Chief and Dansey's main rival for the ear of Menzies.

While the G Sections could feed off the work of the Passport Control Offices in the various countries they covered, the A Sections were forced to run their own agents into occupied territory. The A Sections were split largely for convenience rather than along logical geographical lines.

So Frank was appointed A1, heading a new section of the same name that covered Germany and Norway, the odd pairing of the two countries being an attempt to capitalise on his extensive knowledge of the Nazis and the more recent experience in Oslo. Within the service he was regarded as the 'éminence grise on Germany', while his close relationship with the Norwegians was rightly expected to be invaluable.

Eric Welsh, a Royal Naval Reserve officer who was fluent in Norwegian, was recruited from the Naval Intelligence Division and appointed as his deputy. They were joined by Newill, Mitchell and Margaret Reid, who was to remain as Frank's secretary.

'These A sections choose, recruit, train and despatch agents into occupied territory,' the KGB agent Kim Philby told Moscow Centre in one of his wartime reports. 'The methods used vary widely according to the particular problems involved. Men are landed by boat or parachute or are pushed into occupied territory from neutral countries (in cooperation with the G stations).'

Frank's London flat was a long-standing 'safe house' in Nell Gwynne House, Sloane Avenue, just opposite the Chelsea Cloisters, while Kay and Ursula remained in the relative safety of Stourbridge.

'Kay has been digging for victory,' Owen Lee wrote to his sister Joyce in Miami. 'She really has made her little garden look wonderful. Every inch is growing something. Rita is now a full-fledged nurse and attends at the military hospital, as does Kay twice a week.'

When he could, Frank would travel up to Stourbridge on a Friday evening to spend time with his wife and daughter. 'He would come home occasionally at the weekends and he always used to furiously do a bit of gardening as soon as he arrived,' said Beryl Price, the Foleys' next-door neighbour. If he was forced to stay in London by work, as he all too frequently was, Frank spent his Sundays attending Mass at the Brompton Oratory just a few hundred yards from his flat, before having lunch with one of his colleagues.

It was a difficult period for MI6. The loss of so many stations abroad had caused havoc with its networks. At best, its agents in the occupied countries had no link to Head Office. At worst, they had been compromised and arrested. But the refugees arriving in Britain provided an opportunity to build up new networks and to attempt to renew contacts with those that had been lost, Margaret Reid later recalled, 'When Europe began to disintegrate and refugees poured into this country from Belgium, Holland, France, as well as from Norway, we began to build up an intelligence service and train men to be dropped in their own countries behind the enemy lines.'

The invasion of Norway had presented particular problems for the Royal Navy, making it far more difficult to intercept the German ships that were attempting to break out into the Atlantic. A1's most immediate priority was 'to hold control over the movements of the major units of the German battle fleet along the Norwegian Coast'.

The main source of information on Norway was coming from the Ultra decrypts produced by the code-breakers at Bletchley Park, from aerial photography, and from the debriefing of refugees carried out by Naval Intelligence at the London Reception Centre in Wandsworth, south London.

There was also some intelligence coming out from teams of saboteurs infiltrated by the Special Operations Executive and from the MI6 agents like Reed Olsen who had been put in place by Frank and Leslie Mitchell before they got out. The most pressing need was to work on that. Under Frank's direction, the A1 section began to set up a coast-watching system to monitor the movement of the German ships along the Norwegian coast.

The goodwill built up by Frank with senior Norwegian officers during the retreat through Norway now began to pay huge dividends. King Haakon had set up a government-in-exile in London, and in July 1940 an intelligence office, known as FO II, was established, initially within the Norwegian Foreign Ministry, to work with Frank's section. The MI6 man was to have complete operational control over the agents.

There was no shortage of Norwegians prepared to go back into their homeland as agents. Since the German invasion, a regular flow of refugees had been arriving in Scotland and the Shetland Isles in the traditional Norwegian fishing smacks known as *skoyter* or puffers. Many of them had come to Britain with the specific intention of joining Milorg, the home resistance which worked with the SOE, or the intelligence organisation XU. They were assembled at Lerwick in the Shetland Islands and systematically interrogated by the Norwegians to weed out any plants before being assigned to either SOE or MI6 operations.

The MI6 agents were instructed in intelligence-gathering techniques, the use of codes, and how to operate a radio transmitter at the MI6 training school in London's St James's Street, while the SOE agents were taught at Fawley Court, near Henley-on-Thames. But neither was ideal for training men to go into Norway, and joint MI6/SOE schools were set up near Aviemore in the Cairngorms, in what the records describe as 'wild mountain country more similar to Norway, winter and summer, than any other tract of Britain', and at Toronto, in Canada, where there was a large number of Norwegian refugees.

Infiltration was a difficult problem. 'Dropping operations to the interior of Norway were never popular with the RAF,' the official SOE historian wrote. 'Weather conditions over the mountains were unpredictable and always dangerous to low flying at night, in any case aircraft were hard to come by in the summer of 1940.' But early on in the war, the puffers were able to cross the North Sea pretty much as they pleased, and since most of the agents had come out this way, it seemed to be the most obvious means of putting them back again.

In October 1940, at a meeting with the SOE's Scandinavian representatives, Frank proposed sending an officer acceptable to MI6, SOE and MI5 to the Shetlands with orders to requisition some of the boats and use them to run agents into and out of Norway.

Whoever it was would also need to check the credentials of any Norwegian who arrived there claiming to be an MI6 or SOE agent, in order to prevent the Germans infiltrating their operations; he would also have to debrief refugees arriving from Norway and talent-spot any potential agents who should be sent on to London; and crucially, for security purposes, he would have to keep the crews returning from Norway segregated from the local population to ensure there were no leaks.

The man Frank had in mind for the post of 'liaison officer and chief interrogator' was his long-time colleague from Berlin and Oslo, now working as one of his assistants, Leslie Mitchell.

A few weeks later Mitchell was sent to Lerwick with orders to requisition a flotilla of puffers.

He was a good choice to control the activities of the Norwegians, who were not used to the parade-ground discipline of the British military.

'He had a wise, kindly face, which did not accord well with brass buttons and he had too much sense of the ridiculous and his own fallibility to be a good parade-ground officer,' one of his colleagues said. 'But he had in plenty the much more valuable qualities of sympathy and humour and freedom from prejudice and false pride.'

Mitchell set up his headquarters in a dilapidated but comfortable farmhouse at Flemington, where the agents awaiting infiltration were billeted while the crews lived on board their boats at Lerwick or Cat Firth.

The puffers were sixty-foot wooden drifters powered by single-cylinder semi-diesel engines and with a large exhaust pipe extending out of the top of the wheelhouse. This made a loud popping noise which in calm weather could be heard miles away. Mitchell used the boats to ferry up to ten MI6 or SOE agents across the North Sea at a time at speeds of between 6 and 10 knots.

The crews would set out for sea from their home ports in Norway, ostensibly to fish, but under cover of darkness or bad visibility made for the Shetlands. They had to move fast in order to be back in port before anyone could suspect they might have been involved in anything more complicated than fishing. The operation gradually grew in success, becoming immortalised as the Shetland Bus.

The Norwegian agents were trained in the use of wireless transmitters and sent back home, normally to the districts or villages they had come from, in the hope that this would give them a better support network. From there they were to watch the coastline for German shipping, radioing their sightings back to London. They were warned not to get too ambitious and to keep their messages short. Frank insisted that Landau's old adage from the days of La Dame Blanche – 'little but good' – was drummed into them.

Despite the ultimate success of the operation, it had a difficult start. By the time the first agents had been trained, collaborators operating under cover as members of the resistance had already been put in place across Norway. Many of the early groups were given away by these 'Good Norwegians'. Others were uncovered when they radioed back to England by the German *Peiler* or direction-finding units, which proved to be far more efficient than had been expected.

There is little doubt that the Norwegians were very brave, but in the initial operations were understandably inexperienced, and it was a painful learning process. The Norwegians were 'endowed with exceptional energy and courage', one wartime intelligence officer said, but 'many of them committed grave blunders during the first two years. First and foremost, they were too open and optimistic, and many paid dearly for it.'

The first MI6 ship-watching station, led by Sigurd Jakobsen, was in fact put in place before the agreement on co-operation between British and Norwegian Intelligence, and inherited by Frank from his opposite number in the Admiralty.

Hardware, as it was known, was based in Haugesund, south of Bergen, covering the coastline from Trondheim to Kristiansand. Jakobsen did not just watch the German Navy. He also sent a number of volunteers and refugees across the North Sea. But at the beginning of August 1940, he made the fatal mistake of agreeing to help an 'English sailor' who claimed to be on the run and trying to get back to Britain. The man turned out to be a Gestapo agent.

The second station was far more successful. Oldell, run by Gabriel Smith, a Norwegian naval intelligence officer based in Oslo, was in contact with MI6 from early July. But his transmissions were monitored from the very start and, although Frank and Welsh decided in February 1941 that Smith was too well known locally and would have to be exfiltrated, it was not long before the

German *Peiler* had locked on to his wireless signals and uncovered the rest of the team.

Despite being tortured by the Gestapo, the Norwegian agents did not give anything away. But the captured cipher keys enabled the Germans to decipher the messages they had been monitoring, giving them valuable intelligence on how the coast-watching system operated. Nevertheless, Oldell was replaced by a successor station code-named Beta, which survived until Norway was liberated in May 1945.

By the end of the war, a total of around two hundred Norwegian radio agents had been put in place. They included Torstein Raaby, who was to become better known after the war as the radio operator on Thor Heyerdahl's Kon Tiki expedition, and Bjorn Rorholt, who was based in the Trondheim area.

Commending Rorholt for a medal, Stewart Menzies, the head of MI6, described how the Norwegian had gone into a military base disguised as an insurance agent. At the same time as selling life policies to the German officers, he was looking for the best place to put an illicit MI6 radio station to report on what was going on in the camp. According to 'C', Rorholt's adventures had 'rivalled the most exciting of thrillers'.

The owner of an Oslo bookshop, apparently recruited before the war by Foley or Mitchell, provided the network with logistical support. 'The book seller became our chief contact in Oslo,' recalled Oluf Reed Olsen.

> The work he did was first-class. A whole lot of identity cards and rations cards had to be obtained. In addition to identity cards valid for Oslo and all the inland districts except the frontier zones, frontier dwellers' cards for the various frontier zones had to be obtained. For this purpose, the bookseller had a contact with a quite young lady employed in the police passport office who did this job admirably.

The coast-watchers were not alone. The XU network was the largest Norwegian intelligence-gathering organisation in Norway, with around 1,500 agents controlled from London by the Norwegian High Command. They included farmers, professional drivers, workers on German construction sites, doctors and teachers, all of whom provided invaluable information on the activities and strength of the occupying forces.

By monitoring milk deliveries – individual German soldiers were rationed to a quarter of a litre of milk a day – the XU was able to determine how many soldiers there were in each camp. Supplies of beer and bread were also divided by the individual ration figures to confirm the evidence of the milk supplies.

The SOE, which had sent its first team into Norway during the invasion when it was still part of MI6, also provided large amounts of intelligence on the occupying forces, all of which was fed back to Frank and included along with the XU material and Bletchley Park's Ultra decrypts in the reports emanating from Broadway. Frank's experience and ability to smooth over problems ensured that the relationship with the Norwegians started off on the right note.

'Collaboration between them and MI6 almost entirely lacked the friction experienced with other governments in exile,' one wartime intelligence officer said. 'Even MI6 and the SOE got on with much less than their normal friction. So there must have been something special about Norway.'

Chapter 19

The Hollowed-Out Tennis Racquet

Despite the pressures of his work, Frank had remained in contact with a number of the Jewish refugees he had helped to escape from Nazi Germany. For most, their problems had only continued once they arrived in Britain. In one of the sorriest episodes in the history of British Intelligence, MI5, the domestic Security Service, orchestrated the round-up and incarceration of twenty-two thousand German and Austrian refugees, the majority of whom had fled to Britain to escape the very regime they were now suspected of supporting.

They included many of those German Jews Frank had helped to escape the concentration camps. 'Paula Weber's brother was taken and interned yesterday,' Margaret Reid told her mother in early July 1940. 'She rang me up and told me but there is nothing to be done. Our main concern is that the father who is over 60 and has been in a concentration camp should not be made to endure more than is necessary.'

Frank received letters from a number of relatives of those who now found themselves imprisoned by the British, pleading with him to help them get out of the internment camps. Dr Oscar Fehr was held in one of the five main camps on the Isle of Man, treating those internees with eye problems. But there was little that Frank could do apart from write a sympathetic letter to

Fehr's wife Jeanne. 'I am depressed to hear that your venerable husband has been interned and hope that his case will receive the most sympathetic consideration by the new tribunals which were mentioned in the House of Commons last night,' he said. 'You have indeed suffered greatly.'

The mass internment led to considerable concern over what Churchill himself described as 'the witch-finding activities of MI5', and by the end of 1941 most of the refugees had been released. Dr Fehr had to take his medical exams again, but then managed to set up his own consulting rooms in Harley Street.

Frank was made Commander of the Order of St Michael and St George in the 1941 New Year's Honours list 'for valuable services rendered to the state'. He went with Kay to Buckingham Palace to be decorated by King George VI. The ceremony was held in one of the palace corridors because the room normally used for such occasions had been damaged by a bomb, and Kay was impressed by the fact that 'the palace servants, in place of their normal livery, wore the uniform of the home guard'.

Both Frank and Margaret Reid also kept in touch with Otto Ruge, who had been taken prisoner and was now being held in a PoW camp in Germany. After the war, Ruge wrote to Frank to thank him: 'I have not forgotten how we worked together or how much help you and your lady helpers gave to me during those rather difficult weeks. Nor will I forget the exquisite tobacco parcels you sent me so regularly during all the years I spent in Germany. They were a great help to keep me in form during those rather dreary years.'

But as head of A1, Norway was not Frank's sole concern. When MI6 was forced to evacuate the Oslo station, he had also lost contact with his agents in Germany. The best way for them to get information out was now judged to be via Germany's two neutral neighbours Sweden and Switzerland. The stations in Stockholm and Geneva were both expanded to cope with the difficulties of re-establishing contact with the old agents and building up new networks. Slowly A1 began to re-establish its intelligence networks inside the Third Reich.

It was the Geneva station which enjoyed what was perhaps the greatest coup, making indirect contact with Admiral Wilhelm Canaris, the head of the Abwehr. Canaris was part of the group of senior German officers opposed to Hitler and was later hanged for complicity in an attempt, in July 1944, to assassinate him with a bomb.

At the start of the war, Canaris smuggled Halina Szymanska, the wife of a Polish officer and a close confidante, to Switzerland.

'He had a penchant for attractive ladies,' one former MI6 officer said.

> She was the wife of the Polish military attaché in Berlin. Both of them were very friendly with Canaris. She was rescued by Canaris when her husband was captured by the Russians when they invaded Poland and he got her out to Switzerland where she then became a member of the Polish Government-in-Exile legation to Switzerland.
>
> Canaris maintained contact with Szymanska over the years and indeed he himself visited Switzerland at least a couple of times and, whether he knew what he was doing or not, he said far more than he would otherwise have done to Madame Szymanska about German intentions. All of which ended up back here. To a large degree it was current events in Germany and intentions regarding Hitler's next move.
>
> The most important item Szymanska reported was in January 1941, when she was able to tell us that an irrevocable decision had been made by Hitler, against the advice of his staff, to attack Russia in May of that year.

At the time, Hitler's main preoccupation appeared to be with Operation Sea Lion, the proposed invasion of Britain, so the news that he was about to switch his attention to Operation Barbarossa, the attack on the Soviet Union, was not only an important piece of intelligence for the British, it was also a great relief. MI6 passed the information on to Moscow via Sir Stafford Cripps, the British ambassador there, but Stalin discounted it as disinformation.

The Stockholm station may not have had such a dramatic success as Geneva, but using the Norwegian XU intelligence network and foreign workers as intermediaries, it managed not just to take over control of a number of Frank's agents but also to set up several networks of its own.

Carl Aage Andreasson, a Danish businessman who was able to travel between Germany and Sweden with impunity, was not captured by the Gestapo until early 1944. Under interrogation, he revealed that Victor Hampton, an MI6 officer based in the Stockholm embassy, was running four separate networks inside Germany – based on Hamburg, Bonn, Königsberg and Berlin – as well as a fifth in Austria centred on Vienna.

One Norwegian agent run by MI6 from Stockholm had such good contacts inside the German establishment that he was given the run of its military facilities. Among the intelligence items he provided was the crucial report that the *Bismarck* was leaving the Baltic in May 1941, allowing the Royal Navy to hunt her down.

For the first two years, A1 received high-grade political and military intelligence from Paul Thümmel, a senior Abwehr officer who had been developed initially by the Czech intelligence service as Agent A-54. Thümmel had provided good intelligence on the German invasions of Czechoslovakia and France, in particular the fact that the main thrust of the German attack on France would come through the Ardennes, a report ignored by the military commanders.

Now under the direct control of MI6, he continued to provide detailed intelligence on German intentions, most notably the plans for an invasion of Britain in late 1940 and their subsequent deferment by Hitler. He also gave good information on the planned invasion of the Soviet Union which backed up the evidence from Szymanska and from the code-breakers at Bletchley Park. But he was arrested by the Gestapo shortly afterwards and executed in April 1945.

One of Frank's most important agents inside Germany was his old friend Rosbaud. The principal target for his network

of scientists was the extent of the Nazi atomic weapons programme. There was also concern over the experimental weapons
establishment at Peenemünde in north-eastern Germany, where
– according to the Oslo Report – the Luftwaffe was developing
rocket-driven gliders, controlled by radio for use as air-to-sea
missiles.

Rosbaud had stayed in touch with his wife through letters to the
Jewish scientist Lise Meitner, who was still in Sweden, and via his
brother-in-law Rudolf Frank, who lived in Switzerland. 'Several
times, my father received books by ordinary mail which he was
to forward to my sister,' Frank's son Vincent said. 'He also told
me that once he had a visit from two British gentlemen from the
embassy, but I don't know if they instructed him to send the books
on or whether he was told this in the letters from Rosbaud.'

Another route for getting the information out of Germany was
via the French underground. Two French physicists captured by
the Germans and placed in a prisoner-of-war camp were set to
work in a laboratory in Berlin where they met Rosbaud. One of
them, Henri Piatier, had a brother who was in the resistance. 'I
worked in the laboratory from the end of 1942 until we were
freed in 1945,' Piatier said.

> Obviously we were engaged in very sensitive tasks and the
> information was of use to the allies.
>   We managed to get material out through two routes. Rosbaud
> had an intermediary who smuggled information through Norway
> and Sweden. I was able to smuggle out documents to my brother,
> who was in the resistance. He sent a friend who was supposed
> to be a Vichy official dealing with prisoners of war. In fact, he
> was a member of the resistance himself and he smuggled the
> information out.

But the main control over Rosbaud, or source Griffin as he was
known, appears to have been from the Stockholm station via the
link with Meitner. In one of the letters from his wife, he was
told that a young Norwegian 'friend of the family' was studying

at the Dresdener Technische Hochschule and might visit him. It was therefore no surprise when Sverre Bergh, an XU secret agent sent by MI6, telephoned Rosbaud at the Springer Verlag offices in Berlin's Linkstrasse.

The two men met for a beer in one of the tent restaurants in the Tiergarten, scene of so many of Frank's own pre-war 'Treffs' with Rosbaud. The German scientist handed over some 'important' information, including material he had collected on the experimental station at Peenemünde during a visit to an old acquaintance who worked there.

But Rosbaud had been forced to tread carefully to avoid arousing his fellow scientists' suspicions, and there was not enough detail in his report to satisfy Head Office. It was decided to send Bergh up to Peenemünde himself to find out more about what was going on.

The young Norwegian came back with a description of a 'cigar-shaped projectile' – the A4 rocket, the first guided missile to exceed the speed of sound and the prototype of the V-2 flying bomb that was to cause widespread damage in London. He also produced a plan of the central cluster of experimental buildings where the main work was being carried out under the direction of Wernher von Braun, the top German rocket scientist and later the man behind America's NASA space programme.

The material was passed back via a Swedish diplomat to the Stockholm station. But like so many MI6 agent reports, it was not believed. It was not until 1943, following two corroborative, although far less detailed, reports by another British agent, that the RAF was persuaded to mount major air raids against Peenemünde, forcing the Germans to pull the rocket base back into Poland.

The information on Peenemünde was not by any means the only scientific intelligence produced by Rosbaud. As the man in charge of the country's leading scientific journals, he saw reports on every significant German scientific advance before they were sent to the censors, and was able to pass on anything interesting to the British. He also remained on close terms with all the leading Nazi scientists. They were ever eager to curry favour with him since they needed the publicity provided by the Springer journals in order to enhance or maintain their own reputations and prestige.

Gathering the intelligence was rarely a great problem. The hard part was actually smuggling the information out of the country. Whenever one of the students at the Dresdener Technische Hochschule went home to Norway he would take reports back, one of those involved in the operation recalled.

'They occasionally got some help from Swedish diplomatic couriers, who would take an envelope with them in the bag, and then hand it on to one of the student group who "happened" to be travelling north on the same train, as soon as they reached Swedish territory. But more often they had to carry the material all the way themselves.'

Bergh and Rosbaud developed their own ingenious method of getting the intelligence back to London. One of the Norwegian's friends was the Swedish journalist Olle Ollen, who was known on the diplomatic circuit as a very keen tennis player.

Every so often, he would send his racquets back to Stockholm to have them restrung. Bergh persuaded Ollen to let him hollow out the handle of one of the racquets that needed new strings so material could be smuggled safely out of Germany. The hollowed-out tennis racquet was frequently sent back to Stockholm for restringing, taking with it valuable intelligence for the British, including details of the new jet engine under development for the Messerschmitt Me-262.

But the most important information that MI6 was looking for from Rosbaud was anything on the Nazi atomic weapons programme. A group of prominent German scientists, who included Otto Hahn and were known as the Uranverein, or Uranium Club, had been given the task of creating a German atomic bomb.

They were led by the Nobel prize-winner Werner Heisenberg, but were severely handicapped by lack of funding, shortages of raw materials and by the loss of the Jewish scientists like Einstein, Born, Frisch, Meitner and Bethe, some of whom were to be highly influential in the equivalent Anglo-US atomic weapons programme, the Manhattan Project.

One of the most famous SOE operations was Gunnarside, the raid on the plant in the Norwegian town of Rjukan where the Germans were producing heavy water for use in the production of an atomic bomb. The raid, in February 1943, put the plant out of operation for several months in what seemed like a serious setback for the German atomic weapons programme.

In fact, the British concerns over the potential of the equivalent Nazi programme were ill-founded. The members of the Uranverein had accepted very early on that they would not be able to produce an atomic bomb in time for it to have any impact on the war. 'If the German government had given every possible help, then we would still not have done it as quickly as the Americans,' said Carl von Weizsäcker, one of the German team. 'We were sure we could not do it. We realised this around the end of 1940.'

After the war, friends of Heisenberg and his fellow scientists claimed that they had deliberately delayed the programme because they did not want to build a bomb. But whatever the truth of the matter, Heisenberg continued to persuade the Nazis that the project was '*Kriegsentscheidend*', vital to the war effort, despite privately conceding that while an atomic bomb was theoretically possible, his team was not capable of producing it.

On 4 June 1942, he gave a briefing in Berlin to Albert Speer, the German Minister for Armaments and War Production, and leading members of the armed forces on the potential of such a bomb. Speer, who had been ordered by Hitler to take charge of the project and to inject new urgency into it, recalled being told that the Uranverein was 'a group of scientists who were on the track of a weapon which could annihilate whole cities, perhaps throw the island of England out of the fight'.

Cupping his hands, Heisenberg told the Nazi minister that the bomb would need to be only the size of a pineapple to have the explosive power of fifteen thousand tons of TNT. But it was clear from his explanation of how it might work that he and his team were nowhere near producing such a weapon, and when Speer offered him a three-hundred-strong team of scientists and several million marks to carry out further research, Heisenberg was forced to admit that he could not see how he would be able to make any use of such resources.

A few days later, Rosbaud had a drink with some of the scientists involved in a café on the Ku'damm. He listened intently to their discussion of the meeting with Speer and their predictions of how the German atomic weapons programme would now come to nothing. Shortly afterwards, he persuaded an unsuspecting Nazi scientist with whom he was on close terms to give him a letter that would provide an excuse for him to visit 'an old friend' in Oslo.

On 10 June 1942, wearing the uniform of a Luftwaffe officer, Rosbaud flew by military aircraft to Norway, ostensibly to find raw materials needed by Göring's top secret aerial warfare research organisation, the Luftwaffe Forschungsamt. In fact, he made contact with members of the XU, passing on news of the total lack of progress made by the Uranium Club.

The dangers involved in such activities were obvious. But unlike many of his scientific colleagues, the Austrian was determined not to bow to the Nazis. Samuel Goudsmit, who was sent to Germany after the war to investigate the extent of the Nazi nuclear programme, said:

> Rosbaud is among the few to have kept their integrity throughout the Nazi regime and the war.
>
> His personality and deep understanding gave him the friendship and confidence of all true scientists who came into contact with him and there were many. Everyone knew of his outspoken anti-Nazi feelings. He was living proof that it was possible to continue unmolested without giving in to Nazi pressure.'

The flying visit to Oslo led to more questions for Rosbaud. But by mid-1943, MI6 was able to assure the British government that the German atomic weapons programme had 'ceased to be a source of grave anxiety'. When the first atomic bomb was dropped on

Hiroshima in August 1945, Heisenberg, Hahn, von Weizsäcker and the rest of the Uranverein were incarcerated at Farm Hall, a country house near Huntingdon.

Unbeknown to them, hidden microphones were picking up their reaction to the BBC news reports that their British and American rivals had succeeded in creating an atomic bomb. It ranged from Hahn's dismay at the horrific results of his discovery to Heisenberg's total disbelief that anyone could have succeeded where he had failed.

The taped conversation did not tell British Intelligence anything it did not already know. But without Frank's recruitment of Rosbaud, many more resources would have had to have been diverted away from other more vital projects into countering the German atomic weapons programme.

The friendship between the two men, based initially on a shared experience during the First World War and their common interest in helping the Jews, but later reinforced by their hatred of Hitler, had paid enormous dividends.

'Rosbaud's wartime reports were particularly valuable because they helped us correctly to conclude that work in Germany towards the release of nuclear energy at no time reached beyond the research stage,' wrote R. V. Jones, who headed the MI6 wartime scientific section. 'His information thus calmed fears that might otherwise have beset us. His contributions were considerable and, in nuclear energy at least, approaching crucial.'

Chapter 20

Rudolf Hess

Frank's section was not just involved in collecting intelligence from Germany. Despite the Venlo incident, Menzies remained convinced that MI6 could create splits inside the Nazi camp, chiefly by encouraging the dissidents within the military establishment. The link with Canaris through Madame Szymanska persuaded him that this was a real possibility, and Frank had a continuing brief to look out for any way of exploiting such contacts.

It was not just the dissidents who were trying to get in touch with the British. For some time a few members of Hitler's entourage had believed they could use the former appeasers within the British establishment to broker a peace accord between Britain and Germany. With the need to deal eventually with the Soviet Union uppermost in his mind, Hitler had himself made several attempts to persuade the British that they should unite against the Bolshevik threat. All were ignored.

But Albrecht Haushofer, an English expert at the German Foreign Ministry, remained convinced that it would be possible to find British politicians receptive to the idea of peace with Germany. He received influential backing from a close family friend – Rudolf Hess, the Deputy Führer.

At Christmas 1940, Haushofer's father Karl had a dream in which

Hess triumphantly united Britain and Germany against the Soviet Union. Shortly afterwards, Hess's personal astrologer drew up the Deputy Führer's horoscope for 1941. It appeared to indicate that the circumstances were propitious for Hess to make peace.

The man he and the Haushofers identified as a potential contact was the Duke of Hamilton, whom Albrecht Haushofer had known before the war. Both the Haushofers and Hess believed that as a leading Conservative peer Hamilton would have access to the King and would be an ideal contact inside the British establishment. He was 'the person appointed by destiny' who would help Hess to secure the anti-Bolshevik pact foretold in Karl Haushofer's dream.

Despite his cult status within the Nazi Party, as the cell-mate of the Führer and an influential figure in the formulation of *Mein Kampf*, Hess had been progressively sidelined since Hitler came to power. Although he was the Deputy Führer, he was not regarded as Hitler's chosen successor. If he could set up a peace deal with Britain, he reasoned, his influence would be restored.

In September 1940, Albrecht Haushofer put out an initial feeler to Hamilton, suggesting in a letter posted through the Thomas Cook office in Lisbon that they meet in a neutral country like Portugal. Although it was never stated in the letter, the main German 'negotiator' was to be Hess.

My Dear Douglo,

If you remember some of my last communications in July 1939, you – and your friends in high places – may find some significance in the fact that I am able to ask you whether you could find time to have a talk with me somewhere on the outskirts of Europe, perhaps in Portugal. I could reach Lisbon any time (and without any kind of difficulties) within four days after receiving news from you. Of course, I do not know whether you can make your authorities understand so much that they

give you leave. But at least you may be able to answer
my question.

The letter was intercepted by MI5 and the suggestion came to
nothing, but on Saturday, 10 May 1941, Hess flew to Britain in a
Messerschmitt-110 intent on making contact with Hamilton. By
coincidence, as he headed for Hamilton's Renfrewshire estate, the
Duke was one of the RAF officers tracking his flight.

'At dusk on Saturday May 10th while Wing Commander
The Duke of Hamilton was on duty in the Turnhouse Sector
Operations Rooms an enemy aircraft was plotted off the coast
of Northumberland and made a landfall close to Farne Islands,'
the official account of the incident stated.

Hess bailed out shortly before his aircraft crashed in a field near
Eaglesham, to the south of Glasgow, bursting into flames. 'My
parachute landed me about ten feet in front of the door of a small
farmhouse,' he said. 'The inhabitants took care of me very well.
They helped me to get into the house, put a rocking chair near
the fireplace and offered me tea.'

Claiming to be a Hauptmann Alfred Horn and on a 'special
mission', Hess insisted on speaking to Hamilton, who, along with
a military interrogator, interviewed the Deputy Führer early on
the Sunday morning.

Hess told the Duke that he was on a 'mission of humanity' to
try to make peace between Britain and Germany. 'He asked me
if I could get together leading members of my party to talk over
things with a view to making peace proposals,' Hamilton said.

> I replied that there was now only one party in this country.
> I then told him that if we made peace now, we would be
> at war again certainly within two years. If a peace agreement
> was possible, the arrangement would have been made before
> the war started. But since however Germany chose war in
> preference to peace at a time when we were most anxious
> to preserve peace, I could put forward no hope of a peace
> agreement.

Hamilton flew south to Oxfordshire to brief Winston Churchill, who had replaced Chamberlain as British Prime Minister following the Norway débâcle and was spending the weekend at Ditchley Park. Yes, it was indeed Hess, Hamilton said, and he had photographs to prove it. Churchill, in typically truculent mood, reportedly responded by saying that he was not going to change his plans to watch a film. 'Hess or no Hess, I'm going to see the Marx Brothers,' he said. Hamilton had to wait to brief him until after the film was over, by which time it was deemed too late to do anything until the next day.

First thing on Monday morning, Alexander Cadogan, Permanent Under-Secretary at the Foreign Office, called in Stewart Menzies, the head of MI6, to discuss what should be done about the man claiming to be Hess. He wanted to send Ivone Kirkpatrick, who had known Hess in Berlin, to Scotland to check that it was indeed the Deputy Führer. Menzies agreed.

That morning, the Germans announced that Hess had disappeared. He had apparently lived 'in a state of hallucination, as a result of which he felt he would bring about an understanding between England and Germany. The National Socialist Party regrets that this idealist fell a victim to this hallucination. This however will have no effect on the continuance of the war which has been forced on Germany.'

While Menzies consulted with Frank over what the MI6 position should be, Kirkpatrick flew to Scotland to interview Hess, code-named 'Jonathan' or 'Z'. It was late when he arrived with Hamilton at Buchanan Castle, the military hospital where he was now being held.

Hess and Kirkpatrick recognised each other immediately, and the Deputy Führer launched into a lengthy, rambling speech recalling how badly Britain had always treated Germany. This was about to change because Germany now had the ability to mount mass attacks on Britain with U-boats and aircraft.

'By 3 am, my patience was exhausted,' Kirkpatrick said. 'I cut him short and summarily demanded that he should define the object of his visit. He replied that it was to convince the British Government of the inevitability of a German victory and to bring about peace by negotiation.'

He had not told Hitler about his planned mission but knew from his own conversations with the Führer that he was quite happy to allow Britain to control its empire so long as Germany had a free hand in Europe. Neither country would concern itself with events in the other's sphere of influence.

With rumours rife that Hitler was about to attack the Soviet Union, Kirkpatrick asked how this peace plan would affect Moscow. Hess reacted sharply, saying that Germany had important demands to make of Russia and these would be satisfied by force if necessary. But this did not mean that Germany was about to invade the Soviet Union. For now, the alliance with Moscow was useful to Hitler. He would select his own moment to make his demands.

Kirkpatrick reported this back, adding the caveat that the Deputy Führer was clearly no longer part of Hitler's inner circle and was not very well informed on German plans. 'However, it might be possible for an expert to extract information from him on the subject of U-boat construction and the training of crews and similarly in regard to aircraft and pilots.'

Cadogan told Churchill that from Kirkpatrick's conversations with Hess it was doubtful that he had any detailed military knowledge 'but it seems quite possible that a certain amount of information on political matters might be obtained, by inference, in the course of a number of conversations'.

Churchill, Cadogan and Menzies agreed that Hess should be treated like a defector. He would be debriefed rather than inter-rogated. It was possible that he was a plant, deliberately sent to confuse, to provide 'disinformation' that would lure the British into a trap. But if he was genuine, as a senior member of the Nazi leadership, there had to be a mass of intelligence he could offer.

Menzies stressed that it would not be easy. For any defector there were an infinite number of Rubicons to be crossed before he would give up everything he knew. Hess, with his personal loyalty to Hitler dating back to the 1923 attempted putsch, was likely to be a particularly hard nut to crack.

Churchill ruled that Hess 'should be strictly isolated in a convenient house not too far from London, fitted by "C" with the necessary appliances and every endeavour should be made to study his mentality and get anything worthwhile out of him. Special Guardians should be appointed.'

MI6 was to put its top German expert on the job. 'There will be no hurry about interviewing him and he is to be kept in the strictest seclusion. The public will not stand any pampering except for intelligence purposes of this notorious war criminal.'

Mytchett Place, a forbidding Georgian mansion in Aldershot which was normally the official residence of the garrison commander, was selected as Camp Z, Hess's new home. As the MI6 'éminence grise on Germany', Frank was to be in charge of the debriefing of Jonathan. He would be assisted by a Colonel Wallace, actually Thomas Kendrick, the former head of station in Vienna, who was now working at the Combined Services Interrogation Centre in Cockfosters, where the top Nazi PoWs were held, and a 'Capt Barnes', a pseudonym for another German-speaking MI6 officer.

Jonathan was moved to the Tower of London while Camp Z was fitted out with microphones and a bank of tape recorders. Everything he said was to be recorded. Even the gardens were to be fitted with hidden microphones to catch every word. No one was sure how long it would take. 'As Major Foley is going to be away for a week or two I am going into his flat for the time being,' Margaret Reid told her mother.

Maj-Gen. Alan Hunter, Director of Prisoners of War, took charge of the camp itself, placing Lt-Col. Malcolm Scott in charge of the administration with orders to ensure that no one was allowed anywhere near Jonathan without Cadogan's authority. 'He is not to have any visitors except those prescribed by the Foreign Office,' Scott's written orders stated. 'He is not to have newspapers nor wireless. He is not to have any contacts with the outer world whatsoever.'

Mytchett Place had been turned into a miniature fortress surrounded by barbed wire and trenches. There were machine-gun posts at the entrance and a company of around 120 Coldstream and Scots Guards had been put in place to ensure that Hess was totally secure.

At a quarter to three on Tuesday, 20 May, 1941, Frank, Kendrick and 'Barnes' arrived 'to take up their duties as personal companions to Z'. A couple of hours later, the military ambulance carrying Jonathan and Colonel Gibson Graham, the army doctor attending him, drove through the gates. General Hunter was on hand to introduce the prisoner to the guards and his 'personal companions'.

Asked if he had any particular wishes, Hess replied that he wanted to see Hamilton and Kirkpatrick. He took a brief walk in the garden with his 'companions', but became extremely agitated at the sight of the fortifications surrounding the house and convinced that the Guards were there to murder him.

Hess told Graham that he was 'surrounded by Secret Service agents who were intent on his destruction' either by driving him to suicide or by murdering him in some way, perhaps with poison, so as to be able to stage a suicide. He refused to eat much of his dinner that evening and declined breakfast on the following day, telling Graham that he did not trust any of his guardians, particularly Frank, because he looked too old to be a proper army officer, and 'Barnes', because his ill-fitting uniform betrayed the fact that he was not a real soldier.

'Jonathan is very depressed and wished to be left alone,' Frank and Kendrick said in their first report. 'We are of the opinion that this might be the psychological moment when he might change his attitude if his wish concerning visits by the Duke of Hamilton and Kirkpatrick is complied with. Speed might be highly productive. Doctor says he is moody, "like a spoilt child". His present mood should, if possible, be exploited.'

In his conversations with Graham, Hess continued to talk of mass air and submarine attacks and to insist that he had come of his own volition and without Hitler's knowledge. The doctor became convinced that Hess was 'definitely over the border that lies between mental instability and insanity'. Hess insisted that his peace proposals were genuine but could not be conducted with the present government because the Führer would not do a deal with Churchill. He seemed to believe that a change of British government was imminent but did not know how or why this might occur.

'He is in a high state of depression at the failure of his mission and has hinted that it might be better for him to die (suicide),' Frank wrote. 'He is convinced that he is in the hands of a clique who are preventing him from daily access to the King, and that the only way to gain access to the King is through the Duke of Hamilton.' It would be better if the Duke could come to explain to him that this was not the case. 'The present impasse is likely to continue until he has seen the Duke, who is the only person in whom he appears to have complete confidence.'

The occupants of Mytchett Place slowly settled into a routine. Hess and Frank would frequently walk around the grounds, conversing in German, with the MI6 man stopping for longer chats under trees in which microphones were hidden. Hess said later that Frank 'spoke German without an accent'. But although he evidently warmed to the MI6 officer – describing him as 'an older gentleman and very nice' – their conversations produced little real intelligence.

Nor were Hess's feelings towards Foley reciprocated. 'Frank said he had never come across a man with such revolting personal habits,' one former colleague said. But despite his distaste for Hess, Frank normally dined with him, along with his MI6 colleagues, in the increasingly vain hope that there might be something valuable that could be drawn out of him.

Their meals were dominated by Jonathan's obsession with the idea that he might be poisoned. He would snatch food away from the MI6 officers as they were about to eat, or insist they ate their food first. 'Hess always suspected that his food was being poisoned,' Kay Foley said. 'So Frank exchanged plates with him and also sipped his glass of wine. Frank was sure that he was insane.'

The first concerted effort to debrief Hess for intelligence purposes resulted only in a repeat of the exaggerated claims of German air and submarine capabilities, coupled with nonsensical claims that submarines were being built in every part of the Reich, 'even in Czechoslovakia', and taken down rivers to the sea. Naval Intelligence concurred with Frank's assessment that Jonathan knew nothing of any military significance. 'It sounds like uninformed and probably sincere repetition of current propaganda,' the Admiralty concluded.

All three service intelligence departments provided Frank with a list of questions for Hess. But it soon became clear that he was unable to say anything about German military might other than repeat in very general terms the Goebbels propaganda about vast superiority.

Menzies came down to Mytchett to discuss the situation with Frank, Kendrick and Barnes, who told him they were unlikely to get anything out of Jonathan. He was obsessed with the idea that there was 'a political clique or Secret Service ring which is preventing him from meeting the proper peace people and the King'. All three men were extremely frustrated with their 'boring' task and sick to death of their charge.

There was clearly a need to rethink the situation, and Frank suggested that he might be presented with a 'negotiator'. Alternatively, another senior German prisoner of war might be placed in his room so that their conversations could be recorded.

'The success and progress of the methods we are using depends almost entirely on our being able to record unguarded and unsuspect conversation,' Frank said. 'At present, the special methods (bugging) are functioning solely as an aide memoire. We were hoping that the Gods would deliver into your hands a Nazi of importance who would be sent down to this camp.'

The Guards officers, who had to look after Hess during the night and frequently conversed with him, were as unimpressed as their MI6 counterparts. 'I find it difficult to believe,' one recorded in his diary, 'that this rather broken man – who slouches into his chair careless as to his dress, who swings in mood from cheerfulness to depression in a few hours, whose mind is clouded with delusionary ideas, who believes in second sight and dreams – that this man was the Deputy Führer. He is such a second-rater with none of the dignity, the bearing of a great man.'

Following Graham's concerns over Hess's mental health, the army's top psychologist, Colonel J.R. Rees, examined the prisoner, concluding that he did not appear to be lying. He was not insane, but he was mentally ill and suffering from depression, probably as a result of the obvious failure of his mission. 'I was told that while the troops were parading in the garden he was on the terrace and that he gave the most curious display of doing what was practically a goose step down the path in front of them,' Rees said.

> This probably epitomises the situation.
>
> The man has excellent intelligence but is childish in his outlook and consequently unstable and with bad judgement. He has clearly been dominated by many people, and most markedly by Professor Haushofer whose dreams or visions of his (Hess's) mission have been accepted as prophetic. In my opinion, Hess is a man of unstable mentality and has almost certainly been like that since adolescence. In technical language, I should diagnose him as a psychopathic personality of the schizophrenic type.

Chapter 21

Meeting Philby

The idea of a fake 'official negotiator' was taken up by Churchill. It had to be someone whom Hess would regard as representing the government but at the same time it could not be someone with real power in case news leaked out, giving the public, or indeed the Americans, the idea that the British were really seeking a peace deal. The man chosen for the job was Lord Simon, the Lord Chancellor, who before the war had been a noted appeaser.

'Hess is becoming disillusioned and more useful,' wrote Robert Bruce Lockhart, head of the Political Warfare Executive, in his diaries. 'Now being examined by Kendrick and Foley. Been shown what the Germans say about him. Wants peace. We are to have a pseudo-negotiator, Lord Simon. When idea mooted, Winston roared with laughter – "the very man".'

Hess was not told at this stage, but by Wednesday, 4 June he had become very agitated. He wrote to his wife for the first time since his arrival, including a fatalistic quotation from Goethe. That afternoon, Scott recorded in the camp diary, he sat under one of the trees in the garden 'in the most uncomfortable position, refused to speak to anyone, was morose and in a fit of the deepest depression'.

After dinner, he went out into the garden again, insisting

unusually that Frank did not join him, and 'walked up and down in a very agitated way'. That night he said goodnight to his companions, something he never usually did, and muttered to himself: 'I can't stand this any more.' Frank and Kendrick warned the duty officer to keep a close watch on him. They believed he might be about to commit suicide.

Menzies told Frank that he could let Jonathan know that he would be visited by a representative of the government on the following Monday. He was to be reminded that he had met Lord Simon in 1935, when the then Foreign Secretary had visited Berlin. Simon was to be accompanied by Kirkpatrick and the government had accepted Hess's own condition that a German consular official who had been interned at the outbreak of the war should be present as a witness.

When Frank told him that he was to have talks with a member of the government, Hess seemed at first not to understand. 'After dinner, I walked with him in the garden in the rain,' Frank said. 'He asked me to confirm that my message was serious and not merely a method of soothing him. On being reassured, he talked cheerfully and vividly of general matters, and of his flight to Scotland. He appeared to be a changed man. He told me he had an agreeable recollection of the chief negotiator.'

On the eve of his meeting with Simon, Hess was even more paranoid than normal, insisting on swapping meals with Kendrick and refusing to walk in the gardens after dinner. Frank told Menzies that there appeared to be 'a serious deterioration' in Jonathan's mental health. 'You may care to warn the gentlemen who are visiting him tomorrow that they may find it difficult to conduct reasoned and logically thought out conversations.'

The next day, Simon and Kirkpatrick arrived at Mytchett under the assumed identities of two psychiatrists, Dr Guthrie and Dr McKenzie. 'We drew up at the door and were met by two special officers, both of whom I already knew,' Kirkpatrick recalled.

★   ★   ★

They explained that the plan was for us to have lunch first, alone with them, after which the meeting with Hess would take place.

Hess was apparently in an odd frame of mind. He had that morning displayed a sudden lack of confidence. In consequence, he had childishly declared that he felt unwell and did not propose to get up. He was now in bed but every effort would be made to produce him after lunch. So we ate our lunch quietly, discussed the best method of broaching intelligence matters with Hess and sat down to await developments.

What followed when the German finally agreed to get up was described by Kirkpatrick as 'a Mad Hatter's tea party'. Hess made yet another long statement, Frank said, having sat listening in the recording room. 'This statement contained nothing new, either in its general outline or in detail. He finished by putting forward his known (peace) proposition. During this long performance, he appeared entirely confident, but as soon as the negotiator made any pertinent remark or question, he took refuge in vague generalities.'

Cadogan was already convinced it was all a waste of time. 'Nothing useful transpired,' he recorded in his diary. 'He recited all the rubbish that he's treated us to for the past month.' Churchill was characteristically even more blunt. 'I have read the Guthrie – Jonathan transcripts which seem to me to consist of the outpourings of a disordered mind,' the Prime Minister said. 'They are like a conversation with a mentally defective child who has been guilty of murder or arson.'

After Simon and Kirkpatrick had gone, Hess appeared totally drained, Scott recorded in the camp diary. But he soon perked up considerably. 'For the rest of the evening he seemed relieved, was somewhat arrogant, and strutted about the lawn after dinner with Maj Foley.'

But over the next few days the lack of an official response to his peace terms and the failure of what he evidently saw as an historic mission plunged Hess into despair. On Friday, 15 June Frank sent an urgent message to Menzies.

'Jonathan's mental state has deteriorated seriously during the last 48 hours,' he said. 'During the night his fear of poisoning became more acute than it has ever been. I consider I should advise you to press for the immediate visit of Colonel Rees. It is obvious even to us laymen that he is very ill. Under these conditions, we are precluded from doing any useful work from our angle.'

Menzies relayed the report to Cadogan. 'C came in about Hess, who's going off his head,' the head of the Foreign Office wrote in his diary. 'I don't much care what happens to him. We can use him. There is a meeting tomorrow between Winston and Simon about him at which I hope to be present and to get decisions on how to treat him and how to exploit him – alive, mad or dead.'

That night, Hess told the duty officer that 'he trusted all the members of the Guard but that he was "in the hands of the Secret Service", was being poisoned, and we could do nothing to stop them'.

At four o'clock the next morning, Hess asked to see the doctor. When the guard opened the gate closing off his quarters, he barged out of his room and threw himself over the banister on to the floor below. The attempt at suicide resulted only in a broken leg.

Dr Dicks, a psychiatrist who had taken over from Graham as camp doctor, called in an army surgeon, who set the leg, while Hess screamed in pain and demanded morphia. 'His bearing during first aid was cowardly and childish,' Dicks wrote.

> The patient afterwards was very difficult and was very childish in his exaggeration of the attendant discomfort.
>
> He is now expressing the belief that his medical officer, as well as the special attached officers, is insane or at least under the influence of hypnosis by an evil power which seeks his destruction. In other respects, he thinks them 'very nice men'.

Rees examined him and concluded that there was now no doubt that he was insane. 'Although Hess is secretive about most of this history, it is clear that there must have been similar attacks of this mental trouble previously.' He would have to be attended around

Simon Wertheimer's parents Leopold and Adele on a return visit to Germany after the war (*Simon Wertheimer*)

Willi Preis, one of Foley's Jewish agents, whom he succeeded in getting out of a cell in the Gestapo's Alexanderplatz HQ and put on a flight to Holland (*Ohniel Preis*)

August Weber, leading member of the opposition Staatspartei, whom Foley helped to escape from Germany

Foley's letter to the Fehr family telling them to come to the Tiergartenstrasse to collect their passes. It is addressed to Prof Dr Oskar Fehr, Wife and children Ingeborg and Kitty

BRITISH PASSPORT CONTROL OFFICE,

BERLIN, W.35.

TIERGARTENSTRASSE 17.

Telegrams:
"Pasbrit, Berlin."
Telephone: Lutzow, 4310.

Our Ref. No. BG/68695

Your Ref. No.

TO Herrn Prof. Dr. Oskar Fehr,
Frau u. Kinder Ingeborg
u. Kitty,
Berlin, W. 62,
Keithstrasse 10.

3.1.39

Ich teile Ihnen ergebenst mit, dass
ich die Erlaubnis erhalten habe, Ihren Pässe
zur Einreise nach England zu visieren.

Ich bitte Sie gelegentlich mit einem noch
gültigen Pass bei uns vorsprechen zu wollen, bzw.
denselben an uns durch die Post samt Porto einzu-
senden. Die Visumsgebühr beträgt R.M. 8.30 pro Pass.
Gebühren werden nicht durch Nachnahme erhoben.

Hochachtungsvoll,

F Foley

BRITISH PASSPORT CONTROL OFFICER, BERLIN.

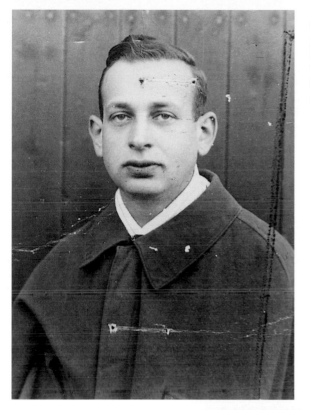

Gunter Powitzer's file photograph from Sachsenhausen. He is wearing a heavy coat to cover the effects of beatings by the camp guards (*Ze'ev Padan*)

Foley pictured in August 1939 in London where he had gone to be briefed on what action he should take in the event of war

Foley's secretary Margaret Reid

Foley (left) relaxing with his
deputy Leslie Mitchell in Oslo

Norwegian agents Oluf Reed Olsen (facing camera) and his friend Kaare Moe (*Oluf Reed Olsen*)

Hellueitner-Graf

Paul Rosbaud, the scientist recruited by Foley who provided invaluable information on the progress of the German atomic programme and the rocket research taking place at Peenemünde (*Lotte Meitner-Graf*)

THE PASSPORT CONTROL DEPT.,
FOREIGN OFFICE,
BROADWAY BUILDINGS,
BROADWAY,
WESTMINSTER,
LONDON, S.W.1.

23rd August, 1940

Dear Madam,

        I am depressed to hear that
your venerable husband has been interned
and hope that his case will receive the
most sympathetic consideration by the
new tribunals which were mentioned in
the House of Commons last night.
You have indeed suffered greatly,

                Yours sincerely,

                F. Fole,

Mrs. Jeanne Fehr,
Hay Lodge Private Hotel,
PEEBLES.

Foley's letter to Dr Fehr's wife expressing sadness at her husband's internment

Foley photographed before going to Buckingham Palace to be appointed Commander of St Michael and St George in March 1941

1. Commander of the Order of St Michael and St George Citation 'for valuable services rendered to the state'

2. British War Medal for World War I

3. Victory Medal for World War I with oak leaf indicating that Foley had been mentioned in dispatches for his actions during the Kaiser's Battle

4. 1939-45 Star, awarded for service in an operational area

5. Defence Medal for World War II, awarded for service at home

6. 1939-45 War Medal with oak leaf indicating that he had been mentioned in dispatches for his actions during the Norwegian campaign

7. Knights Cross of St Olau (First Class) awarded to Foley by King Haakon of Norway. The citation said Foley 'spared no effort to assist the Norwegian forces in their fight against the Germans and was repeatedly very dangerously exposed to enemy fire'

Ursula holding a neighbour's child outside the Foley's home in Stourbridge after the war

Adolf Eichmann
listening to evidence
during his 1962 trial in
Israel

(Below) Benno Cohn,
the former chairman of
the German Zionist
Organisation who told
the Eichmann trial that
Foley 'rescued
thousands of Jews from
the jaws of death'

the clock by psychiatric orderlies. 'We have got another – and a rather awkward – lunatic on our hands for the duration,' Cadogan recorded in his diary.

From that point on, the attitude towards Hess changed considerably. He was allowed access to *The Times*, and a few days later both 'Barnes' and Kendrick returned to London, leaving Frank alone with the prisoner. Two days later, the Germans invaded the Soviet Union, removing the most important of the considerations in trying to obtain intelligence from Jonathan, and leaving Frank feeling increasingly marginalised.

During the summer, Frank's depression at the situation was eased by a short break with Kay and Ursula and by letters from Hans Friedenthal, the former President of the German Zionist Organisation, and Georg Landauer, head of the Jewish Agency's German department, who both congratulated him on his CMG. 'I take this occasion to tell you how thankful I and all those who had contact with you in Berlin before the outbreak of the war are to you for all you have done in favour of my co-religionists,' Friedenthal said.

> You, my dear Captain Foley, have always stood for me as a representative of British freedom. I have always felt it a great privilege and consolation to have made your acquaintance, and your genuine humane activities, especially in such times, made a deep impression on us. We Jews have no order to award, but we have a good and long memory and you may be assured that the German Jews will not forget how often you have helped them.

Landauer wrote in similar terms. In his response, Frank thanked him for his congratulations and commiserated with him on the plight of the Jews. 'I am sorry to read of the immense amount of suffering your people are experiencing in Europe,' the MI6 officer said. 'The Teutonic beast is never satiated: the only solution is extermination. We in this country are working hard to that end and the time will come when they will plead for mercy. I hope that those who have suffered so much will be heard and revenged.'

The political warfare experts of the newly formed Special Operations Executive had been urging for some time that Jonathan should be used for propaganda purposes, and when, in early July, he appeared to be 'comparatively sane', Frank broached the possibility of his broadcasting to Germany.

'He is ready to read his own script, provided the authorities – the higher authorities – agree,' Frank told Menzies.

> He told me he had been thinking things over and had slowly come to the conclusion that suspicion of those appointed to look after him was probably unjustified and that it came from his own psychosis.
>
> He then went on to say that someone had suggested to him that his fear of us was based on his experience of Gestapo methods. He denied strongly that there was any cruelty or torture in German concentration camps and prisons. He had visited them. He knew the Führer also was decidedly opposed to such barbaric practices. I happen to know a great deal about concentration camps and I have probably met as many victims as anyone. But I pretended to have only an academic and detached knowledge and let him speak.
>
> The strange thing is that one gained the impression that he honestly believes his own opinion to be the true one and that he is genuinely opposed to the infliction of suffering and cruelty. We know from previous statements that he will not take part in blood sports of any description. His own anxiety has been so acute that he is interested in putting an end to any kind of cruelty, even in Germany, if it is proved to exist.

Hess had asked Frank to provide him with evidence of what was happening in the camps.

> He went so far as to say that he would accept the evidence of a Jew of credibility. There must be many Aryans and Jews who could say much.
>
> I suggest that these two conversations are not without importance as they may be made to lead to the first serious stage in destroying his faith in his friends, provided we are able to convince him that he had been deceived and cheated by them, even in this matter.

There must be a number of unbiased books that would describe what was going on in the camps, Frank said.

> We could produce actual victims whose testimony would be even more effective.
>
> I am thinking it must be possible progressively to convert him into an active instrument of propaganda against Hitler if he is proceeded with quietly and gradually. I would thank you to be good enough to consider plans on these lines and to direct me if you agree.

In a further attempt to draw Hess out of himself, he was allowed more access to the press, and in particular to magazines. 'At present, he reads *The Times* and *Tatler*,' Frank told Menzies. It would be better if he were allowed to follow the progress of the war in the illustrated journals current at the time which would be easier for Hess to read. 'The *Tatler* is too silly and is more liable to induce contempt than admiration for British life,' Frank said. 'I am thinking of *Picture Post*, *Illustrated London News*, etc. My object is to make him more amenable to intellectual intercourse and subtly to foster opportunities for us to introduce various subjects in which you are interested.'

Despite the intermittent periods of 'comparative sanity', Hess's condition continued to deteriorate, and the plans to use him for propaganda purposes against Hitler were never taken up, to the astonishment of the experts both in Britain and Germany. 'It apparently has not occurred to London to do the obvious thing and to make statements in Hess's name without reference to Hess himself,' Goebbels noted in his diary. 'It seems we have a guardian angel.'

But Churchill, who was keen to cement his new-found alliance with Moscow and at the same time bring America into the war, was anxious not to give any impression that Britain was willing even to contemplate a deal with the Nazis.

Nevertheless, Menzies remained convinced that it might still be possible to use Hess in some way to cause a split in the Nazi camp, an argument which Frank did not accept. 'The evidence one has collected leaves no doubt that Jonathan is absolutely and entirely devoted to the Führer, that he would not participate in any intrigue against him,' he said.

Frank became involved in a series of conferences at the Foreign Office, Broadway, and the headquarters in St Albans, a small town north of London, of Section V, the MI6 counter-intelligence department which was now heavily involved in the burgeoning British deception operations against Germany. It was during this period that he had his first encounter with one of the new intake of bright young officers who had joined during the war – Kim Philby, who was to become infamous as the Third Man in the Cambridge spy ring.

'I first met Frank in November 1941, in Broadway,' one of Philby's former colleagues said.

> We met in the grinding lift. We had both shown our passes at the entrance door and again in the lift. He was well-known to the liftman who had been employed years before the war, but I was a new boy. We chatted and he being older than I, and clearly "an old hand", I treated him with the respect I thought was due to him and he and I became firm friends.
>
> Nevertheless, it was soon obvious to me that Frank was uneasy about something or other. By this time, he was 'looking after' the famous Rudolf Hess. He suggested that the implications of this were at first bewildering to the political powers. They, unlike him, had not served in Germany under Hitler and it seemed to him that their lack of understanding of the Germans was astonishing.
>
> Frank's sessions with Hess would be discussed at a meeting between Felix Cowgill, the head of Section V; the head of its German section; and none other than Kim Philby. FF clearly became aware during the various top-level meetings that were had a propos of Hess that there was no question of making any kind of bargain with any of the Germans but he told me that a staunch anti-bargain man, if not the staunchest, was Kim Philby.
>
> During one of Frank's visits to St Albans, I invited him to spend the night in a spare room which my landlady had – Philby and

family living up the road. FF decided that Kim was to be avoided
that evening. He already had his suspicions, or maybe I should say
'feelings', and during the course of the evening, he asked me –
his words – 'How well do you know Philby?''. It was only later
of course that I realised the significance of this remark.

The question of what the British should do with Hess remained
unresolved throughout the latter part of 1941. A visit by Lord
Beaverbrook, the Minister of Supply, failed to provide any new
ideas. Convinced that there was nothing useful Hess could tell
them, and no doubt missing his involvement in the real war,
Frank had repeated arguments with Menzies over the Deputy
Führer's continued incarceration at Mytchett.

Quite apart from the fact that it did not have the appropriate
facilities for someone in Hess's condition, if he was regarded as
a prisoner of war it was against the Geneva Convention to hold
him so close to obvious military targets, Frank said. But despite
backing for Frank's view from the psychiatrists, the head of MI6
was adamant that it was too early to transfer Hess either to a hospital
or a PoW camp.

Shortly before Christmas, Hess demanded to see the Swiss
Minister, Walther Thurnheer, handing him a letter for King
George VI in which he repeated the allegation that he was being
poisoned by MI6. In his report on Thurnheer's visit, made after
listening to the conversation through the concealed microphones,
Frank again stressed Hess's mental instability.

'Jonathan brought up all the usual poisoning suspicions,' he
said.

> He complained that he suffered from intestinal trouble, loss of
> memory and broken nerves. He told the Minister that he was
> convinced that drugs had been added to his food within the
> last two weeks in order to make it difficult for him to carry
> on a rational conversation with him. I think I may say that the
> Minister gained the impression that Jonathan was suffering from
> delusions.

Early in the new year, Frank's patience finally snapped. The two men had eaten lunch together in Hess's room when the German opened a box to reveal a collection of biscuits, Ryvita, cocoa, sugar and various types of pills which he said contained poison and were proof that the British were trying to murder him. He would be taking them back to Germany with him after the war for analysis.

Frank reacted furiously, telling Hess that he was talking non-sense. 'I offered to consume the tablets and swallowed them then and there to his utter amazement, although he was not able to say whether they were sleeping draughts or laxatives,' Frank said. He then stood in front of Hess eating the Ryvita before putting the kettle on and making cocoa, which he insisted Hess shared. Later that afternoon, he returned to the German's cell to show him that the so-called poison had had no adverse effect on him.

The incident left Hess even more depressed. The camp commandant noted in his diary that Jonathan now 'admitted that he must have been mistaken about the poison in his collection. He has given all the balance of his hoard of so-called poisoned foods etc to the medical orderly to be thrown away. He now realises that all this poisoning mania must be psychosis and consequently is in a dreadful state over it.'

Hess wrote to the King, retracting his previous allegations of poisoning. 'Today, Major Foley, whom I mentioned in my letter, ate before my eyes some of the food and tablets which I had assumed to contain noxious substances,' he said. 'The incident has forced me to conclude that my complaints were the result of auto-suggestion brought on by my captivity.'

Shortly afterwards, Churchill and Menzies finally accepted that there was nothing to be done with Hess other than to place him in a hospital, and in June 1942 he was moved to Maindiff Court Hospital, Abergavenny, in South Wales, while Frank was recalled to London to take a leading role in one of the greatest intelligence operations of all time – the Double-Cross System.

Chapter 22

The Twenty Club

Menzies told Frank that he desperately needed an officer with real operational experience for a committee that was in charge of double agents. It was embroiled in a bitter turf war in which MI6 had somehow managed to range itself against MI5 and the intelligence services of all three armed forces. The present MI6 representative, a desk man, had dug himself into a hole. The only sensible option was to bring in a new man, and Frank was ideal.

The double agent network, known as the Double-Cross System, had originated from a plan devised by a member of MI5. Dick White, a future head of both MI5 and MI6, suggested that any German agents uncovered during the war should be left in place and 'turned' to work as double agents for British Intelligence. MI5 would be able to keep complete control over all German espionage activities in Britain, and as a welcome side-effect, the information the agents asked for would tell the British what the Abwehr did and did not know.

The first opportunity to turn a German agent came when Arthur Owens – a businessman and part-time MI6 agent or 'stringer' – was found to be working for the Germans. He was arrested and agreed to work as a double agent under the cover name of SNOW. His controller was Lt-Col. Tommy 'Tar' Robertson of MI5. Through

SNOW, Robertson acquired a number of other agents, and a new section, B1a, was set up to run them.

Then, in March 1940, the cipher used by the Abwehr's agents to communicate with their controllers was broken by the code-breakers at Bletchley Park. The deciphered material enabled MI5 to keep track of the messages of the double agents and spot any other German spies arriving in the country. It also meant that the agents' reports could be designed to allow the code-breakers to follow them through the Abwehr radio networks. Hopefully, this would help them break the keys for the more complicated Enigma cipher used on the radio links between the Abwehr outstations and their headquarters in Hamburg.

By the end of 1940, Robertson had a dozen double agents under his control. At the same time, MI6 was running a number of German spies abroad. 'Basically, MI5 was responsible for security in the UK and MI6 operated overseas,' one of the agent runners said. 'Obviously there was a grey area as far as double agents was concerned because they were trained and recruited overseas and at that point were the concern of MI6 while once they arrived here they became the responsibility of MI5.'

If the double agents were to maintain their credibility with the Abwehr, they needed information they could feed back to Hamburg. The problem was how to do this without damaging the British cause. Initially it was decided that the 'intelligence' provided by the double agents should be aimed purely at demonstrating how strong Britain's defences were. But by the beginning of 1941, it was clear that more could be done with the double agents. They could be used to deceive the Germans, to provide them with misleading information that would give Allied forces an advantage in the field.

A 'Most Secret' committee was set up to decide what information should be fed back to the Germans. Its small select membership included representatives of MI5, MI6, naval, military and air intelligence, HQ Home Forces and the Home Defence Executive, which was in charge of civil defence. The committee was called the XX Committee, although it swiftly became known as the Twenty Committee, or more colloquially the Twenty Club, from the Roman numeral suggested by the double-cross sign. It met every Wednesday in MI5 headquarters, initially in Wormwood Scrubs prison, but subsequently at 58 St James's Street.

'The XX Committee was chaired by J C Masterman,' one of the MI5 agent handlers said. 'Tar Robertson, who ran B1A, really developed the whole thing. He was absolutely splendid, a marvellous man to work for. He and Dick White were the two outstanding people I suppose and Tar collected around him some very bright people who actually ran the agents for him.'

The MI5 and MI6 officers handling the double-cross agents desperately needed to know what information they could give them to pass on to the Germans. Much of it was built around 'chicken-feed', unimportant information that would give the Abwehr a feel that its agents were doing something and had access to real intelligence without telling them anything really harmful to the war effort. But to make the system work properly, the Twenty Committee would need to build up a false picture of what the British were doing, and this could only be achieved slowly if it was not to make the Germans suspicious.

The committee's task was to co-ordinate the construction of this false intelligence picture. They supervised the system. They did not run the individual agents. 'They approved the overall plan,' the former agent handler said.

> I was in touch with the Germans probably two or three times a day by radio and so I had to move fairly quickly. So the approving authorities were not the actual Twenty Committee because it only sat once a week. But I would get approval from people who were on the committee and every week I and others who were actually active would prepare a short report for the committee saying what we were doing and what we had done.

The Twenty Club's confidence in their double agents was considerably enhanced in December 1941 when Bletchley Park broke the Abwehr's Enigma cipher. This told them that the Germans believed the false intelligence they were feeding them. It also showed whether or not individual double agents were trusted or under suspicion, in which case steps could be taken to remedy the situation.

This was an important breakthrough. Early on, the Twenty Club members could not be sure that they were not themselves being taken in by the Germans. The captured agents were dismissed as plants and 'too amateurish' to be genuine German spies. 'The position at the beginning was largely experimental as no one knew very much about the working of double agents or about the working and general incompetence of the Abwehr,' wrote Ewen Montagu, the Naval Intelligence representative on the committee. 'Later on, after we had had experience of the German Intelligence Service, no incompetence would have surprised us.'

By the spring of 1942, the information collected from the Bletchley Park decrypts had built up such a good picture of Abwehr operations in Britain that Robertson was able to state categorically that MI5 now controlled all the German agents operating in Britain. The Twenty Club was able to watch the Germans making arrangements to send agents to Britain and discussing the value of their reports, Robertson wrote. 'In two or three cases we have been able to observe the action (which has been rapid and extensive) taken by the Germans upon the basis of these agents' reports.'

But the breaking of the Enigma cipher had brought a new problem for the committee. The release of any material from Bletchley Park was controlled extremely strictly by MI6 in order to safeguard the Ultra secret. The fact that the 'unbreakable' Enigma ciphers had been broken had to be protected at all costs.

The MI6 representative on the committee was Felix Cowgill, the head of Section V, the MI6 counter-espionage division. A former Indian Police officer, Cowgill was a shy, slightly built man in his mid-thirties. 'His face gives the impression of intensity coupled with a great weariness,' Philby wrote in one of his reports to Moscow. 'Although normally quiet in manner, due to shyness, he is combative in his work, always prepared to challenge an office ruling.'

Cowgill defended the Ultra secret vigorously to the extent of refusing to allow the Home Forces and Home Defence Executive representatives on the Twenty Committee to see Ultra material at all, while anything that referred to MI6 agents was held back even from MI5. 'Cowgill was so imbued with the idea of security that when he was put in charge for C of this material, he was quite willing to try entirely to prevent its use as intelligence lest it be compromised,' Montagu said. 'These views inevitably caused friction.'

While there was no doubt that MI5 was paying scant regard to some of the necessary restrictions on the Bletchley Park decrypts, Cowgill's attitude made the Twenty Committee's operations almost impossible. Some members were not privy to vital information about the agents on which the others were basing their decisions. The controls were soon being ignored on a wholesale basis. 'A good deal of bootlegging of information had to take place,' said Montagu. 'Many undesirable "off the record" and "under the table" practices were essential unless work was to stop entirely.'

The situation came to a head over the case of a man who was to become the most valuable of all the Double-Cross agents – Juan Pujol Garcia, better known as Garbo.

The Enigma decrypts had revealed an Abwehr agent who claimed to be running a network of agents in Britain. His reports were ridiculously inaccurate. He was clearly a fraud, reporting 'drunken orgies and slack morals in amusement centres' in Liverpool, and Glasgow dockers who were 'prepared to do anything for a litre of wine'. It ought to have been obvious to the Germans that not only had he never met a Glasgow docker in his life, he had never been to Britain. Yet they believed him whole-heartedly. MI6 became concerned that his false reports might damage the Twenty Club's own plans.

Then in early February, the MI6 head of station in Lisbon

reported that he had been approached by a Spaniard claiming to be a top Abwehr secret agent. He said he had been disaffected by the Spanish Civil War and was keen to help Britain fight the Germans. Having been turned down by the MI6 station in Madrid, he had gone to the Germans, persuading them that he was a Spanish intelligence officer who had been posted to Britain and offering to act as a German spy.

In fact, Pujol went to Lisbon, where armed with a Blue Guide to Britain, a Portuguese book on the British fleet and an Anglo-French vocabulary of military terms, he produced a series of highly imaginative reports built on the alleged network of agents.

Pujol was vehemently anti-Nazi and his reports were apparently designed to disrupt the German intelligence service; he was in effect a freelance double-cross operation in miniature. Cowgill kept him secret from MI5, on the basis that although sending reports ostensibly from British territory and therefore notionally under MI5 jurisdiction, he was actually abroad and the responsibility of MI6.

In fact, at the lower levels, MI6 officers did discuss him with their MI5 counterparts. But when, at the end of February, the senior officers in MI5 found out about Pujol, they reacted furiously, using him as a peg on which to hang all the anger that had been building up over a number of issues, most notably the distribution of the Bletchley Park decrypts.

MI5 insisted that he should be brought back to Britain. Cowgill said no, he was abroad and therefore an MI6 agent. Sir David Petrie, the head of MI5, used the row to lobby for MI5 to take over control of Section V. He added all the arguments over the distribution of deciphered intercepts and the fact that Section V was based in St Albans, too far away from London to make liaison with MI5 as easy as it should have been.

Menzies decided that he would have to do something about the situation. He was spending too much time arbitrating between Cowgill and the other members of the Twenty Committee, which was clearly not operating to its full potential anyway, and he was determined to fight off the MI5 takeover bid.

In the spring of 1942, he proposed a compromise. While it was not practicable to move Section V from St Albans to London as MI5 was demanding, he was happy to set up a new department with offices in London and St Albans to improve liaison with MI5 over Double-Cross.

At the same time, he was taking Cowgill off the Twenty Committee and replacing him with an officer with more extensive operational experience. The man he had in mind had spent the past twenty years concentrating on Germany. He knew the German mind and how it would react to any deception. His name was Frank Foley.

From that point on, Frank came up to London from Mytchett Place every Wednesday to attend the Twenty Committee meeting in tandem with Cowgill, splitting his time between watching Hess and learning the details of the Double-Cross operation. In June, he took over the new department full time, attending the meetings of the Twenty Committee in Cowgill's place.

'There was an obvious qualitative difference in the way in which the committee worked from then on,' one former MI5 officer said. 'For the first time, the MI6 representative was speaking authoritatively because he was a real operational officer. He knew what he was talking about and it showed.'

J.C. Masterman, the secretary of the Twenty Committee, also pointed to June 1942 as the moment that the Double-Cross System really began to take off. 'Broadly speaking, bad men make good institutions bad and good men make bad institutions good,' Masterman said. 'It cannot be denied that there was some friction between MI5 and MI6 in the early days, but this disappeared when the MI6 representative on the committee was changed.'

Frank was relieved to be rid of Hess and back in the real war. He divided his time between his London offices at 5 St James's Street, a short walk away from the MI5 headquarters, and Glenalmond, the large surburban house in St Albans where Section V was based.

At the back of the house was a bar, known as the Snakepit, which looked out over a lawn and an overgrown rose garden, where the MI6 officers gathered after work to discuss the various cases.

The new department, code-named VX, took over the task of building up a complete picture of the activities of the German intelligence services. But its most important role was controlling the MI6 double-cross agents and liaising with the rest of the Twenty Committee.

One of the major problems faced by the Double-Cross officers was that when the British tried to work out what the Germans would do next, they based their judgments on what they would have done in the same situation. But their opponents, and in particular Hitler, had a different view of things.

'It is necessary for the deception staff to think as the enemy thinks and to divorce themselves entirely from being influenced by what we would do if placed in what we imagine to be the enemy's position,' one former deception officer said. 'Again and again, what the deceivers suggested was plausible to the enemy. But both our operations and intelligence staffs maintained that it was not because they were governed strictly by their appreciation of what we would think was plausible in the enemy's place.'

Masterman had been a prisoner of war in Germany during the First World War. But his knowledge of the German way of thinking was nowhere near as sharply developed as Frank's.

'Foley knew the Germans backwards,' one former MI6 officer said. 'So if people wanted to know how the Germans would react to any particular deception plan, they would naturally ask him.' Frank swiftly succeeded in turning around the committee's attitude to MI6, which had been so heavily tarnished by Cowgill's restrictions.

'He was not a member of the establishment clique,' another of his former colleagues said. 'But he was a pretty serious chap, feet on the ground, solid, very much the elder statesman, giving useful advice whenever called upon. His exceptional knowledge of the workings of, and personalities in, the Abwehr, acquired during years of service in Berlin, made him a tower of strength.'

Shortly after Frank took up his new post, Margaret Reid was awarded her Krigsmedalje by King Haakon. Much to her annoyance, the Foreign Office had not yet agreed to allow Frank to receive his Knight's Cross of St Olav.

'It was a source of great chagrin to me not to receive my decoration at the same time as my chief,' she told her mother. 'I believe he will be decorated later when the Foreign Office have ceased quibbling about what they will allow him to accept. Do not congratulate me. I feel rather sick of the whole affair. People who do nothing at all get all the limelight and the real men who do the job underground get no reward and may be shot in the end.'

Much of Frank's work was based on German espionage activities in the Iberian peninsula and in particular the Portuguese capital Lisbon, from where the Abwehr was attempting to infiltrate its agents into Britain. 'Portugal was neutral and so to Portugal came the agents official and unofficial of countries on both sides,' said John Masterman. 'It was not possible to learn in Berlin what was happening in London, but it might be possible to hear, or guess, or deduce in neutral Portugal what was happening in both. So Lisbon became a kind of international clearing ground, a busy ant-heap of spies and agents, where political and military secrets and information – true and false, but mainly false – were bought and sold.'

Foley made several trips to Lisbon to check people out. One of his first was to question the double agent known as Hamlet, who like Garbo provided the Abwehr with reports from Britain. Hamlet was an Austrian Jew who had owned property in Germany until 1936, when it was confiscated as part of the Aryanisation programme and he was briefly imprisoned. On his release, he moved to Italy to set up a new business and sent his children to England to be educated. When war broke out, he went to Belgium where he was recruited by the Abwehr and sent to Lisbon, using his extensive business interests as cover for espionage.

His reports to Brussels, ostensibly obtained from agents in Britain, were much in the manner of Garbo's – highly valued by the Germans but mainly based on newspaper reports and bar gossip in Lisbon. In late 1941, he met a penniless expatriate Englishman attempting to make his way home. Hamlet bought him dinner for several weeks, taking him on as his business representative in London and asking him to take some jewellery to his children. More importantly, he asked him to set up contacts between London and senior German officers anxious to make peace.

'Hamlet declared, as early as 1941, that there was strong military opposition to Hitler and that he himself believed that this opposition could be assisted and made effective for the benefit of the Allies as well as Germany,' Masterman said. On his return to London, Hamlet's new employee reported the approach to MI5 and, code-named Mullet, was recruited into the Double-Cross stable.

But curiously nothing further was done about the case until nine months later, a few weeks after Frank took over the MI6 Double-Cross files. At least one former intelligence officer suggested that this might have had something to do with the fact that the man on whom Cowgill had relied for information on double-cross operations in Spain and Portugal was Kim Philby. 'The last thing the Russian sympathisers wanted was the German resistance working with the British towards negotiating a peace thus uniting the West against one common enemy – the Soviet Union.'

Whatever the reasons behind the delay, Mullet was sent back into Lisbon in August 1942 for talks with Hamlet, who now claimed to have a direct line to Admiral Canaris and General Alexander von Falkenhausen, the military governor of Belgium. Frank discussed the case with Menzies and they decided that Frank should go to Lisbon himself to check Hamlet out.

He flew from Whitchurch, near Bristol, in a BOAC airliner. His meetings with Hamlet convinced him that much of what the Austrian was saying was true. He really did have a good link to von Falkenhausen through a mutual friend, code-named Puppet. But there was no direct link to Canaris.

Hamlet, Mullet and Puppet would have provided a useful double agent network. But they might in the future become more useful as a link to the German opposition. The Twenty Committee agreed that it might be better to keep them in reserve until things became clearer. Despite Hamlet's exaggeration of his relationship with Canaris, he appeared genuine, his motivation was credible, his children were in England and he had put himself at the mercy of the British by offering to betray the Germans.

Frank returned from Lisbon laden with bananas and oranges for Ursula and his niece Patricia, who lived in London. 'My father was teaching at a naval training school in Highgate,' Patricia Dunstan said.

> Uncle Frank would come and see us quite frequently. Mother would cook him Sunday lunch. We would visit his London flat and I was always intrigued by his scrambler phone and very disappointed that the voice on the phone sounded normal and not all scrambled up.
>
> If we went to see him on a Sunday we would go to mass at Brompton Oratory. I remember Ursula and Auntie Kay coming down for the day and we went to Trafalgar Square and sat on the steps feeding the pigeons. When Uncle Frank had to go away, we didn't know where or why he was going, but when he returned I remember him standing at the door in civvies – he always seemed to be dressed in smart suits – carrying a very colourful straw bag full of oranges and bananas for me.

Chapter 23

Like a Spider Spinning His Web

Frank's star communist agent Jonny X was also brought into the Double-Cross System. Having been exonerated by Moscow, he was back in Brazil and about to leave for Japan on another mission when the Second World War broke out. The time was now right, he decided, to end his own role as a double agent and 'come in from the cold'. MI6 asked him to stay in Brazil, maintaining his cover as Franz Gruber and gathering information on Nazi activities there.

But in January 1940 he was arrested by the Brazilian authorities, who threatened to deport him to his country of origin – Germany. As a known communist, this would have meant a one-way ticket to a concentration camp. The Foreign Office successfully intervened with the Brazilians on Jonny's behalf, citing 'the services he rendered in denouncing the communist movement of 1935'. He was freed and recalled to London for debriefing.

Then, on 9 November 1943, an Abwehr agent was landed in Canada by U-boat. Werner Janowski was put ashore near New Carlisle in Quebec. He buried his German uniform and next morning hitched a lift into town, where he took a room in the Carlisle Hotel. With spy fever rampant, Janowski was soon spotted. 'His shoes were quite different from anything I had ever seen,' the hotel-owner's son said. 'His dark gabardine topcoat was not quite like the Canadian style.'

When Janowski tried to pay with old Canadian dollar bills that had been largely replaced and lit his cigarette with a Belgian box of matches, the police were informed and he was arrested at the station as he tried to leave town. Provided with the opportunity to extend their network to North America, the Twenty Committee sent two representatives to Canada to help to play Janowski back at the Germans. One of them was Jonny X.

Janowski was given the code-name Watchdog and succeeded in establishing radio contact with Hamburg in January 1943. For the next nine months he and Jonny were holed up in a cellar in Montreal, with Jonny supervising his messages to ensure that Janowski did not try to warn Hamburg that he was compromised. But the case was neither yielding enough intelligence nor providing sufficient scope for deception, so the Twenty Committee attempted to expand it by getting Janowski to ask his Abwehr controllers to send him some assistants.

Unfortunately, Janowski's arrest had been reported both in the Canadian and American press and in the Quebec state parliament. When there was a three-week delay in Hamburg responding, it was decided that Watchdog must be compromised and he was closed down. Given the pathetic nature of the Abwehr's intelligence operations in North America, this was probably premature, and indeed Hamburg came back up almost immediately and continued calling Watchdog for a further six months. But the members of the Twenty Club were not prepared to take the risk.

By the spring of 1943, they had developed the Double-Cross System into a fine art. But one of their most famous pieces of deception did not involve a double agent at all. Operation Mincemeat was designed to persuade the Germans that the Allies were about to launch the invasion of southern Europe through Sardinia and Greece, thereby drawing attention away from the real target – Sicily.

Charles Cholmondley, an RAF officer attached to MI5, told

the committee that the Spanish authorities had recently given the Germans a number of documents found on the body of a dead British airman which had been washed ashore. He suggested planting documents that would draw attention away from Sicily on another body and dropping it off the coast of Spain as if it too had come from a crashed aircraft. The Spanish authorities would no doubt repeat their previous trick and the Germans would reinforce their garrisons in the notional target at the expense of the real one.

Montagu took charge of the operation. He acquired a suitable body from a London hospital and gave it the identity of Major William Martin, Royal Marines, an official courier. Attached to Martin's wrist by a chain was a briefcase containing a number of documents, including a letter from one senior British general to another discussing planned assaults on Greece and an unspecified location in the western Mediterranean, for which Sicily was to be a cover. A further letter from Lord Mountbatten, the Chief of Combined Operations, referred jocularly to sardines, which was rightly thought enough of a hint to make the Germans believe the real attack was going to be on Sardinia.

The members of the Twenty Club were highly inventive in their choice of other documents to be planted on the body. Two 'used' West End theatre tickets for a few days before the intended launch of the body were in his pocket to show that he must have been travelling by air. A photograph of Martin's 'fiancée', actually that of a female MI5 clerk, was placed in his wallet. For several weeks, Cholmondley carried two love letters from the 'fiancée' around in his pocket to give them the proper crumpled look. There was even an irate letter from Martin's bank manager.

The body was floated ashore near the southern Spanish town of Huelva at the end of April from the Royal Navy submarine HMS *Seraph*, and, as expected, the documents found their way to the Germans. They swallowed the deception completely, giving top priority to the reinforcement of Sardinia and the Balkans. Even two months later, when the invasion of Sicily had been launched,

German intelligence continued to insist that the original plan had been to attack Sardinia and Greece and that it had only been switched to Sicily at the last moment.

Frank's family always understood that he was involved in the preparations for Mincemeat, in particular the search for a suitable body. *The Man Who Never Was*, Montagu's own account of the operation, gave him all the credit. But it is now clear that this was partly to hide the involvement of MI5 and MI6. Certainly, Frank would have been asked for advice on how the Germans might react, and would have had to ensure that the MI6 stations in the area did not inadvertently disrupt the operation on the ground. But the precise extent of his and Robertson's contributions to the operation remains shrouded in mystery.

Possibly the best of the double-cross agents controlled by Frank's section was Artist, a senior Abwehr officer whose real name was Jonny Jebsen. One of his top recruits was Dusko Popov, an urbane Yugoslav thought by many to be the model for James Bond. He and Jebsen had been at university together. The German sent him to London in December 1940 to gather intelligence for the Abwehr. Popov reported the recruitment to the British and became one of MI5's most important double agents under the codename Tricycle.

Jebsen was unaware of this when two years later he approached the British in Madrid claiming that the Gestapo was on his tail. Kenneth Benton, the Section V man in Spain, interviewed the German spy whom he described as 'a small man, chain-smoking and looking rather sweaty and apprehensive, who told me he was an officer in the Abwehr and wished us to protect him from the Gestapo'.

In return, Jebsen said he was prepared to tell the British what he knew about the Abwehr operations in Lisbon, adding that he was a *Forscher*, a talent-spotter or recruiter of potential agents. He told Benton about Popov, 'who has either been turned already or would go over to your side at the drop of a hat'.

That night Benton sent a Most Immediate message to St

Albans. The following morning, he received confirmation that Artist was telling the truth. 'Popov is one of our most successful double-agents, pseudonym Tricycle,' the message from St Albans read. 'This contact has great potential value. Use utmost caution, but try to obtain names of other agents he has recruited, in case there is one we have missed.'

Benton placed Artist in a safe house for a more detailed debriefing. 'He told me that he suspected the Gestapo of lining their pockets with forged British bank notes, but I was never quite sure that it was not the other way around. If so, he ran a lot of risks, not least because he had a great liking for pornographic films and admitted that one of the reasons why he came so frequently to Madrid was the existence of two clandestine cinemas which specialised in this kind of film.'

Frank discussed the case with Cowgill and Philby, and they decided it would be better if Artist was returned to Lisbon where the secret police were more sympathetic and there was less danger of Gestapo surveillance. So Benton handed Jebsen over to his counterpart in Lisbon, who arranged to meet the German at Montserrat, a tropical garden in Estoril. 'We didn't know what each other looked like and so we said we would meet under a certain tree,' the Lisbon-based officer said. 'To my amazement, when he turned up, he was dressed in Anthony Eden attire, complete with pinstripe trousers and hat.'

For fifteen months, Jebsen stayed in Lisbon, where the MI6 representative interrogated him thoroughly. He pointed the British in the direction of a number of useful agents and described the havoc caused inside the Abwehr as a result of its rivalry with the Nazi Party's Sicherheitsdienst which would shortly take it over. But Benton was right in his assessment of Jebsen's difficulties with the Gestapo. He was wanted for handling forged currency and the Germans suspected he was about to defect. In April 1944, Frank received information from Bletchley Park that showed that Jebsen was about to be arrested and snatched back to Germany.

On 28 April, the Section V representative in Lisbon had a

meeting with Jebsen, who had good news for him. There had
been problems with the Tricycle case and the Twenty Committee
had become concerned that he might be compromised. But Jebsen
could confirm that Hamburg remained convinced of his loyalty.
Despite the good news, the MI6 man was puzzled by something.
'I had received a telegram from Head Office which at the end
said: "Tell Artist to be careful",' he recalled. 'I told him this and
he said: "Ha, ha. You know I'm always careful." That afternoon,
he was due to travel from Lisbon to Oporto. On the way, he was
kidnapped by the Sicherheitsdienst.' Jebsen was bundled into the
false bottom of a trunk and smuggled back to Germany. He was
sent to Oranienburg concentration camp, where he died.

The Lisbon-based officer blamed Frank for Jebsen's demise.
'This had all come through on the decodes,' he said. 'Foley knew
it. All he said was: "Tell Artist to be careful". They should have
told me. I could have said: "We've had a tip from Madrid." I
always felt bitter about that part of it.'

The decision to send the message was almost certainly Frank's.
But the situation must have been discussed with Cowgill and
Philby, possibly even with Menzies himself. Whatever the arguments in Jebsen's favour, and there is no doubting his bravery or his
contribution to the Allied cause, to have issued a stronger warning
would have risked compromising the all-important Bletchley Park
operation. There was simply no choice.

Throughout 1943, Frank continued to make intermittent trips
to Portugal to debrief agents and defectors. At the beginning of
June, he was on his way back to England when he met up with
his old friend Wilfred Israel at Lisbon airport. Israel had been
in Spain on behalf of the Jewish Agency, attempting to help
Jewish refugees coming down the escape lines through France.
By coincidence, there was also someone else Frank knew from
his time in Berlin waiting at the airport – Gordon Thompson
Maclean, Inspector-General of His Majesty's Consulates.

The BOAC flight to Whitchurch that morning had a VIP
passenger on board. Leslie Howard, the actor and film star, had

been on a British Council lecture tour in Spain and Portugal. He had illustrated his talk on 'How to Make a Film' with scenes from one of his most recent pictures, *Pimpernel Smith*, curiously the story of an academic turned spy who is sent to Germany and while there becomes involved in helping Jewish children to escape.

Maclean was not booked on that particular flight. 'He asked Uncle Frank if they could change places,' said Patricia Dunstan. 'He said Leslie Howard was his wife's favourite actor and he wanted to get his autograph.' Frank happily agreed. Shortly before ten o'clock, the DC3 took off for Whitchurch with thirteen passengers and four crew on board. A few hours later, as it was crossing the Bay of Biscay, it was shot down by a squadron of German fighter aircraft. All of those on board were killed.

The closer co-ordination between MI5 and MI6 over the double agents was helped immensely in July 1943 when Section V moved from St Albans to Ryder Street, just off St James's Street and a stone's throw from both MI5 headquarters and the offices of the London Controlling Section run by Colonel Johnny Bevan, which was co-ordinating all deception operations. Now whenever problems arose, MI5 officers could simply walk across the road to discuss them with Frank.

'One always gets the impression of a tremendous rivalry and that sort of thing,' a former double-cross agent handler said.

> And I suppose at the top, there can be rivalry. But at the lower level, one just has to get on with the job and I always found everybody very helpful. Even at the top, one can exaggerate the degree of thigh-grabbing. The time-scale was so short, you couldn't really have a long battle with anybody. I don't think there was really enough time for bad blood to be created.
>
> I suppose the ongoing common ground was in discussing with people like Foley the training methods, the German controllers, and the equipment with which they were providing our agents and this was a two-way exchange. I would go over and have a chat with them in their offices or ring them up on the scrambler. We told them what we knew and they told us what they knew.

A few weeks after the move to Ryder Street, the Foreign Office finally agreed that the Norwegians could award Frank the Knight's Cross of the Order of St Olav. He was invested with the order at the Norwegian embassy by King Haakon on 17 August. 'I remember Uncle Frank getting my mother to sew a new medal ribbon on to his uniform,' said Patricia Dunstan.

By now the main thrust of the Twenty Club's operations was in preparing for D-day. Churchill was as fascinated with deception as he was with espionage. At the Teheran Conference in November 1943, when the final decision was made to launch the invasion of Europe in mid-1944, the British Prime Minister told Stalin that 'in wartime, truth is so precious that she should always be attended by a bodyguard of lies'.

From that point on, the overall deception plan for D-day was known as Operation Bodyguard. In dealing with any of the double agents, Frank always had to have at the back of his mind what part they might play in Bodyguard. Everything had to be directed towards that. The Double-Cross System became like a game of chess with the agents resembling pieces, each being carefully moved into a position where it could contribute to the opponent's demise.

Frank now had to liaise not only with MI5 and Bevan's London Controlling Section, but also with SHAEF, the Supreme Headquarters Allied Forces in Europe, which was co-ordinating the invasion plans from Norfolk House in nearby St James's Square. 'Foley was tremendously involved in the preparations for the invasion,' a former MI6 officer said. 'He was in charge of one of the most prestigious sections of the service, sitting in Ryder St like a spider spinning his web.'

His ability to merge into the background did not prevent him earning the respect of his fellow intelligence officers, even if some of them saw him as someone who was solid rather than brilliant. 'Foley struck one very much as being a good plain cook, fairly straightforward,' one of the agent handlers said. 'He was a fairly nondescript individual and he had around him at different times some quite colourful characters like Philby, Tommy Haris – who was in MI5 but at one time was working with Foley – and Dick Brooman-White, who was a very colourful character.'

Tommy Haris was Garbo's handler. Although Garbo was based in Britain, his network was so large and so vital to the overall deception picture that virtually everything had to be closely co-ordinated on a day-to-day basis. Hence the close link with Frank.

A number of agents would, in the parlance of the Twenty Club, 'come up for D-Day'. Apart from Garbo, the most important was the triple agent Brutus. Roman Garby-Czerniawski, a Pole, had led the Interallie resistance network in France and, once it was uncovered, volunteered to work for the Abwehr in London in order to save the other members of his group from execution handing himself over to MI5 on arrival in Britain.

But Hamlet and Mullet were also involved, as were Tricycle and Tate, the Dane Wulf Schmidt, who was one of the longest-serving double agents. Schmidt, who parachuted into Britain in September 1939, acquired his code-name from his striking resemblance to the famous music-hall artist Harry Tate. He was so successful that the Abwehr described him as 'the pearl' in their British network and awarded him two Iron Crosses.

All of these helped in building up Fortitude South, the false picture of the intended target of D-Day. But by far the most important and complex role was played by Garbo. At one point he had a network of twenty-seven agents, some of whom had survived from his freelance period before the British recruited him. They included a Swiss businessman based in Bootle who had reported the 'drunken orgies and slack morals in amusement centres' in Liverpool and an enthusiastic Venzuelan living in Glasgow who had noted the willingness of Clydeside dockers to 'do anything for a litre of wine'.

The Swiss businessman died of cancer in the autumn of 1942. But his widow continued working for Garbo, becoming virtually his personal assistant. The Venezuelan also grew in stature, developing his own ring of agents and effectively assuming the number-two position in the Garbo network.

Other agents included Moonbeam, the Venezuelan's brother, who returned home via Canada where he stopped off and, with the assistance of Jonny X, wrote a number of reports in secret ink to Garbo's controllers in Madrid. Moonbeam was soon settled in Canada, developing his own network which included an American travelling salesman who provided reports from the USA. So successful was this network that Garbo sent another of his agents, a Gibraltarian waiter, code-named Fred, to Canada to operate a radio transmitter for Moonbeam, again aided by Jonny X.

With the exception of Jonny, none of these agents actually existed. Nevertheless, they all contributed to the German dependence on Garbo as their most reliable source for intelligence on the Allied plans and set the scene for his key role in Fortitude. This was designed to make the Germans believe that the Normandy landings in early June were simply a feint. The real invasion of Europe was to be mounted a few weeks later in the Pas de Calais. It would be led by General Patton's First United States Army Group.

Like the agents who reported its activities, the First United States Army Group did not exist. It had been built up by false reports from the double-cross agents, dummy invasion craft left in the open in east coast ports and mobile wireless vehicles travelling around south-east England broadcasting messages from a number of different locations to fool the German radio interception units.

On D-Day, Garbo reported that the Allied forces were on their way before they hit the beaches, but too late for the Germans to do anything about it. This helped to persuade them that his intelligence was accurate and paved the way for the next stage of the deception.

A few days later, as the Allied advance faltered and with the élite 1st SS Panzerdivision on its way, together with another armoured division, to reinforce the German defences in Normandy, Garbo sent his most important message, reporting troops massed across East Anglia and Kent and large numbers of troop and tank transporters waiting in the eastern ports.

'From the reports mentioned, it is perfectly clear that the present attack is a large-scale attack but diversionary in character to draw the maximum of our reserves so as to be able to strike a blow somewhere else with ensured success,' Garbo said. 'The constant aerial bombardment which the area of the Pas de Calais has suffered and the strategic disposition of these forces give reason to suspect an attack in that region of France which at the same time offers the shortest route for the final objective of their illusions, which is to say, Berlin.'

Garbo's warning went straight to Hitler, who ordered the two divisions back to the Pas de Calais to defend against what he expected to be the main invasion thrust and awarded Pujol the Iron Cross. Had the two divisions continued to Normandy, the Allies might well have been thrown back into the sea.

A few weeks later, as the Allies advanced across northern France, Frank wrote to his brother Andy in Canada telling him about the V-bombs that were being aimed at Britain. 'The landing was a marvellous operation,' he said.

> I don't want to hear anybody tell me again that the old country cannot organise and fight too. We are bearing the brunt of it and not only in France too. We stuck the bombings of London for 50 consecutive nights in 1940 and now we are taking it again on and off during the 24 hours of every day. The V-bombs are nasty things though as they travel fast and hit hard. But the Government is getting the children away and life and work goes on in this city of London as if nothing is happening.

Operation Crossbow, the attempt to counter the V-bombs, was now occupying much of the Twenty Committee's time. The double agents were being repeatedly asked for information on where the missiles were falling. This posed a dilemma, recalled Professor R. V. Jones, who advised the double-cross team on scientific matters. 'If the agents sent back false reports the deception might be detected by photographic reconnaissance which would show the Germans that there was no damage where the agents had said that there was. In that event the whole Double Cross system would be unmasked.'

The mean point of impact of the V-bombs was in south-east London, four miles short of their target. But by carefully manipulating the times and locations of the blasts reported back by the double agents, the committee succeeded in persuading the Germans that they were overshooting and the range of the V-bombs was shortened, moving the danger still further out of London. Operation Crossbow was the last major deception in which Frank participated. On 14 December 1944, he attended his final meeting of the Twenty Club.

Chapter 24

Hunting for Nazis

As the Allies advanced on Berlin, Frank was one of the many intelligence officers selected for work in the Allied Control Commission that was to govern occupied Germany. It was to be divided into four zones – American, French, Russian and British. Frank was to be the MI6 representative in the Public Safety Branch, the organisation controlling the police. His official title was to be Assistant Inspector-General of the Public Safety Branch. But his actual role was to take charge of the Special Branch, hunting for Nazis.

Shortly before his departure, Frank wrote to Werner Senator, one of his Jewish contacts in Berlin, expressing regret that he had been unable to see him when he visited London a few months earlier.

'I am afraid the circumstances of this war have left one little time for one's friends,' he said.

> It cannot last much longer. We shall soon be in Berlin. Now the sunshine has returned both really and figuratively. Although it is still April, we are enjoying midsummer weather. The tulips in the parks are making a glorious display. Perhaps it is the beginning of dawn not only for us but also for thousands and thousands of the persecuted as the British and American armies are overrunning

the concentration camps and freeing the unfortunate people in them who are still alive.

We are reading about and seeing photographs of those places the names of which were so well known to us in the years before the war. Now the people here really and finally believe that the stories of 1938–39 were not exaggerated. They were understated in fact. It is all too horrible. Looking back, I feel grateful that our little office in Tiergartenstrasse was able to assist some – far too few – to escape in time.

Frank expressed deep interest in the work Senator was now engaged in, ensuring that the many orphans created by the Holocaust were being looked after. 'I am particularly sympathetic towards children because my only child is very ill and is causing my wife and me a great deal of worry and anxiety,' Frank said. 'I have often hoped that as I helped so many doctors, fate would arrange for me to meet the doctor who would cure her. We feel that some such man exists.'

When Frank arrived back in Berlin in the summer of 1945, it was barely recognisable from the city that he had known before the war. The Russians had spent twelve days pulverising the capital. Most of the inner-city offices and apartment blocks had been reduced to rubble among which the surviving inhabitants sought shelter.

Whole fronts of apartment blocks had been ripped off, with the residents continuing to live in their furnished, open-fronted flats on all floors, as if they were doll's-houses. The value of the Reichsmark had collapsed. Barter was the only way for many Germans to get hold of the necessities of life.

Cigarettes became the most common form of currency, with one cigarette worth the equivalent of ten marks. With people prepared to exchange their most treasured possessions for tins of cigarettes or coffee, the black marketeers, or *Schieber*, flourished just as they had when Frank first arrived in Berlin in the wake of the First World War.

'The spectacle of misery pervaded one's life,' said Noel Annan, one of the British intelligence officers attached to the Control Commission. 'In Berlin, the trees of the Tiergarten were cut down for firewood. A familiar sight was of some wizened old man hauling a little cart with a few sticks in it and of chains of men and women passing chunks of rubble from hand to hand in an attempt to clear a site.'

One of the first things Frank did was visit the former MI6 station at Tiergartenstrasse 17, which had long since been flattened by Allied bombing. Prodding among the rubble with his walking stick, he found his old safe still intact and containing some of the valuables he and Kay had been forced to leave behind in August 1939. After their departure from Berlin, the German authorities had apparently opened the safe, removed everything, tagged it, catalogued it and put it back again.

The role of the Public Safety Branch was to build up a civilian police force and to oversee the process of denazification. The British, Americans and Russians had agreed at the Potsdam Conference that all traces of the Nazi Party were to be eradicated. All top Nazis should be arrested and interned while 'all members of the Nazi Party who have been more than nominal participants in its activities and all other persons hostile to allied purposes' should be removed from any public or semi-public posts or positions in important businesses.

In practice, this was far from easy. During the Third Reich it had been virtually impossible to hold on to any responsible job other than as a member of the Nazi Party. All public sector officials had to be party members. Businessmen who declined to join were denied both contracts and the raw material they needed to make their products. It was impossible to run the country without the assistance of people who had been Nazis. The authorities were forced either to allow many junior party members to go free or to give them very light sentences more appropriate to minor driving offences.

As head of the Special Branch, Frank was more interested in catching the former members of the SS and the German intelligence services who were on the automatic arrest list as threats to the creation of a new non-Nazi Germany.

At the end of 1944, Heinrich Himmler, the head of the SS, had ordered the creation of an underground guerrilla network to resist an Allied occupation of Germany. Dubbed Werewolf, it was to be based around Hitler's former retreat in the Bavarian Alps, with the eventual aim of re-establishing a Nazi regime. By the time Frank flew into Berlin it had already carried out a number of assassinations of Allied personnel and Germans working with the Allies. Two German mayors had been killed by suspected Werewolf terrorists.

Frank's men uncovered and infiltrated a series of underground networks aimed at restoring a Nazi state. The first major successes came against an organisation code-named Nursery, based on former members of the Hitler Jugend and its female equivalent, the Bund Deutscher Madel. Nursery's aim was 'the long-term penetration of German political and economic life, with the ultimate intention of re-establishing the Nazi system'.

Nursery was uncovered by the British and Americans at the end of 1945, and they co-operated to infiltrate the organisation and find out the names of the key members. It planned to create a network of German companies with Nazi directors who under cover of co-operation with the occupying powers would provide support and escape lines for more senior Nazis who had gone underground to avoid arrest. Funds were mainly drawn from a company that it controlled in the American zone, but most of its support came from within the British zone. Nursery was finally broken up in the spring of 1946 with several hundred arrests in both the British and American zones.

Hitler Youth had also been involved in the Edelweiss Pirates, groups of young people whose main objective seemed to be beating up Polish refugees and discouraging fraternisation between German women and British soldiers, one intelligence officer reported. 'It is probable that Nursery attracted the more competent and older members of the Hitler Youth and that it is only the young and irresponsible who swell the ranks of the Edelweiss.'

Frank's biggest operation was against the neo-Nazi umbrella organisation Deutsche Revolution, which contained a number of groups run by former senior Waffen SS officers, including Klaus Barbie, the so-called Butcher of Lyons.

'Several groups of ex-Waffen SS members have been, and are, under observation,' the intelligence officer reported. They had set up a courier system and had links across all three western zones and within group in one other unnamed West European country. 'One feature of SS activity has been the planning and successful operation of an escape route from a civilian internment camp. There are also reports that SS officers are being hidden in monasteries and possibly also in hospitals and clinics.'

Deutsche Revolution claimed to want to form an anti-communist bulwark against the Soviet Union in conjunction with the British and Americans. This offered good opportunities for a sting code-named Operation Selection Board, and at the beginning of 1947, Kurt Ellersiek, one of the group's leaders and a former SS major-general, was put in touch with a British officer who expressed secret sympathies with the aims of National Socialism He then set up a meeting between Ellersiek and some of his colleagues and a British 'Foreign Office specialist' who claimed to support the aims of the Deutsche Revolution.

The meeting went well and the 'Foreign Office specialist' suggested that the British might back the group, but they would need to know more details – how big was the movement and who and where were its main members? Ellersiek obligingly provided the details the British had requested and in return the 'Foreign Office specialist' promised to pass the group's proposals on to London and Washington.

Ellersiek threatened that if the Allies did not agree to the group's proposals, it would unleash a 'devastating new weapon' on the occupying forces. Given that the members of Deutsche Revolution included Colonel Hans Eismann, a former officer in the Wehrmacht High Command's Bacteriological Warfare Department, this threat appeared to have some credibility.

The Americans were in favour of calling a halt to the operation and rounding the groups up, but the British were keen to play them along further in order to get as much information as possible. At the same time, other groups within Deutsche Revolution began to make contact with the Allies, although less tentatively than Ellersiek's group.

But by late February, both the British and the Americans agreed that it was time to wrap the groups up before they could begin to build up a following among the general population. At 2 a.m. on the morning of Sunday, 23 February 1947, amid heavy snowstorms, British and American soldiers raided homes across the two zones and arrested more than 120 suspects, the vast majority of them in the British zone.

Ellersiek's wife was arrested at their home in Hamburg while he was picked up at his mistress's flat in Fulda in the US zone. American soldiers had to kick their way through four heavily barred doors before finding Ellersiek and his mistress, Frau Katischeff, clad in silk pyjamas. One of those who evaded capture was Klaus Barbie, who shortly afterwards was controversially recruited by the Americans as an intelligence contact.

The British authorities revealed that Deutsche Revolution's actual aims were the restoration of a Nazi government, the revival of the German Army and an attempt to regain territory in East Prussia and Silesia that had been incorporated into Poland by Stalin.

'The aims of these people and their threats are of course as silly as they are pretentious,' a British statement said. 'But there comes a point beyond which silliness cannot be allowed to continue unchecked. These are desperate characters who have no hope for the future in any decent society. Some of the leaders are war criminals wanted for crimes against humanity.'

But despite Nursery and Selection Board, Himmler's Werewolf organisation failed to materialise in any strength, and it soon became clear that the main problem for those SIS officers posted to the Control Commission was the huge number of Russian espionage agents who had been infiltrated into the British sector. In the summer of 1947, responsibility for uncovering former Nazis was handed over to the Germans and Frank was posted back to London.

At the end of the war there had been a tendency within MI6 to sit back and think: 'Well, we won.' German Intelligence was rightly viewed as having been 'Ill-directed, badly organised and corrupt'. But nevertheless there had been some notable German successes. Head Office decided that it needed an experienced officer to pore over the Abwehr and Sicherheitsdienst documents captured by the British to see what mistakes had been made, what lessons could be learned.

Although officially Frank should have retired in 1944, he had stayed on for the duration of the war, first to manage the MI6 end of the Double-Cross System and then to help hunt down Nazis in Germany. Now he returned to the little flat in Chelsea and continued working. 'I draw my pension and work again,' he told his brother Andy.

> I did not expect that I should be called upon to go through two wars in a fighting capacity. I hope that we are not on the verge of a third, but things do not look too promising.
>
> Russia is a cruel and bloody country, at least their government is. I had quite a lot to do with high-ranking Russian officers in Berlin and liked them but they were terrified of their own government. I am sick and tired of these tyrannical dictators. Without them Europe would settle down easily.

In 1949, Frank retired from MI6, returning to Stourbridge to Kay, Ursula and Jonny, his ageing spaniel. Kay's sister Rita had died of cancer. But another sister, Ruth, now moved to Stourbridge following the death of her husband, a wealthy Latin American businessman. Frank's mother Isabella had died when he was in

Germany, and they had moved out of the rented house and bought a similar one a few houses along the road. Frank spent much of his time gardening, reading and corresponding with the many people he had helped to flee Germany.

He had files full of letters thanking him for what he did, Kay Foley said. 'They all say things like this one from a businessman in America: "You gave visas to my sister, her husband and her daughter for Palestine. Without your visas my relatives would have perished. I shall never forget you".' Every Christmas, he received a canned turkey from New York from a Jewish doctor he had helped to get out of Nazi Germany.

Ernst Ruppel senior, who Frank had got out of Buchenwald, had bought a house just around the corner in Norton Road, and the two men became firm friends. Ruppel had built up two new businesses from scratch, making lighting and lampshades.

Frank was also close friends with both the Prices and the Berlyns and with another neighbour – Chris Gittins, the actor who played Walter Gabriel in *The Archers*. But he knew few other people in the area outside of Kay's family. 'He was quite a nondescript little man,' said Beryl Price. 'You would pass him in a crowd. But I suppose this was all to the good when he was doing his undercover work.' Others in the street found him distant and difficult to get to know. But Mrs Berlyn said this was because they did not know him. 'Frank was fairly quiet,' she said.

> But he was a charming man. You could tell he had been a gentleman and done a lot of things. But he never spoke about it.
>
> He and Kay did lead a very quiet life. She joined in with the local coffee mornings. He didn't seem to do much. He used to read a lot and potter about in the garden. But that was his life. He was always very nice to everyone, particularly to the children in the road. Kay used to go into the community more than he did. But we were all very fond of him because he was a gentleman.

Frank kept in touch with old friends from his intelligence days and in particular Val Vivian and Ian Colvin. In August 1951, he wrote to his niece Margaret describing how he had recently spent some time in London looking up people he had known in Berlin.

'I had two very enjoyable evenings,' he said. 'One was with Ian Colvin who has just written a book called *Chief of Intelligence*. It deals with the part the German Admiral Canaris played in the war. His wife was formerly a member of my staff in Berlin. He is one of the three men Churchill mentions in the first volume of his wonderful memoirs.'

It seems likely that Frank was one of Colvin's sources for the Canaris book and more particularly for two other books he wrote on incidents in which Frank had been involved: *Flight 777* on the shooting down of the aircraft containing Wilfred Israel and Leslie Howard which Frank had been fortunate not to be on; and *The Unknown Courier*, about Operation Mincemeat, in which Colvin described being briefed on the operation by a mysterious 'Hush Man'.

When Frank and Colvin had dinner in August 1951, Duff Cooper had just published *Operation Heartbreak*, a fictional account of Mincemeat, and rumours were rife that it was based on a real event. Shortly afterwards Colvin began researching his own book. When he approached the authorities to ask if they could help him, they encouraged Ewen Montagu to publish his own sanitised account in order to spike Colvin's guns.

The other old Berlin hand whom Frank had seen during his visit to London was Norman Ebbutt, 'who was the correspondent of *The Times* in Berlin and was expelled by the Nazis for telling the truth and for warning the world what was coming. Unfortunately, he got a stroke and is no longer able to work.'

In letters to his brother Andy in Canada, Frank expressed continued concern that there might be a third world war. 'There are far too many blackguards in the world and the biggest of all is the Soviet Union. If only the war in Korea could be stopped. It was a bad idea to begin it, I think. I hate war and all the suffering it causes to the weak and innocent. God only knows what the next one will be like.'

Andy's grandson Dennis visited Frank and Kay in the mid-1950s. They talked long into the night, drinking wine. 'He was down to earth,' Dennis said. 'He had no pretensions and no side.' The two men discussed the possibility of another war and Frank told him that he was a pacifist, 'unless some tyrant gets busy trying to rob people of their mental and physical liberty'. He also said he had faced considerable difficulties in persuading other officials to help him to get Jews out of Germany, 'but I just pounded on the desks until I got what I wanted'.

On Thursday, 8 May 1958, Kay and Ursula went into Birmingham shopping. When they returned Frank, now seventy-three, had gone back to bed. He told Kay he had not been feeling too good all afternoon. Perhaps he would feel better after a good hot bath. Shortly after getting into the bath, Frank suffered a heart attack. His head slipped under the water but he managed to haul himself up before suffering a second fatal attack.

It was some time before Kay realised that he had been in the bath longer than normal. She went upstairs, walked into the bathroom and found him lying there unconscious. Ursula ran out of the house to get neighbours to help her mother lift Frank out of the bath. They laid him on his bed and a doctor was called. But it was too late. The man who had saved many thousands of Jews from certain death at the hand of the Nazis was himself dead.

Frank's passing went almost unnoticed in Britain. The Ruppel family attended his funeral at Stourbridge Cemetery, along with a number of relatives and friends. The only sign of his secret past was the flowers sent by Valentine Vivian, the legendary former Assistant Chief of MI6. But as news of the death of 'Captain Foley' reached Israel, tributes began to pour in, and former leaders of the Jewish community in Germany decided that the quiet Englishman must be remembered by those he saved.

In a letter to the *Daily Telegraph,* Robert Weltsch, the former editor of the *Jüdische Rundschau,* and a constant thorn in the Nazis' side during the 1930s, wrote that Frank deserved a special tribute for his work in getting Jews out of Germany. 'In the most sympathetic and humane manner, and shunning bureaucracy, this indefatigable man was always prepared to help wherever possible. Nobody who lived in Berlin during those days of horror will ever forget what an island of comfort Mr Foley's office was to thousands of harassed and suffering people; to some he appeared as a saint. Many remember today that it is this British representative to whom they owe their life.'

Hubert Pollack, Frank's old friend and secret agent in Berlin, organised a special fund to plant a grove of trees in Israel in his memory. Money poured in. One of those who wrote to the fund was Emmy Hirschberg. She and her mother had decided to emigrate to Palestine in 1935, but soon realised they would have problems. They only had enough money for one 'Capitalist Visa'. Emmy was not fit enough to get work and her mother was too old.

'My mother was 80 years old,' Emmy said. 'I was only 50 but I was crippled and dependent on my mother.' So they asked a German lawyer to draw up the application. Two years passed before they reached the end of the queue. 'Then a letter arrived telling me that since I had £1,000, I could go on a Kapitalistenzertifikat but my mother would have to go first to England from where I could "claim" her. This was impossible.' Emmy was too crippled to do anything without her mother's help.

> I was terrified. What were we to do? The lawyer advised me to set out my position precisely in a letter to the head of the British Passport Control Office, Capt Foley.
>
> I wrote the letter and a short time later the visa arrived marked 'Emmy Hirschberg and Mother'. Foley had registered us as if we were a married couple. The visa caused a sensation among those on board the ship taking us to Palestine and when we got there it was passed from hand to hand among the port

immigration officers and the Jewish Agency representatives. Had I known that Foley would have lived so long, I would like to have thanked him while he lived. I would like now, despite my own straitened circumstances, to contribute to the Foley Grove.

Among those who gathered near Kibbutz Harel just over a year after Frank's death to plant the grove of trees and to pay tribute to him was Wim van Leer, the young Jew sent to Germany by the Quakers. He remembered those harrowing scenes outside the British Passport Control Office and how Frank had given him his personal escape route through Holland to help him to get Jews out.

'Speakers recalled Foley's noble deeds, his motivation stemming from deeply felt Christian principles and his simple humanity far beyond the call of duty,' van Leer said. 'Some of the participants doubtless thought of friends and relatives who had not managed to disentangle themselves from the closing net, or those innocents hoping against hope that the advent of Nazi terror was but a passing phenomenon. And what a miracle it was that we were standing there, a handful of Jewish transplants paying homage, that afternoon among the pine trees on a windswept hill on the road to Jerusalem.'

A year later, a team of Mossad officers staged a daring raid on Argentina to kidnap Adolf Eichmann, taking him back to Israel to stand trial for his part in the Final Solution. The person they chose to identify Eichmann, to ensure they had the right man, was the same grey-haired old lawyer who had addressed the small group clustered around the Francis Edward Foley Memorial Grove – Benno Cohn, the former Chairman of the German Zionist Organisation. When Eichmann went on trial on Monday, 2 April 1962, Cohn described the reign of terror that followed Kristallnacht and how few people had reached out to help the Jews.

'There was one man who stood out above all others like a beacon,' Cohn said. 'Captain Foley, Passport Officer in the British Consulate in the Tiergarten in Berlin, a man who in my opinion was one of the greatest among the nations of the world. He brought his influence to bear to help us. It was possible to bring a great number of people to Israel through the help of this most wonderful person. He rescued thousands of Jews from the jaws of death.'

Postscript

Kay and Ursula Foley moved to Devon after Frank's death, together with Kay's sister Jane. They lived initially in Colestocks near Honiton before moving to Sidmouth. Kay worked in a nearby nursing home. Some of the Jews helped by Frank set up a small trust fund for her, and between them Hubert Pollack and Ernst Ruppel senior arranged for her to go to Israel to see the memorial grove. She died in April 1979. Her will directed that her ashes be scattered at the top of Peak Hill, a local beauty spot overlooking the English Channel in much the same fashion as Gallant's Bower, the hill above Dartmouth where Frank proposed to her. Ursula worked with disabled children. She never married and died as a result of an epileptic fit in April 1982, just three years after her mother.

Margaret Reid continued to work in the MI6 Norwegian section after Frank left to look after Hess. In August 1942, she married Lt-Col. Edward de Renzy-Martin, who had been Inspector of the Albanian Gendarmerie and subsequently MI6 head of station in Madrid. Margaret retired from MI6 in 1943 and had two children. After the war, she and her family moved to the Lake District. She returned to Norway for several holidays and remained in contact with Norwegian friends. She died in

April 1974. Her diaries are held in the Brotherton Library at the University of Leeds and were published in Norwegian in 1980.

Hubert Pollack became a member of the Israeli military intelligence service Aman. After Frank's death, he acted as secretary for the group of prominent German Jews, including Benno Cohn, Hans Friedenthal and Siegfried Moses, who created the memorial grove. For several years, Pollack attempted to persuade the Israeli Government to fund a visit by Kay to see the grove, complaining that 'the Jewish communities here and in England have not shown much appreciation for the fact that Major Foley saved the lives of thousands of Jews'. In a letter to Teddy Kollek, a former member of Mossad LeAliyah Bet who was then Ben Gurion's intelligence adviser, Pollack complained that the Israeli authorities were behaving 'like a bunch of beggars' in their treatment of Foley's widow. He added: 'A British officer who knew in 1939 about the operations of Mossad LeAliyah Bet and did not inform the mandate police did more for the state of Israel than most of the rich Jews or important non-Jews who received the red carpet treatment from our state'.

Jonny X went to Germany at the end of the war to assist the Control Commission. Quite possibly he was working with Frank, although there is no firm evidence to support this. He then returned to Canada settling in Ontario where he ran a caravan site. He resurfaced during the 1950s, embarassing the authorities by revealing his past and embarking on a string of lectures and newspaper interviews in which he warned of the dangers of Soviet subversion of western society. He died in the 1970s.

Paul Rosbaud helped to set up an affiliate of the Springer publishing company in London after the war, before moving on to a new scientific publishing venture with a young British Army captain who had served in postwar occupied Germany. Rosbaud suggested the company be called Pergamon, and his colleague Robert Maxwell agreed. But the two soon fell out and Rosbaud left, working for a number of European scientific publishers. In 1961, the American Institute of Physics awarded him its first Tate Medal for services to scientific publishing. He died of leukaemia at St Mary's Hospital, London, in January 1963.

Rudolf Hess remained at Maindiff Court Hospital until the end of the war, when he was put on trial at Nuremberg and sentenced to life imprisonment. He was incarcerated in Spandau Prison in Berlin where he hanged himself in 1987 at the age of ninety-three. The circumstances of his flight to England and his death remain embroiled in a plethora of conspiracy theories. Frank's views were encapsulated in a newspaper interview given by Kay Foley after her husband's death. She said: 'Frank felt the man was mad and should never have been tried.'

Author's Note

I first came across Frank Foley while researching a history of British espionage. A former MI6 officer told me of a wartime spy whose brilliant operational ability was still held up as an example to new recruits but whose most important claim to fame was that he had helped thousands of Jews to escape from Nazi Germany.

'One of the most interesting things about Foley was that normally, to be a good case officer, you have to be a bit of a shit,' he said. 'But Foley managed to be a brilliant case officer and a near saint. He was a quite outstanding character. Schindler pales into insignificance alongside his work on getting Jews out of Germany. He was a very, very able man, who I don't think ever got the recognition he should have done.'

It was an impressive testimonial. But if Foley had done so much to help the Jews why wasn't he better known? There had been a few newspaper articles about him, claiming him as 'Britain's Schindler' but with little in the way of evidence.

One report suggested Foley was being considered by Yad Vashem, the Israeli organisation dedicated to ensuring that the 'martyrs and heroes' of the Holocaust are not forgotten, for the distinction of Righteous Among the Nations, the accolade accorded to a number of Gentiles, most notably Schindler, who helped to rescue Jews from the clutches of the Nazis. But when I spoke to the officials at Yad Vashem, they said there was insufficient evidence to consider Foley for the award.

I was therefore somewhat surprised when a copy of a document I had requested from the Yad Vashem archives arrived in the post. It was the memoirs of Hubert Pollack and it described how Foley had saved 'tens of thousands' of Jews from the Holocaust. It was just one piece of the substantial body of evidence backing up Foley's claim to be regarded as Righteous Among the Nations. Much of it comes from Israeli sources, indeed from the most senior members of Germany's Jewish community.

One of those Jewish leaders, Hans Friedenthal, President of the German Zionist Organisation, promised Foley that his efforts on behalf of the Jews would not be forgotten. 'We Jews have no order to award, but we have a good and long memory,' he said. 'You may be assured that the German Jews will not forget how often you have helped them.'

Those who knew that Foley had helped them never did forget. But the vast majority were unaware of the identity of the man who had saved them from the Holocaust and now it seems that when the Jews did get an award with which to honour those who had helped them, Foley's case was dismissed for alleged lack of evidence.

The German Jews who arrived in Palestine had done what they could, entering his name in the Golden Book of the Keren Kayemeth, the Jewish National Fund, and planting the grove of trees in his memory. But the most widely recognised honour accorded to those who helped the Jews has been denied Foley for what seem quite spurious reasons. If having read this book you agree with that judgement, you should write to the following address: Department for the Righteous, Yad Vashem, P.O.B. 3477, Jerusalem 91034, Israel.

Notes

Chapter 1

Pages 3–4

Information on Frank's early life comes from his birth and baptism certificates; the files of the Somerset Record Office; the 1891 Census in the General Register Office; the files of St Joseph's RC School, Burnham, and St John's C of E School, Highbridge; PRO WO374/24816 (British Army record of Capt. F. E. Foley); and from the following two books: Geoffrey Maslen, *Burnham-on-Sea and Highbridge in Old Photographs*, Alan Sutton, Stroud, 1988, and Dr N. Worth, *Tourist's Guide to Somersetshire Rail and Road*, Edward Stanford, London, 1894. Walrow Terrace still exists. I am grateful to Mr Maslen for his advice on the history of Highbridge and Burnham and to Dr J. A. Harding, archivist of the Roman Catholic diocese of Clifton, for his assistance on Frank's early schooling

Page 4

Frank's sister Margaret was a member of the order of the Sisters of Mercy and as Mother Gerard was Mother Superior of the order's convent in Dighton Rd, Bristol

Page 5

Details of Frank's secondary education in France and university career come from his family and from PRO WO374/24816 (British Army record of Capt. F. E. Foley)

Pages 5–6

Details of Foley's escape from Germany from interview with his niece Patricia Dunstan, dated 18 July 1997; PRO WO374/24816 (British Army record of Capt. F. E. Foley); and from Wim van Leer, *Time of My Life*, Carta, Jerusalem, 1984

Page 6

Frank's post as an assistant master from PRO WO374/24816 (British Army record of Capt. F. E. Foley)

Pages 6–8

Details of the Inns of Court Officer Training Corps come from PRO WO374/24816 (British Army record of Capt. F. E. Foley) and from the Imperial War Museum: the papers of Capt. H. C. Meysey-Thompson, IWM92/19/1, and Sir Percy McElwaine, IWM92/35/1

Pages 7–15

Details of the battle on 21 March 1918 come from the following sources: PRO WO374/24816 (British Army record of Capt. F. E. Foley); the unpublished memoirs of Pte Frank Beardsall, 2/6th Bn, the North Staffordshire Regt; Gen. Sir James E. Edmonds, *Military Operations France and Belgium 1918*, Macmillan, London, 1935; Martin Middlebrook, *The Kaiser's Battle*, Penguin, London, 1983; Ernst Jünger, *Storm of Steel*, Constable, London, 1994; Battalion War Diary, 2/6th North Staffordshires; John Buchan, *A History of the Great War*, Vol. IV, Thomas Nelson, London, 1920; Malcolm Brown, *The Imperial War Museum Book of the Somme*, Sidgwick and Jackson, London, 1996; *The Times* and the *Daily Telegraph* for 22 and 23 March 1918. (I am very grateful to Dr Tristran Pointon for his research on Foley's military career while working at the Regimental Museum of the Staffordshire Regiment and to Martin Middlebrook and Ross

Davies for supplying material from the unpublished memoirs of
Frank Beardsall)

Pages 14–15

The story of Frank questioning his faith comes from an interview with his nephew, the Revd John B. Kelley, dated 28
July 1997

Pages 8–15

Details of Frank's army career from PRO WO374/24816 (British
Army record of Capt. F. E. Foley) and from the Army Lists for
the period

Page 15

Details of what happened in front of the medical board and the
transfer to the Intelligence Corps from PRO WO374/24816
(British Army record of Capt. F. E. Foley) and from the memoirs
of Sir Ivone Kirkpatrick IWM79/50/1

Chapter 2

Pages 17–18

Details of the transfer to the Intelligence Corps and its operations
from PRO WO374/24816 (British Army record of Capt. F. E.
Foley); the memoirs of Sir Ivone Kirkpatrick IWM79/50/1; Sir
Ivone Kirkpatrick, *The Inner Circle*, Macmillan, London, 1959;
Henry Landau, *Spreading the Spy Net*, Jarrolds, London, 1932.
See also Christopher Andrew, *Secret Service*, Sceptre, London,
1985; Anthony Clayton, *Forearmed: A History of the Intelligence
Corps*, Brassey's, London, 1993; Michael Smith, *New Cloak,
Old Dagger: How Britain's Spies Came in from the Cold*, Gollancz,
London, 1996

Page 18

Instructions on how to recruit an agent from 'Memorandum on the work of the Section of Civil Affairs and Security, General Staff, British Army of the Rhine', written by Lt-Col. R. W. Oldfield, 12 December 1929, Intelligence Corps Museum

Page 18

Details of Intelligence Corps toys from the memoirs of Sir Ivone Kirkpatrick IWM79/50/1

Page 19

Foley's First World War encounter with anti-Semitism from Christopher Andrew, *Secret Service*, Sceptre, London, 1985; PRO FO372/2706

Pages 18–19

Details of Frank's army career from PRO WO374/24816 (British Army record of Capt. F. E. Foley) and the Army Lists for the period

Page 19

Information on work of Intelligence Corps in Cologne from 'Memorandum on the work of the Section of Civil Affairs and Security, General Staff, British Army of the Rhine', written by Lt-Col. R. W. Oldfield, 12 December 1929, Intelligence Corps Museum; Henry Landau, *Spreading the Spy Net*, Jarrolds, London, 1932; Anthony Clayton, *Forearmed: A History of the Intelligence Corps*, Brassey's, London, 1993; Lt-Col. C à Court Repington, *After the War*, Constable, London, 1922

Pages 19–20

Details of Owen Lee pieced together from information supplied by Beryl Price, a neighbour of Frank in Stourbridge, and RAF Lists for that period.

Page 20

Information on Tiergartenstrasse offices from Henry Landau, *Spreading the Spy Net*, Jarrolds, London, 1932; Karl Baedeker, *Berlin und Potsdam*, Karl Baedeker, Leipzig, 1936

Pages 20–2

Frank's recruitment into MI1c and details of typical recruitments from Henry Landau, *Spreading the Spy Net*, Jarrolds, London, 1932; Sir Paul Dukes, *The Story of ST-25*, Cassell, London, 1938

Pages 22–4

Information on matters relating to Passport Control, including attitudes towards its use for intelligence collection, need to keep out Bolsheviks and protect jobs, Frank's salary, etc., see: PRO FO371/10480; T161/501; FO372/1624; FO372/3284; FO372/2799; FO372/2975; Henry Landau, *Spreading the Spy Net*, Jarrolds, London, 1932, Michael Smith, *New Cloak, Old Dagger*, Gollancz, London, 1996; Phillip H. J. Davies, *Organisational Development of Britain's Secret Intelligence Service 1909–1979*, University of Reading, 1998; Christopher Andrew, *Secret Service*, Sceptre, London, 1985

Pages 24–5

Relationship between Frank and Kay from various interviews with family and neighbours

Pages 25–7

Information on Berlin in the wake of the war from Otto Friedrich, *Before the Deluge: A Portrait of Berlin in the 1920s*,

Harper and Row, New York, 1972; Giles MacDonogh, *Berlin*, Sinclair-Stevenson, London, 1997; Roger Eatwell, *Fascism: A History*, Virago, London, 1996; Marvin Lowenthal, *The Jews of Germany*, Lindsay Drummond, London, 1939; Greg Lacey and Keith Shephard, *Germany 1918–1945*, John Murray, London, 1997

Chapter 3

Page 29

Information on Tiergartenstrasse offices from Henry Landau, *Spreading the Spy Net*, Jarrolds, London, 1932; Sir Nevile Henderson, *Failure of a Mission*, Hodder and Stoughton, London, 1940; interview with Margaret Forbes-Robertson; Karl Baedeker, *Berlin und Potsdam*, Karl Baedeker, Leipzig, 1936

Pages 29–31

Information on early SIS operations from Henry Landau, *Spreading the Spy Net*, Jarrolds, London, 1932; John Whitwell, *British Agent*, Frank Cass, London, 1996; Phillip H. J. Davies, *Organisational Development of Britain's Secret Intelligence Service 1909–1979*, University of Reading, 1998; C. G. McKay, *From Information to Intrigue*, Frank Cass, London, 1993; Michael Smith, *New Cloak, Old Dagger*, Gollancz, London, 1996; Kenneth Benton, 'The ISOS Years: Madrid 1941–43', *The Journal of Contemporary British History*, Vol. 30, No. 3, July 1995

Pages 31–2

Information on Russians in Berlin and on Berlin in the 1920s generally from: 'Russian Colony in Berlin', *The Times*, 20 February 1923

Pages 31–3

Information on Berlin from Otto Friedrich, *Before the Deluge: A*

Portrait of Berlin in the 1920s, Harper and Row, New York, 1972; Giles MacDonogh, *Berlin*, Sinclair-Stevenson, London, 1997; Bella Fromm, *Blood* and *Banquets: A Berlin Social Diary*, Geoffrey Bles, London, 1942; 'Berlin after all the Wickedness and the Wall', *Independent*, 9 January 1993

Page 33

Information on Frank's participation in Berlin nightlife from interview with Margaret Forbes-Robertson, 12 December 1996

Pages 33–4

Information on Frank and Kay's wedding from *Dartmouth and South Hams Chronicle*, 1 July 1921. I am grateful to the staff of the Cookworthy Museum, Kingsbridge, Devon, for tracking this item down

Pages 34–8

Information on Germany in the 1920s and the emergence of Hitler from PRO CAB101/70; Roger Eatwell, *Fascism: A History*, Virago, London, 1996; Marvin Lowenthal, *The Jews of Germany*, Lindsay Drummond, London, 1939; Greg Lacey and Keith Shephard, *Germany 1918–1945*, John Murray, London, 1997; Saul Friedlaender, *Nazi Germany and the Jews: The Years of Persecution 1933–39*, Weidenfeld, London, 1997; Otto Friedrich, *Before the Deluge: A Portrait of Berlin in the 1920s*, Harper and Row, New York, 1972; 'Daily Life in Berlin', *The Times*, 23 August 1922; 'Shopping in Berlin', *The Times*, 16 October 1923; 'Berlin Food Riots', *The Times*, 17 October 1923

Page 35

Frank papering toilet walls with Reichmarks from interview with Revd John B. Kelley, Foley's nephew, 28 July 1997

Chapter 4

Pages 39–40

Information on Berlin from Otto Friedrich, *Before the Deluge: A Portrait of Berlin in the 1920s*, Harper and Row, New York, 1972; Giles MacDonogh, *Berlin*, Sinclair-Stevenson, London, 1997; Bella Fromm, *Blood and Banquets: A Berlin Social Diary*, Geoffrey Bles, London, 1942; 'Berlin after all the Wickedness and the Wall', *Independent*, 9 January 1993

Pages 40–4

Information on rise of Hitler from PRO CAB101/70; Roger Eatwell, *Fascism: A History*, Virago, London, 1996; Marvin Lowenthal, *The Jews of Germany*, Lindsay Drummond, London, 1939; Greg Lacey and Keith Shephard, *Germany 1918–1945*, John Murray, London, 1997; Martin Gilbert, *The Holocaust*, Fontana, London, 1987

Pages 42–9

Information on treatment of the Jews from Marvin Lowenthal, *The Jews of Germany*, Lindsay Drummond, London, 1939; Martin Gilbert, *The Holocaust*, Fontana, London, 1987; Greg Lacey and Keith Shephard, *Germany 1918–1945*, John Murray, London 1997; Saul Friedlaender, *Nazi Germany and the Jews*, Weidenfeld, London, 1997; Benno Cohn, testimony to Eichmann trial, Session 14, 25 April 1961

Pages 44–5

Information on activities of Hubert Pollack from: Hubert Pollack, *Captain Foley, der Mensch und anderen Berichte*, Yad Vashem Archives YVS 01/17

Page 45

Kay Foley on concentration camps from *Sunday Mercury*, 7 May 1961

Page 46

Frank Foley on office overwhelmed from PRO FO371/16721

Page 46

Lady Rumbold on persecution of the Jews from Martin Gilbert, *The Holocaust*, Fontana, London, 1987

Pages 46–7

Benno Cohn from transcript of Eichmann trial, Session 14, 25 April 1961

Page 47

Robert Weltsch from *Jüdische Rundschau*, 4 April 1933

Pages 47–8

Delmer report in PRO FO30/69/282

Page 48

Nazi official's explanation of the behaviour towards the Jews PRO FO30/69/282

Page 49

Hankey report in PRO FO30/69/282

Page 50

Commercial attaché on position of Jew in Germany PRO FO371/16721

Chapter 5

Page 51

German authorities questioning Foley's position from PRO
FO372/2975; FO372/2706

Page 51

OGPU uses Berlin as centre of operations from Nigel West and
Oleg Tsarev, *The Crown Jewels*, HarperCollins, London, 1998

Page 51

GRU cover from PRO CAB81/134; Jan Valtin, *Out of the Night*,
Fortress Books, London, 1988

Page 52

Quotes on Comintern operations in Germany from Jan Valtin,
Out of the Night, Fortress Books, London, 1988

Page 52

Indian communists' use of Berlin as centre of 'secret conspiracy' from India Office Library and Records L/P&J/12/45;
L/P&J/12/47

Page 52

Movement of Westbureau to Copenhagen from Jan Valtin, *Out
of the Night*, Fortress Books, London, 1988

Pages 53–4

DeGraff approach to Foley from the *Ottawa Citizen*, 12 January
1954; MI6 file passed to the Russians by John Cairncross and

now in the KGB Archives (File 72240, Vol. 6, p.93); information provided to the author in confidence; Robert Moss, *Carnival of Spies*, Hodder and Stoughton, London, 1987. Although *Carnival of Spies* is a work of fiction, it is based loosely on the Jonny case.

Page 53

Quotes on training of Comintern agents from Jan Valtin, *Out of the Night*, Fortress Books, London, 1988

Pages 53–4

Further details of DeGraff recruitment from MI6 file passed to the Russians by John Cairncross and now in the KGB Archives (File 72240, Vol. 6, p.93); information provided to the author in confidence

Page 54

DeGraff life history from the *Ottawa Citizen*, 12 January 1954; the *Ottawa Journal*, 12 January 1954; MI6 file passed to the Russians by John Cairncross and now in the KGB Archives (File 72240, Vol. 6, p.93); information provided to the author in confidence; Robert Moss, *Carnival of Spies*, Hodder and Stoughton, London, 1987.

Pages 54–5

Details of Hamburg uprising from: A. Neuberg, *Armed Insurrection*, NLB, London, 1970; Gordon Brook-Shepherd, *The Storm Petrels*, Collins, London, 1977

Pages 55–6

Further details of DeGraff life history and recruitment by Foley from the *Ottawa Citizen*, 12 January 1954; the *Ottawa Journal*, 12 January 1954; MI6 file passed to the Russians by John

Cairncross and now in the KGB Archives (File 72240, Vol. 6, p.93); Information provided to the author in confidence

Page 55

Information on problems experienced by the British Communist Party in early 1930s from: E. H. Carr, *The Twilight of Comintern, 1930–1935*, Macmillan, London, 1982; K. Morgan, *Harry Pollitt*, MUP, Manchester, 1993

Pages 56–7

Details of Shanghai mission and background from: the *Ottawa Citizen*, 12 January 1954; information provided to the author in confidence; India Office Library and Records L/P&J/12/45; Charles A. Willoughby, *Sorge: Soviet Master Spy*, William Kimber, London, 1952; *All about Shanghai: A Standard Guidebook*, University Press, Shanghai, 1934; Frederick S. Litten, 'The Noulens Affair', *The China Quarterly*, No. 138, June 1994; E. H. Carr, *The Twilight of Comintern, 1930–1935*, Macmillan, London, 1982

Page 59

DeGraff quotes on Brazilian attempted uprising from the *Ottawa Citizen*, 12 January 1954, and from the MI6 report on his mission which was passed to the Russians by John Cairncross and is now in the KGB Archives (File 72240, Vol. 6)

Pages 58–61

Other details of his Brazilian mission from: Fernando Watson, *Olga*, Peter Halban, London, 1990; information provided to the author in confidence; MI6 file passed to the Russians by John Cairncross and now in the KGB Archives (File 72240, Vol. 6); *Daily Telegraph*, 26–29 November 1935; *The Times*, 26 November – 7 December 1935 and 26 March 1936; *Independent*, 10 March 1990; *Guardian*, 12 March 1990

Page 61

Moscow inquest into failure of Brazilian revolution from the *Ottawa Citizen*, 12 January 1954; PRO HW17/21

Page 61

Vivian praise for Foley's handling of the deGraff case from MI6 file passed to the Russians by John Cairncross and now in the KGB Archives (File 72240, Vol. 6, p.93); for a demonstration of the extent to which MI6 knew the inner workings of the Comintern during this period see India Office Library and Records L/P&J/12/144

Chapter 6

Page 63

Death of Frank's father from Office of National Statistics

Page 63

Ursula Foley's fall triggers epilepsy from interview with Revd John B. Kelley dated 28 July 1997 and interview with Patricia and Richard Dunstan dated 18 July 1997

Pages 63–4

Information on activities of Jewish organisations and on Wilfred Israel from Naomi Shepherd, *Wilfred Israel: German Jewry's Secret Ambassador*, Weidenfeld and Nicolson, London, 1984; A. J. Sherman, *Island Refuge: Britain and Refugees from the Third Reich 1933–39*, Frank Cass, London, 1994; Christopher Isherwood, *The Berlin Novels*, Minerva, London, 1992; Saul Friedlaender, *Nazi Germany and the Jews*, Weidenfeld, London, 1997

Pages 64–6

Information on activities of Hubert Pollack from: Hubert Pollack, *Captain Foley, der Mensch und anderen Berichte,* Yad Vashem Archives YVS01/17; Hubert Pollack, 'Personal and Confidential Note on the late Major Francis E Foley', Central Zionist Archives CZA K11/391; Naomi Shepherd, *Wilfred Israel: German Jewry's Secret Ambassador,* Weidenfeld and Nicolson, London, 1984; interview with Arnold Horwell (formerly Horwitz), 28 November 1996

Pages 66–7

Information on British official policy and public attitude towards Jewish refugees from A. J. Sherman, *Island Refuge: Britain and Refugees from the Third Reich 1933–39,* Frank Cass, London, 1994; PRO FO371/16740; FO371/16758; CAB23/33

Page 67

For information on MI6 financial difficulties see F.H. Hinsley *et al, British Intelligence in the Second World War,* Vol. 1, HMSO, London, 1979; Christopher Andrew, *Secret Service,* Sceptre, London, 1987; Michael Smith, *New Cloak, Old Dagger,* Gollancz, London, 1996

Page 67

Details of increasing lack of regard for Third Country Rule from Phillip H. J. Davies, *Organisational Development of Britain's Secret Intelligence Service 1909–1979,* University of Reading, 1997; and information provided to the author in confidence

Pages 67–70

Information on visit of Kay's sister Joyce Kelley to Berlin from private papers of Kelley family and correspondence with Revd John B. Kelley

Pages 68–9

Information on Rosbaud from Arnold Kramish, *The Griffin*, Macmillan, London, 1986; Ernest Volkman, *Espionage: The Greatest Spy Operations of the 20th Century*, Wiley, New York, 1995; R. V. Jones, *Reflections on Intelligence*, Mandarin, London, 1990; Thomas Powers, *Heisenberg's War: The Secret History of the German Bomb*, Cape, London, 1993; Mark Walker, *German National Socialism and the Quest for Nuclear Power, 1939–1949*, CUP, Cambridge, 1990

Pages 70–71

Foley report on situation for Germany's Jews in PRO FO371/18861

Pages 71–2

Background to Night of the Long Knives from Roger Eatwell, *Fascism: A History*, Virago, London, 1996; Marvin Lowenthal, *The Jews of Germany*, Lindsay Drummond, London, 1939; Greg Lacey and Keith Shephard, *Germany 1918–1945*, John Murray, London, 1997

Pages 72–3

William Shirer comments throughout from William L. Shirer, *Berlin Diary: The Journal of a Foreign Correspondent 1939–1941*, Alfred A. Knopf, New York, 1941

Pages 73–4

Reports by Smallbones and Foley on anti-Semitic actions by German authorities in PRO FO371/18861

Pages 74–5

Fate of Fehr family from correspondence with Inge Samson (née Fehr) dated 2 April 1997 and 28 May 1997

Page 75

Foley on anti-Semitic actions by German authorities in PRO FO371/18861

Chapter 7

Pages 77–82

Information on Meyer-Michael from his unpublished memoir kindly supplied by his daughter Sabine Komberti and from interviews with Mrs Komberti and her sister Susan Meyer-Michael dated 19 December 1996 and 24 February 1997.

Page 81

Foley remarks on emigration possibilities for Jews from PRO FO371/18861

Page 82

William Shirer comments throughout from William L. Shirer, *Berlin Diary: The Journal of a Foreign Correspondent 1939–1941*, Alfred A. Knopf, New York, 1941

Page 83

Foley contact with Luftwaffe colonel from information supplied to the author in confidence; F. H. Hinsley, *British Intelligence in the Second World War* (abridged edition), HMSO, London, 1994

Pages 83–4

Information on SIS budgets and flouting of the Third Country Rule from information provided to the author in confidence; Michael Smith, *New Cloak, Old Dagger*, Gollancz, London, 1996; Phillip H. J. Davies, *Organisational Development of Britain's Secret*

Intelligence Service, 1909–1979, University of Reading, 1998; Nigel West and Oleg Tsarev, *The Crown Jewels*, HarperCollins, London, 1998

Pages 84–5

Foley contact with foreign correspondents and close relationship with Colvin and Ebbutt from Foley letter to his niece Margaret Foley dated 17 August 1951; Naomi Shepherd, *Wilfred Israel: German Jewry's Secret Ambassador*, Weidenfeld and Nicolson, London, 1984

Pages 85–6

Nazi regional leaders' attacks on the Jews and Frick announcement from PRO FO371/18861

Page 86

Picton letter to Ramsay MacDonald from PRO FO30/69/282

Pages 86–7

Reports of violence in Berlin in July 1935 from PRO FO371/18861 and Martin Gilbert, *The Holocaust*, Fontana, London, 1987

Page 87

Foley anecdote on kosher butcher and comments on situation for Germany's Jews in PRO FO371/18861

Page 87

Hitler announcement of law on Reich Citizenship from Martin Gilbert, *The Holocaust*, Fontana, London, 1987; Saul Friedlaender, *Nazi Germany and the Jews*, Weidenfeld, London, 1997; Roger Eatwell, *Fascism: A History*, Virago, London, 1996

Page 87

Foley quote on situation for Germany's Jews in PRO FO371/18861

Chapter 8

Page 89

Dr Serelman's arrest from Martin Gilbert, *The Holocaust*, Fontana, London, 1987

Pages 89–90

Mills letter and details of the difficulties in transferring money from PRO FO371/19919

Pages 91–3

Frank's assistance to Elsbeth Kahn and her family from correspondence with Elsbeth Kahn (now Elisheva Lernau) dated 9 November 1997 and 3 February 1998

Page 93

Frank's assistance to Miriam Rabow and family from letters from Miriam Posner (née Rabow) dated 31 August 1997 and 16 October 1997

Page 94

Frank's assistance to Heinz Romberg from Romberg letters dated 29 July 1997 and 29 August 1997

Page 94

Resignation of Berlin's Lord Mayor from *Daily Telegraph*, 10 December 1935

Page 95

MacDonald resignation letter from *Daily Telegraph*, 30 December 1935

Page 95

Foreign office assessment of MacDonald letter from PRO FO371/20482

Pages 95–6

Shirer commentary on the reoccupation of the Rhineland from William L. Shirer, *Berlin Diary: The Journal of a Foreign Correspondent 1939–1941*, Alfred A. Knopf, New York, 1941

Pages 96–7

Daily Mail reaction to reoccupation of the Rhineland from Franklin Reid Gannon, *The British Press and Germany 1936–1939*, Clarendon Press, Oxford, 1971

Page 97

Background on reoccupation of the Rhineland and the lull in anti-Semitism coinciding with the 1936 Olympics, see Martin Gilbert, *The Holocaust*, Fontana, London, 1987; Saul Friedlaender, *Nazi Germany and the Jews*, Weidenfeld, London, 1997; Roger Eatwell, *Fascism: A History*, Virago, London, 1996

Page 97

Frank on persecution as relentless as ever from PRO FO371/19919

Page 97

On British reaction to the Arab revolt see A. J. Sherman, *Island Refuge: Britain and Refugees from the Third Reich 1933–39*, Frank Cass,

London, 1994; Dalia Ofer, *Escaping the Holocaust: Illegal Immigration to the Land of Israel 1939–1944*, OUP, Oxford, 1990

Pages 97–8

Benno Cohn comments from Central Zionist Archives CZA K11/391 and from transcript of Eichmann trial, Session 14, 25 April 1961

Page 98

Landau disclosure of PCO cover from Henry Landau, *All's Fair: the Story of British Secret Service behind German Lines*, Putnam, New York, 1934

Pages 98–9

German crackdown on foreign spies from *Daily Telegraph*, 11 November 1935; *Daily Telegraph*, 14 November 1935

Page 99

Frank's treatment of the Gestapo from information provided to the author in confidence

Chapter 9

Page 101

Continued persecution of the Jews from PRO FO371/21635; FO371/21692; FO371/21693; A. J. Sherman, *Island Refuge: Britain and Refugees from the Third Reich 1933–39*, Frank Cass, London, 1994

Pages 101–2

Munich SA member's letter of protest over Aryanisation from Saul

Friedlaender, *Nazi Germany and the Jews*, Weidenfeld, London, 1997

Page 102

Confiscation of passports from FO371/21693

Page 102

Winterbotham visit to Berlin from Frederick Winterbotham, *Secret and Personal*, William Kimber, London, 1969

Page 102

Inge Fehr's confirmation from correspondence with Inge Samson (née Fehr) dated 2 April 1997 and 28 May 1997

Page 103

Details of Niemöller arrest and creation of the Confessional Church from Anton Gill, *An Honourable Defeat: A History of German Resistance to Hitler*, Heinemann, London, 1994; Greg Lacey and Keith Shephard, *Germany 1918–1945*, John Murray, London, 1997

Page 103

Expulsion of Ebbutt from Foley letter to Margaret Foley dated 17 August 1951; interview with Margaret Forbes-Robertson dated 3 December 1996; William L. Shirer, *Berlin Diary: The Journal of a Foreign Correspondent 1939–1941*, Alfred A. Knopf, New York, 1941

Page 104

Further confiscations and increased drive against Jews following Funk appointment from FO371/21693; Martin Gilbert, *The Holocaust*, Fontana, London, 1987; Saul Friedlaender, *Nazi Germany and the Jews*, Weidenfeld, London, 1997

Page 104

Gedye on Schnussnig-Hitler meeting from the *Daily Telegraph*, 16 February 1938

Pages 105–6

Information on Anschluss from G.E.R. Gedye, *Fallen Bastions*, Gollancz, London, 1939; Naomi Shepherd, *Wilfred Israel: German Jewry's Secret Ambassador*, Weidenfeld and Nicolson, London, 1984; A. J. Sherman, *Island Refuge: Britain and Refugees from the Third Reich 1933–39*, Frank Cass, London, 1994; Martin Gilbert, *The Holocaust*, Fontana, London, 1987; Saul Friedlaender, *Nazi Germany and the Jews*, Weidenfeld, London, 1997

Page 106

British consul general on situation in Vienna PRO FO371/21635

Pages 106–7

Description of situation at British Passport Control Offices in Vienna from interview with Kenneth Benton dated 3 December 1996

Pages 106–7

Consulate-general report on Jews being forced to wash SA and SS cars in FO371/21635

Page 107

Fate of Jewish business leaders from Saul Friedlaender, *Nazi Germany and the Jews* Weidenfeld, London, 1997

Pages 107–8

Hoare on MI5 report and decision to set up Cabinet subcommittee on Austrian refugees from CAB23/93; A. J. Sherman, *Island Refuge: Britain and Refugees from the Third Reich 1933–39*, Frank Cass, London, 1994

Page 108

Introduction of visas from PRO FO371/21693; FO372/3284; FO371/21748

Page 109

Departure of Hilde Rosbaud to London from Arnold Kramish, *The Griffin*, Macmillan, London, 1986

Pages 109–10

Foley assistance to young communist from CZA11/391; Hubert Pollack, *Captain Foley, der Mensch und anderen Berichte*, Yad Vashem Archives YVS 01/17

Chapter 10

Pages 111–12

Foley assistance to Wertheimer family from interview with Simon Wertheimer, 2 December 1996

Page 113

Henderson report on renewed campaign against the Jews in Germany from PRO FO371/21635

Page 113

Göring confiscation of Jewish funds and press reaction from PRO371/21693; *The Times*, 28 April 1938

Page 113

SA-Mann call for further measures against the Jews from Marvin Lowenthal, *The Jews of Germany*, Lindsay Drummond, London, 1939

Page 114

Details of Frank's tour of the East End from PRO FO371/21693 with additional information from Saul Friedlaender, *Nazi Germany and the Jews*, Weidenfeld, London, 1997

Page 114

Details of renewed campaign against the Jews in Germany from PRO FO371/21635; FO371/21693; FO371/21706; FO371/21749

Page 115

Goebbels order to Berlin police from Saul Friedlaender, *Nazi Germany and the Jews*, Weidenfeld, London, 1997; *The Goebbels Diaries*, Part I, Vol. 3, K. G. Saur, London, 1987

Page 115

Frank quote on persecution of the Jews from PRO FO371/21635

Pages 115–16

Kendrick expulsion interview with Kenneth Benton, 3 December 1996; Michael Smith, *New Cloak, Old Dagger*, Gollancz, London, 1996; Phillip H. J. Davies, *Organisational Development of Britain's Secret Intelligence Service, 1909–1979*, University of Reading, 1998

Pages 116–17

Sinclair report backing appeasement from PRO FO371/21659

Page 117

Chamberlain quotes from J. M. and M. J. Cohen, *The Penguin Dictionary of Quotations*, Penguin, London, 1978 and J. M. and M. J. Cohen, *The Penguin Dictionary of Modern Quotations*, Penguin, London, 1978

Page 117

Kirkpatrick quote from Sir Ivone Kirkpatrick, *The Inner Circle*, Macmillan, London, 1959

Page 118

Daily Express and *Daily Herald* reactions to arrival of Jewish refugees from Franklin Reid Gannon, *The British Press and Germany 1936–1939*, Clarendon Press, Oxford, 1971

Page 118

London magistrate sentencing of Jewish refugees from A. J. Sherman, *Island Refuge: Britain and Refugees from the Third Reich 1933–39*, Frank Cass, London, 1994

Page 118

Willi Preis from correspondence with Ohniel Preis dated 26 July 1997 and telephone conversation dated 31 July 1997

Pages 118–19

Martyl Karweik's story from R. V. Jones, *Reflections on Intelligence*, Mandarin, London, 1990

Chapter 11

Pages 121–2

Details of Grynszpann and aftermath from PRO FO371/21791;

Eichmann trial, Session 14, 25 April 1961, testimony of Zindel Grynszpann; Saul Friedlaender, *Nazi Germany and the Jews*, Weidenfeld, London, 1997, Martin Gilbert, *The Holocaust*, Fontana, London, 1986

Pages 122–3

Details of initial aftermath of von Rath's death from Saul Friedlaender, *Nazi Germany and the Jews*, Weidenfeld, London, 1997; Martin Gilbert, *The Holocaust*, Fontana, London, 1986

Page 123

Inge Fehr details from correspondence with Inge Samson (née Fehr) dated 2 April 1997 and 28 May 1997

Page 123

Frank journey around Berlin during Kristallnacht from correspondence with Ohniel Preis dated 26 July 1997 and telephone conversation dated 31 July 1997

Page 123

Kay Foley presence and quotes from *Sunday Mercury*, 7 May 1961

Pages 124–5

British newspaper reports of Kristallnacht from *The Daily Telegraph* and *The Times*, 8–16 November 1938

Page 125

Goebbels glee from *The Goebbels Diaries*, Part I, Vol. 3, K. G. Saur, London, 1987

Page 125

Fate of Wittlich synagogue from Saul Friedlaender, *Nazi Germany and the Jews*, Weidenfeld, London, 1997

Pages 125–6

Wim van Leer testimony from Wim van Leer, *Time of My Life*, Carta, Jerusalem, 1984

Page 126

Round-ups and Gestapo orders from Martin Gilbert, *The Holocaust*, Fontana, London, 1986; Saul Friedlaender, *Nazi Germany and the Jews*, Weidenfeld, London, 1997

Page 126

Benno Cohn quotes from transcript of Eichmann trial, Session 14, 25 April 1961

Pages 126–7

Foley sheltering Leo Baeck and other Jews in his own home from Kay Foley quotes from *Sunday Mercury*, 7 May 1961 and Naomi Shepherd, *Wilfred Israel: German Jewry's Secret Ambassador*, Weidenfeld and Nicolson, London, 1984

Page 127

Fehr quotes from correspondence with Inge Samson (née Fehr) dated 2 April 1997 and 28 May 1997

Pages 127–30

Ruppel family story from interview with Ernest Ruppel junior dated 20 December 1996

Page 128

Treatment of Jews in Buchenwald from PRO371/21692 and from Naomi Shepherd, *Wilfred Israel: German Jewry's Secret Ambassador*, Weidenfeld and Nicolson, London, 1984

Chapter 12

Page 131

Foley appeals to Mills and London from Hubert Pollack, *Captain Foley, der Mensch und anderen Berichte*, Yad Vashem YVS 01/17; PRO T161/501

Pages 131–2

Benno Cohn quotes on Foley from CZA K11/391

Page 132

Extra commissionaires drafted in from Hubert Pollack, *Captain Foley, der Mensch und anderen Berichte*, Yad Vashem YVS 01/17

Pages 132–3

Reid arrival from Brotherton Library, University of Leeds MS708/9/2; MS708/9/3

Page 133

Mills dispatch of Youth Aliyah certificates and Foley response from the *Jerusalem Post*, 20 June 1958; Naomi Shepherd, *Wilfred Israel: German Jewry's Secret Ambassador*, Weidenfeld, London, 1984; Hubert Pollack, *Captain Foley, der Mensch und anderen Berichte*, Yad Vashem YVS 01/17

Pages 133–4

Problems facing Jews trying to obtain exit permits from PRO T161/501; Wim van Leer, *Time of My Life*, Carta, Jerusalem, 1984

Page 134

Kay Foley on Frank's efforts to obtain visas from *Sunday Mercury*, 7 May 1961

Page 134

Details of passport control procedures in Berlin from interview with Ann Forbes-Robertson dated 3 December 1996

Pages 134–5

Kay Foley on hours worked by Frank from *Sunday Mercury*, 7 May 1961

Page 135

Margaret Reid on Foley and difficulties of the Jews from Brotherton Library MS708/9/2–6

Pages 135–7

Weber family story from interview with Paula Weber dated 16 December 1996

Pages 137–8

New measures taken against the Jews from PRO FO371/22539; FO371/21753; FO371/21696; Martin Gilbert, *The Holocaust*, Fontana,

London, 1986; Saul Friedlaender, *Nazi Germany and the Jews*, Weidenfeld, London, 1997; correspondence with Inge Samson (née Fehr) dated 2 April 1997 and 28 May 1997

Pages 138–9

Wim van Leer account of the treatment of the Jews outside the British PCO and of Foley's assistance in false passports and escape routes from Wim van Leer, *Time of My Life*, Carta, Jerusalem, 1984

Page 139

Foley ordered to drop Luftwaffe agent from information provided to the author in confidence

Pages 140–41

Atomic intelligence and Rosbaud from Arnold Kramish, *The Griffin*, Macmillan, London, 1986; Thomas Powers, *Heisenberg's War: The Secret History of the German Bomb*, Cape, London, 1993; Mark Walker, *German National Socialism and the Quest for Nuclear Power, 1939–1949*, CUP, Cambridge, 1990; 'Focus on 50th Anniversary of Splitting the Atom', Associated Press, 15 December 1988

Page 141

Foley association with Mossad leAliyah Bet from CZA K11/391

Chapter 13

Pages 143–4

Information on illegal immigration and Mossad LeAliyah Bet from

Dalia Ofer, *Escaping the Holocaust: Illegal Immigration to the Land of Israel 1939–1944*, OUP, Oxford, 1990; Jon and David Kimche, *The Secret Roads*, Secker and Warburg, London, 1954; Ephraim Dexel, *Shai: The Exploits of Hagana Intelligence*, Thomas Yosellof, London, 1959

Pages 144–5

Involvement of Eichmann, Heydrich and Göring from Dalia Ofer, *Escaping the Holocaust: Illegal Immigration to the Land of Israel 1939–1944*, OUP, Oxford, 1990; Martin Gilbert, *The Holocaust*, Fontana, London 1987; Saul Friedlaender, *Nazi Germany and the Jews*, Weidenfeld, London, 1997

Pages 145–6

Information on Frank's knowledge of Mossad operations from CZA K11/391

Pages 145–6

Details of Mossad LcAliyah Bct intelligence collection role from Ronald Payne, *Mossad: Israel's Most Secret Service*, Corgi, London, 1991

Page 146

Horwitz comments from interview with Arnold Horwell (formerly Horwitz), dated 28 November 1996

Pages 146–8

Information on Vienna from interview with Kenneth Benton, 3 December 1996; interview with Marjorie Somers Cocks (née Weller), 28 January 1998; 'With the Jews in Vienna', *The Spectator*,

19 August 1938; PRO FO371/21635; FO371/21696; FO371/21748; FO371/21749; FO371/21751; FO372/3284

Pages 148–9

Testimony of Ann Forbes-Robertson from interview dated 3 December 1996

Pages 149–50

Georg Landauer letter from Saul Friedlaender, *Nazi Germany and the Jews*, Weidenfeld, London, 1997

Pages 150–52

Information on problems in Shanghai and Foley response from FO371/24079

Chapter 14

Page 153

Hitler sixteenth anniversary speech from Saul Friedlaender, *Nazi Germany and the Jews*, Weidenfeld, London, 1997; Martin Gilbert, *The Holocaust*, Fontana, London, 1987

Pages 153–5

For Frank's involvement in sending refugees to the Richborough transit camp, see Hubert Pollack, *Captain Foley, der Mensch und anderen Berichte*, Yad Vashen YVS 01/17; PRO HO213/115; FO371/21753; Louise London, 'British Immigration Control Procedures and Jewish Refugees 1933–1939', in Werner E. Mosse (ed.), *Second Chance: Two Centuries of German-Speaking Jews in the United Kingdom*, J. C. B. Mohr, Tübingen, 1991

Page 156

Testimony of Ann Forbes-Robertson from interview dated 3 December 1996

Page 156

Role of David MacEwen from C. G. McKay, *From Information to Intrigue: Studies in Secret Service Based on the Swedish Experience*, Frank Cass, London, 1993; Nigel West, *MI6: British Secret Intelligence Service Operations 1909–1945*, Weidenfeld and Nicolson, London, 1983; PRO FO371/39143

Pages 156–157

Kay Foley on pressure on Frank and conditions in Germany from *Sunday Mercury*, 7 May 1961; *County Express*, 28 October 1939

Page 157

Testimony of Arieh Handler from *Sunday Times*, 26 February 1995; *Jewish Chronicle*, 3 March 1995

Page 158

Testimony of Ann Forbes-Robertson from interview dated 3 December 1996

Pages 158–9

Lachs family story from correspondence and interview with Werner Lachs, March and April 1997

Pages 159–60

Refusal of British Medical Association and General Medical

Council to take more refugees from FO371/21752; A. J. Sherman, *Island Refuge: Britain and Refugees from the Third Reich 1933–39*, Frank Cass, London, 1994

Page 160

Chamberlain quote from Martin Gilbert, *The Holocaust*, Fontana, London, 1987

Page 160

Fehr family story from interview with Inge Samson (née Fehr) dated 2 April 1997

Page 161

Pollack story of Foley and the German spy from *Palestine Post*, 29 June 1941

Chapter 15

Page 163

Kay Foley on Frank getting Jews out of the camps from *Sunday Mercury*, 7 May 1961

Pages 163–5

Rescue of the Powitzer family from interviews and correspondence with Padan, *Daily Mail*, 6 October 1996; *Sunday Times*, 26 February 1995

Pages 165–6

Invasion of Czechoslovakia from PRO CAB81/132; FO371/22958;

John Keegan, *The Second World War*, Viking Penguin, New York, 1990

Pages 166–7

Testimony of Ann Forbes-Robertson from interview dated 3 December 1996

Pages 167–8

White Paper from A. J. Sherman, *Island Refuge: Britain and Refugees from the Third Reich 1933–39*, Frank Cass, London, 1994; Dalia Ofer, *Escaping the Holocaust: Illegal Immigration to the Land of Israel 1939–1944*, OUP, Oxford, 1990; Martin Gilbert, *The Holocaust* Fontana, London, 1987

Page 168

Quota suspensions over illegal immigration from PRO FO371/24079; A. J. Sherman, *Island Refuge: Britain and Refugees from the Third Reich 1933–39*, Frank Cass, London, 1994; Dalia Ofer, *Escaping the Holocaust: Illegal Immigration to the Land of Israel 1939–1944*, OUP, Oxford, 1990; Martin Gilbert, *The Holocaust*, Fontana, London, 1987

Pages 168–9

Arian family story and Dr David Arian's correspondence with Foley from private papers of Bat-sheeva Arian and correspondence and interviews with Mrs Arian. I am grateful to Shlomo Shpiro for his assistance in these interviews

Page 169

Frank's journey to Norway and Sweden from entry and exit

stamps in his passport, a photocopy of which is held in the Brotherton Library, University of Leeds, MS708/8

Pages 169–70

Oster's role from F. H. Hinsley et al., *British Intelligence in the Second World War*, Vol. I, HMSO, London, 1979

Page 170

Evacuation of embassy from interview with Ann Forbes-Robertson dated 3 December 1996

Page 170

Departure of Pollack and friends of Israel from Hubert Pollack, *Captain Foley, der Mensch und anderen Berichte*, Yad Vashen YVS 01/17; Naomi Shepherd, *Wilfred Israel: German Jewry's Secret Ambassador*, Weidenfeld, London, 1984

Page 170

Rosbaud briefing message indicator from Arnold Kramish, *The Griffin*, Macmillan, London, 1986; R. V. Jones, *Reflections on Intelligence*, Mandarin, London, 1990

Page 170

Story of eighty visas handed to Borchardt from correspondence with Chanan Baram, formerly known as Hans Borchardt, dated 10 February 1998, and telephone conversation on 22 February 1998

Page 170

Kay Foley's departure from interview with Ann Forbes-Robertson dated 3 December 1996; *Sunday Mercury*, 7 May 1961

Pages 170–71

Margaret Reid quotes from Brotherton Library, University of Leeds MS708/14/24

Page 171

Youth Aliyah certificates signed by Frank given to US Consulate from Naomi Shepherd, *Wilfred Israel: German Jewry's Secret Ambassador*, Weidenfeld, London, 1984

Page 171

Pollack quotes from CZA K11/391 and Hubert Pollack, *Captain Foley, der Mensch und anderen Berichte*, Yad Vashem YVS 01/17

Chapter 16

Page 173

Information on Kay Foley's arrival in England and reasons for choosing Stourbridge from interviews with Irene Berlyn, dated 10 January 1997, Beryl Price, dated 4 March 1997, and Gwen Evers, dated 27 March 1997

Pages 173–6

Information on Foley movements, dissatisfaction with Oslo set-up and journey to Oslo, via Copenhagen, with Margaret Reid from photocopy of his passport and Margaret Reid letters in the Brotherton Library MS708/8; MS708/14/24; MS708/9/7; MS708/9/8

Page 175

Information on agents in Germany from C. G. McKay, *From Information to Intrigue: Studies in Secret Service Based on the Swedish Experience 1939–45*, Frank Cass, London, 1993; PRO ADM223/475; Ernest Volkman, *Espionage: The Greatest Spy Operations of the 20th Century*, Wiley, New York, 1995

Page 176

Foley problems with Newill, state of office and frustration at non-arrival of intelligence from Margaret Reid letters, Brotherton Library MS708/14/24; MS708/9/8

Pages 176–9

For details of the Oslo Report, see R. V. Jones, *Reflections on Intelligence*, Mandarin, London, 1990; Arnold Kramish, *The Griffin*, Macmillan, London, 1986; R. V. Jones, *Most Secret War: British Scientific Intelligence 1939–45*, Coronet, London, 1979; F. H. Hinsley et al., *British Intelligence in the Second World War*, Vol. I, HMSO, London, 1979. Kramish's otherwise excellent book is unfortunately wrong in concluding that Rosbaud was the author of the Oslo Report, as shown by the investigations of the late Professor R. V. Jones and in particular Mayer's letter of 1967 to Jones describing how and why he wrote the letters.

Page 178

For details of the Venlo débâcle and Sinclair's death see Michael Smith, *New Cloak, Old Dagger*, Gollancz, London, 1996; Christopher Andrew, *Secret Service*, Sceptre, London, 1986

Page 179

Sheila St Clair diagnosed as having terminal cancer and Foley's reaction from Brotherton Library MS708/9/13

Pages 179–80

Paula Weber's application for a visa and accompaniment of Sheila St Clair to England from interview with Paula Weber dated 12 December 1996

Page 180

Rosbaud passing of documents via Odd Hassell from Arnold Kramish, *The Griffin*, Macmillan, London, 1986; R. V. Jones, *Reflections on Intelligence*, Mandarin, London, 1990. Kramish suggests that the documents passed by Hassell on Rosbaud's behalf were the Oslo Report, but as Jones points out Kramish ignores Rosbaud's own testimony that his first contact with Hassell after the outbreak of war was in December, a month after the Oslo Report arrived at the British embassy.

Pages 180–81

Reports from agents in Germany's northern ports from PRO PREM1/435; ADM223/794; Basil Collier, *Hidden Weapons: Allied Secret or Undercover Services in World War Two*, Hamish Hamilton, London, 1982

Page 181

Abwehr officers sent to Norway from Heinz Hoehne, *Canaris*, Secker and Warburg, London, 1979

Pages 181–2

Intelligence failures and Edward Thomas quotes on disgrace to British Intelligence from Edward Thomas, 'Norway's Role in British Wartime Intelligence,' in Patrick Salmon (ed.), *Britain and Norway in the Second World War*, HMSO, London 1995.

Frank's remarks were made to Ian Colvin and reproduced in Ian Colvin, *Canaris, Chief of Intelligence*, George Mann, London, 1973. See also Wesley K. Wark, 'Beyond Intelligence: The Study of British Strategy and the Norwegian Campaign, 1940', in Michael Graham Fry, *Power, Personalities and Policies: Essays in Honour of Donald Cameron Watt*, Frank Cass, London, 1992; Basil Collier, *Hidden Weapons: Allied Secret or Undercover Services in World War Two*, Hamish Hamilton, London, 1982

Page 182

Admiralty report from T. K. Derry, *The Campaign in Norway*, HMSO, London, 1952

Page 182

War Office report from PRO WO190/891

Pages 182–183

Frank's contact flying in from Copenhagen from PRO PREM1/435

Page 183

Transfer of control of German agents to Stockholm from C. G. McKay, *From Information to Intrigue: Studies in Secret Service Based on the Swedish Experience*, Frank Cass, London, 1993

Page 183

Recruitment of Reed Olsen and Moe from Oluf Reed Olsen, *Two Eggs on My Plate*, Companion Book Club, London, 1954

Pages 183–4

Events at MI6 Oslo station on morning of 9 April from Brotherton Library MS708/17/4 and Margaret Reid and Leif C. Rolstad, *April 1940: En Krigsdagbok*, Gyldendaf Norsk Forlag, Oslo, 1980

Chapter 17

Page 185

Departure of legation staff for Hamar from Brotherton Library MS708/17/4 and Margaret Reid and Leif C. Rolstad, *April 1940: En Krigsdagbok*, Gyldendaf Norsk Forlag, Oslo, 1980

Page 185

Frank's orders from information provided to the author in confidence

Page 185

Dispatch of Newill and Mitchell to Stockholm for more wireless transmitter equipment from PRO WO373/109

Page 185

Pollack testimony of Foley involvement in departure of Jews from CZA K11/391

Pages 185–6

Events of the afternoon and evening of 9 April from François Kersaudy, *Norway 1940*, Arrow, London, 1991; Brotherton Library MS708/17/4; Margaret Reid and Leif C. Rolstad, *April 1940: En Krigsdagbok*, Gyldendaf Norsk Forlag, Oslo, 1980

Page 186

Foley description of evacuation of Hosbjor from Brotherton Library MS708/17/4

Pages 186–7

Decision to make for coast from PRO FO371/24834

Pages 186–8

Description of journey to Andalsnes, including quotes from Margaret Reid, from Margaret Reid and Leif C. Rolstad, *April 1940: En Krigsdagbok*, Gyldendaf Norsk Forlag, Oslo, 1980

Page 189

Texts of messages to and from London from PRO FO371/24834 and WO106/1912

Pages 189–90

Margaret Reid quotes, description of journey to Oyer and Ruge's statement to Foley from Margaret Reid and Leif C. Rolstad, *April 1940: En Krigsdagbok*, Gyldendaf Norsk Forlag, Oslo, 1980

Page 190

Foley description of Reid role in council of war from Brotherton Library MS708/17/4

Pages 191–3

Texts of messages to and from London from PRO FO371/24834 and WO106/1912

Page 192

Reid description of Norwegians' reaction to Foley and herself from Brotherton Library MS708/14/29

Page 192

Rolstad impressions of Foley from Margaret Reid and Leif C. Rolstad, *April 1940: En Krigsdagbok*, Gyldendaf Norsk Forlag, Oslo, 1980

Pages 192–3

Frank and Ruge reactions to first British landing from Margaret Reid and Leif C. Rolstad, *April 1940: En Krigsdagbok*, Gyldendaf Norsk Forlag, Oslo, 1980; PRO FO371/24834

Page 193

Arrivals of military attachés, and of Newill and Mitchell, acquisition of Pontiac from PRO WO 208/3297; Margaret Reid and Leif C. Rolstad, *April 1940: En Krigsdagbok*, Gyldendaf Norsk Forlag, Oslo, 1980

Page 194

King-Salter meeting with Morgan from François Kersaudy, *Norway 1940*, Arrow, London, 1991

Page 194

Dudley Clarke impressions of Ruge from Dudley Clarke, *Seven Assignments*, Cape, London, 1948

Page 194

Morgan agreement to Norwegian plans from François Kersaudy, *Norway 1940*, Arrow, London, 1991

Page 194

Foley's concern over his position from Margaret Reid and Leif C. Rolstad, *April 1940: En Krigsdagbok*, Gyldendaf Norsk Forlag, Oslo, 1980

Pages 194–5

Dormer comparison between British and German troops from PRO FO371/24834

Page 195

Use of Foley Mission to pass intelligence to London from PRO WO106/1904; WO106/1912; Edward Thomas, 'Norway's Role in British Wartime Intelligence', in Patrick Salmon (ed.), *Britain and Norway in the Second World War*, HMSO, London, 1995

Page 195

Use of Foley Mission to pass intelligence derived from Bletchley Park intercepts from PRO HW3/95; HW5/1; Edward Thomas, 'Norway's Role in British Wartime Intelligence', in Patrick Salmon (ed.), *Britain and Norway in the Second World War*, HMSO, London, 1995; F. H. Hinsley, *British Intelligence in the Second World War* (abridged version, revised edition), HMSO, London, 1994

Pages 195–6

Military appointments of various members of Foley mission from PRO WO106/1912

Page 196

Foley and Reid evacuation from Margaret Reid and Leif C. Rolstad, *April 1940: En Krigsdagbok*, Gyldendaf Norsk Forlag, Oslo, 1980

Page 196

Gold reserves taken to Britain and King journey to Tromso from PRO FO371/24834

Page 196

Foley fight to get Margaret Reid decoration and testimonial written for head of MI6 from Brotherton Library MS708/17/4; MS708/14/24

Page 196

Foley decoration and citation from PRO WO373/109

Chapter 18

Page 197

Lessons from Foley Mission for transmission of Ultra material to forces in the field from Edward Thomas, 'Norway's Role in British Wartime Intelligence', in Patrick Salmon (ed.), *Britain and Norway in the Second World War*, HMSO, London, 1995

Page 197

Evidence of Foley's departure for France from Brotherton Library MS708/10/3; Arnold Kramish, *The Griffin*, Macmillan, London, 1986

Pages 197–199

Role of Special Signals Unit in battle for France from Edward Thomas, 'Norway's Role in British Wartime Intelligence', in Patrick Salmon (ed.), *Britain and Norway in the Second World War* HMSO, London, 1995; F. H. Hinsley *et al.*, *British Intelligence in the Second World War*, Vol. I, HMSO, London, 1979; F. W. Winterbotham, *The Ultra Secret*, Dell, New York, 1974

Page 198

Information on the evacuation from France provided to the author in confidence; Arnold Kramish, *The Griffin*, Macmillan, London, 1986; Geoffrey Cox, *Countdown to War: A Personal Memoir of Europe 1938–40*, William Kimber, London, 1988; Andrew Lycett, *Ian Fleming*, Weidenfeld and Nicolson, London, 1995

Pages 199–200

MI6 reorganisation in wake of fall of France to produce A Sections from Nigel West and Oleg Tsarev, *The Crown Jewels*, HarperCollins, London, 1998

Page 199

Welsh recruitment from Brotherton Library MS708/14/24

Page 200

Philby quote from Nigel West and Oleg Tsarev, *The Crown Jewels*, HarperCollins, London, 1998

Page 200

Foley safe house from Foley letter to brother Andy Foley dated 10 July 1944

Page 200

Quotes from Owen Lee from *Miami Herald*, 25 August 1940

Page 200

Quotes from Beryl Price from interview with her dated 4 March 1997

Page 200

Foley attendance at Brompton Oratory from interview with Patricia and Richard Dunstan dated 18/July 1997

Page 200

For MI6 problems in wake of fall of Norway and France, see F. H. Hinsley et al., *British Intelligence in the Second World War*, Vol. 1, HMSO, London, 1979; Christopher Andrew, *Secret Service*,

Sceptre, London, 1987; Michael Smith, *New Cloak, Old Dagger*, Gollancz, London, 1996

Page 200

Margaret Reid quote from Brotherton Library MS708/14

Page 201

Priority for Frank's section from Arnold Kramish, *The Griffin*, Macmillan, London, 1986

Pages 201–206

Information on A1's activities against Norway comes from PRO CAB102/650; CAB102/652; ADM223/475; ADM223/481; HS2/238; HS2/240; Oluf Reed Olsen, *Two Eggs on My Plate*, Companion Book Club, London, 1954; David Howarth, *The Shetland Bus*, Thomas Nelson, London, 1951; Patrick Salmon (ed.), *Britain and Norway in the Second World War*, HMSO, London, 1995, C. G. McKay, 'The SIS Network in Norway, 1940–1945, Intelligence and National Security,' Vol. 10, No. 3 (July 1995); Nigel West and Oleg Tsarev, *The Crown Jewels*, HarperCollins, London, 1998

Chapter 19

Pages 207–8

Foley continued contact with Jewish refugees and their internment from Brotherton Library MS708/10/6; interview with Inge Samson dated 2 April 1997; Fehr family private papers; interview with Paula Weber dated 16 December 1996; Richard C. Thurlow, 'Internment in the Second World War', *Intelligence and National Security*, Vol. 9, No. 1 (January 1994); A. W. Brian Simpson, *In the Highest Degree Odious: Detention without Trial in Wartime*

Britain, Clarendon, Oxford, 1992; Richard Thurlow, *The Secret State: British Internal Security in the Twentieth Century*, Blackwell, Oxford 1994

Page 208

Foley made CMG from *London Gazette*, 1 January 1941. Citation from unidentified family papers in the possession of William Kelley, nephew of Frank Foley; date of decoration and Kay Foley's impressions of Buckingham Palace from *Stourbridge County Express*, March 1941

Page 208

Ruge letter to Foley from Brotherton Library MS708/8

Pages 208–209

Details of Madame Szymanska from Michael Smith, *New Cloak, Old Dagger*, Gollancz, London, 1996

Page 210

Agents run from Stockholm from PRO CAB102/649; ADM223/475; C. G. McKay, *From Information to Intrigue*, Frank Cass, London, 1993

Page 210

Paul Thümmel run by MI6 German section from Phillip H. J. Davies, *Organisational Development of Britain's Secret Intelligence Service 1909–1979*, University of Reading 1997

Page 210

Thuemmel's activities from F. H. Hinsley et al., *British Intelligence in the Second World War*, Vol. 1, HMSO, London, 1979; Christopher Andrew, *Secret Service*, Sceptre, London, 1987

Pages 210–16

Information on Rosbaud from Arnold Kramish, *The Griffin*, Macmillan, London, 1986; C. G. McKay, *From Information to Intrigue*, Frank Cass, London, 1993; *After the Battle*, No. 74, 1991; R. V. Jones, *Reflections on Intelligence*, Mandarin, London, 1990; Ernest Volkmann, *Espionage: The Greatest Spy Operations of the 20th Century*, Wiley, New York, 1995; information supplied to the author in confidence

Pages 213–16

Information on the German atomic weapons programme from Arnold Kramish, *The Griffin*, Macmillan, London, 1986; Thomas Powers, *Heisenberg's War: The Secret History of the German Bomb*, Cape, London, 1993; Mark Walker, *German National Socialism and the Quest for Nuclear Power, 1939–1949*, CUP, Cambridge, 1990; 'Focus on 50th Anniversary of Splitting the Atom', Associated Press, 15 December 1988.

Page 216

Jones quote on Rosbaud's contribution from R. V. Jones, *Reflections on Intelligence*, Mandarin, London, 1990

Chapter 20

Page 217

Activities of A1 and Menzies enthusiasm for contacts with dissident Germans from information provided to the author in confidence; 'Wartime Head of Secret Service Dies', by Ian Colvin, *Daily Telegraph*, 30 May 1968

Pages 217–18

Background to Hess arrival in Britain from *After the Battle*, No.

58; Lord James Douglas-Hamilton, *The Truth about Rudolf Hess*, Mainstream, Edinburgh, 1993; I. C. B. Dear (ed.), *The Oxford Companion to the Second World War*, OUP, Oxford, 1995

Pages 217–18

Karl Haushofer dream and Hess horoscope from PRO FO1093/15

Page 218

Hamilton 'appointed by destiny' from PRO FO1093/12

Pages 218–19

Haushofer letter from PRO FO1093/11

Page 219

Details of Hess arrival from PRO FO1093/1

Page 220

Hamilton briefing of Churchill from Lord James Douglas-Hamilton, *The Truth about Rudolf Hess*, Mainstream, Edinburgh, 1993

Page 220

Cadogan meeting with Menzies and dispatch of Kirkpatrick to Scotland from David Dilks (ed.), *The Diaries of Sir Alexander Cadogan O.M. 1938–1945*, Cassell, London, 1971

Pages 220–21

Kirkpatrick meeting with Hess from Ivone Kirkpatrick, *The Inner Circle*, Macmillan, London, 1959; PRO FO1093/11; PREM3/219/7

Pages 221–22

Hess treated like a defector from information provided to the author in confidence

Page 222

Churchill orders on Hess seclusion and interrogation from PREM3/219/7

Pages 222–3

Preparation of Camp Z from PREM3/219/7; *After the Battle*, No. 58; papers of Lt-Col. A. M. Scott IWM69/66/1

Page 222

Identity of guardians from papers of Lt-Col. A. M. Scott IWM69/66/1

Page 222

Reid letter on Foley from Brotherton Library MS708/17

Pages 222–3

Orders for Scott from PRO FO1093/8; papers of Lt-Col. A. M. Scott IWM69/66/1

Page 223

Fortifications of Mytchett Place from *After the Battle*, No. 58

Page 223

Arrival of Foley and Hess at Mytchett from papers of Lt-Col. A. M. Scott IWM69/66/1

Page 223

Hunter introduction and Hess response from PRO FO1093/8; papers of Lt-Col. A. M. Scott IWM69/66/1

Page 223

Hess suspicions over guardians from PRO FO1093/8

Pages 223–4

Graham conversations with Hess from PRO FO1093/8; papers of Lt-Col. A. M. Scott IWM69/66/1

Page 224

Hess view of Foley from J. Bernard Hutton, *Hess: The Man and His Mission*, David Bruce & Watson, London, 1970

Page 224

Foley disgust with Hess habits from information provided to the author in confidence

Page 225

Kay Foley on Hess fears of poison and insanity from *Sunday Mercury*, 7 May 1961

Page 225

Failure of intelligence debriefing from PRO FO1093/10; FO1093/11

Page 225

Menzies visit and Foley's assessment that only way of getting anything out of Hess is through negotiator or placing another German in his room from papers of Lt-Col. A. M. Scott IWM69/66/1; PRO FO1093/11

Page 226

Guards officer diary entry from Peter Padfield, *Hess: The Führer's Disciple*, Papermac, London, 1994; David Irving, *Hess: The Missing Years 1941–1945*, Macmillan, London, 1987

Page 226

Rees conclusions from PRO FO1093/10

Chapter 21

Page 227

Churchill on selection of Simon as 'negotiator' from Kenneth Young (ed.), *The Diaries of Sir Robert Bruce Lockhart*, Macmillan, London, 1980

Pages 227–8

Hess thought to be suicidal from David Irving, *Hess: The Missing Years 1941–1945*, Macmillan, London, 1987; PRO FO1093/10; papers of Lt-Col. A. M. Scott IWM69/66/1

Page 228

Hess told of meeting with Simon and reaction from PRO FO1093/10

Pages 228 9

Kirkpatrick recollections of meeting between Simon and Hess from Ivone Kirkpatrick, *The Inner Circle*, Macmillan, London, 1959

Page 229

Foley reaction to meeting between Simon and Hess from PRO FO1093/10

Page 229

Cadogan and Churchill reaction from David Dilks (ed.), *The Diaries of Sir Alexander Cadogan O.M. 1938–1945*, Cassell, London, 1971; PRO FO1093/10

Page 229

Hess reaction from papers of Lt-Col. A. M. Scott IWM69/66/1

Pages 229–30

Foley warning from PRO FO1093/10

Page 230

Cadogan reaction from David Dilks (ed.), *The Diaries of Sir Alexander Cadogan O.M. 1938–1945*, Cassell, London, 1971

Page 230

Hess remarks to duty officer from papers of Lt-Col. A. M. Scott IWM69/66/1

Pages 230–231

Dicks and Rees reports on Hess's health from PRO FO1093/10

Page 231

Cadogan reaction from David Dilks (ed.), *The Diaries of Sir Alexander Cadogan O.M. 1938–1945*, Cassell, London, 1971

Page 231

Return of Barnes and Kirkpatrick to London from papers of Lt-Col. A. M. Scott IWM69/66/1

Page 231

Correspondence with Hans Friedenthal and Georg Landauer from YVS01/225

Pages 231–2

Foley on Hess attitude to broadcasting and disbelief of Holocaust from PRO FO1093/10

Page 233

Hess access to magazines from PRO FO1093/10

Page 233

Goebbels surprise over lack of propaganda from *The Goebbels Diaries*, Part I, Vol., 3, K. G. Saur, London, 1987

Pages 234-5

Foley doubt that Hess would ever become involved in 'intrigue' against Hitler from PRO FO1093/13

Pages 234-5

Foley meetings at Foreign Office, Broadway and St Albans and distrust of Philby from information provided to the author in confidence and papers of Lt-Col. A. M. Scott IWM69/66/1

Page 235

Foley concerns over suitability of Mytchett Place from papers of Lt-Col. A. M. Scott IWM69/66/1

Page 235

Visit of Swiss Minister from papers of Lt-Col. A. M. Scott IWM69/66/1

Page 236

Incident in which Foley ate all of Hess's 'poisons' and subsequent decision to move Hess to a psychiatric hospital from papers of Lt-Col. A. M. Scott IWM69/66/1; PRO FO1093/14

Chapter 22

Page 237

Menzies tells Foley he wants to put an operational officer on to the Twenty Committee from information provided to the author in confidence

Page 237

White memo from Tom Bower, *The Perfect Englishman*, Heinemann, London, 1995

Pages 237–42

Origins and progress pre-Foley of the Double-Cross System from J. C. Masterman, *The Double Cross System in the War of 1939 to 1945*, YUP, London, 1972; F. H. Hinsley and C. A. G. Simkins, *British Intelligence in the Second World War*, Vol. 4, HMSO, London, 1990; Michael Howard, *British Intelligence in the Second World War*, Vol. 5, HMSO, London, 1990; PRO ADM223/793; ADM223/794

Pages 238–239

Quotes from former double-agent handler from interview with Hugh Astor, 23 January 1998

Page 240

Montagu quotes from PRO ADM223/464; ADM223/792; ADM223/793; ADM223/794

Page 240

Robertson quotes from Michael Howard, *British Intelligence in the Second World War*, Vol. 5, HMSO, London, 1990

Pages 240–42

Cowgill difficulties from PRO ADM223/464; ADM223/792; ADM223/793; ADM223/794; F. H. Hinsley and C. A. G. Simkins, *British Intelligence in the Second World War*, Vol. 4,

HMSO, London, 1990; Michael Howard, *British Intelligence in the Second World War*, Vol. 5, HMSO, London, 1990

Pages 240–41

Philby quotes from Nigel West and Oleg Tsarev, *The Crown Jewels*, HarperCollins, London, 1998

Page 241

Montagu quotes from PRO ADM223/464; ADM223/792; ADM223/793; ADM223/794

Pages 241–2

Turf war brought to a head over Garbo from F. H. Hinsley and C. A. G. Simkins, *British Intelligence in the Second World War*, Vol. 4, HMSO, London, 1990; Michael Howard, *British Intelligence in the Second World War*, Vol. 5, HMSO, London, 1990

Page 242

Fact that MI6 and MI5 did discuss Garbo at lower levels from Desmond Bristow (with Bill Bristow), *A Game of Moles*, Warner, London, 1994

Pages 242–3

Menzies decides to put an operational officer on to the Twenty Committee from information provided to the author in confidence

Page 243

Foley's attendance at Twenty Committee while Hess still at Mytchett and quotes from former MI5 officer from information provided to the author in confidence

Page 243

Masterman quotes from J. C. Masterman, *The Double-Cross System in the War of 1939 to 1945*, YUP, London, 1972

Page 243

Foley offices at 5, St James's Street from correspondence in the possession of Dennis Foley

Pages 243–4

Description of Glenalmond from Desmond Bristow (with Bill Bristow), *A Game of Moles*, Warner, London, 1994

Page 244

Role of VX in building up a complete picture of German intelligence services from Robert Cecil, 'Five of Six at War', *Intelligence and National Security*, Vol. 9, (April 1994); information provided to the author in confidence

Page 244

Problems of accepting that German perception different from that of the British from PRO DEFE28/49

Pages 244–5

Quotes from MI6 officers over Foley contribution to the Twenty Committee from information provided to the author in confidence and Arnold Kramish, *The Griffin*, Macmillan, London, 1986

Page 245

Margaret Reid quotes from Brotherton Library MS708/11/13

Page 245

Masterman on Lisbon from J. C. Masterman, *The Double-Cross System in the War of 1939 to 1945*, YUP, London, 1972

Pages 245–7

The story of Hamlet from J. C. Masterman, *The Double Cross System in the War of 1939 to* 1945, YUP, London, 1972; F. H. Hinsley and C. A. G. Simkins, *British Intelligence in the Second World War*, Vol. 4, HMSO, London, 1990; David Mure, *Master of Deception*, William Kimber, London, 1980

Page 247

Foley brings fruit back for neighbours' children from interview with Beryl Price dated 3 March 1997

Page 247

Patricia Dunstan quotes from interview dated 18 July 1997

Chapter 23

Page 249

Jonny's activities on MI6's behalf in Brazil from *Ottawa Citizen*, 12 January 1954; Fernando Watson, *Olga,* Peter Halban, London, 1990

Page 250

Jonny and the Watchdog case from *Ottawa Citizen*, 12 January 1954; Dean Beeby, *Cargo of Lies: The True Story of a Double Agent in Canada*, University of Toronto, 1996; F. H. Hinsley and C. A. G. Simkins, *British Intelligence in the Second World War*, Vol. 4, HMSO, London, 1990. I am grateful to Mr Beeby for his assistance on further information unearthed since the publication of his book.

Pages 250–51

Details of Mincemeat from PRO ADM223/794; interview with Patricia Dunstan dated 18 July 1997

Pages 252–3

Details of the Artist case from Kenneth Benton, 'The ISOS Years: Madrid 1941–3, *Journal of Contemporary History*, Vol. 30, No. 3 (July 1995); Information provided to the author in confidence; F. H. Hinsley and C. A. G. Simkins, *British Intelligence in the Second World War*, Vol. 4, HMSO, London, 1990

Pages 254–5

Details of Wilfred Israel and Leslie Howard flight from interview with Patricia Dunstan dated 18 July 1997; *The Times* and the *Daily Telegraph*, 3 June 1943 and 4 June 1943; Ian Colvin, *Flight 777*, Evans, London, 1951

Page 255

Move to Ryder St from F. H. Hinsley and C. A. G. Simkins, *British Intelligence in the Second World War*, Vol. 4, HMSO, London, 1990

Page 255

Quotes from former agent handler from information provided to the author in confidence

Page 256

Award of Knight's Cross of St Olav from PRO WO373/109 and interview with Patricia Dunstan dated 18 July 1997

Page 256

Genesis of Bodyguard from Michael Howard, *British Intelligence in the Second World War*, Vol. 5, HMSO, London, 1990

Page 256

Quote on Foley involvement in D-Day preparations from information provided to the author in confidence

Pages 256–7

Quotes on Foley 'good plain cook' and liaison with Haris over Garbo from information provided to the author in confidence

Pages 257–8

Descriptions of other double-cross agents from J. C. Masterman, *The Double Cross System in the War of 1939 to 1945*, YUP, London, 1972; F. H. Hinsley and C. A. G. Simkins, *British Intelligence in the Second World War*, Vol. 4, HMSO, London, 1990; Michael Howard, *British Intelligence in the Second World War*, Vol. 5, HMSO, London, 1990; I. C. B. Dear (ed.), *The Oxford Companion to the Second World War*, OUP, Oxford, 1995; Michael Smith, *New Cloak, Old Dagger*, Gollancz, London, 1996

Pages 257–258

Garbo network from Michael Howard, *British Intelligence in the Second World War*, Vol. 5, HMSO, London, 1990; F. H. Hinsley and C. A. G. Simkins, *British Intelligence in the Second World War*, Vol. 4, HMSO, London, 1990

Page 258

Jonny role from correspondence with Dean Beeby dated 17 April 1998; information provided to the author in confidence

Pages 258–9

Fortitude from PRO DEFE28/47; DEFE28/48; DEFE28/49; CAB81/78; ADM223/794; Michael Howard, *British Intelligence in the Second World War*, Vol. 5, HMSO, London, 1990; F. H. Hinsley and C. A. G. Simkins, *British Intelligence in the Second World War*, Vol. 4, HMSO, London, 1990

Pages 259–260

Crucial Garbo message from PRO DEFE28/49

Page 260

Foley letter to brother Andy dated July 1944 in possession of Dennis Foley

Pages 260–61

Crossbow from ADM223/794; R. V. Jones, *Reflections on Intelligence*, Mandarin, London, 1989; Michael Howard, *British Intelligence in the Second World War*, Vol. 5, HMSO, London, 1990

Chapter 24

Page 261

Foley's role in Germany from *Who's Who*, 1952; FO1032/956; information provided to the author in confidence

Pages 261–2

Letter from Frank Foley to Werner Senator dated 19 April 1945, CZA S7/915

Pages 262–3

Information on Berlin in wake of war from Noel Annan, *Changing*

Enemies: The Defeat and Regeneration of Germany, HarperCollins, London, 1996; Giles MacDonogh, *Berlin*, Sinclair-Stevenson, London, 1997

Page 263

Foley's visit to the site of Tiergartenstrasse 17 from *Sunday Mercury*, 7 May 1961

Page 263

Role of Public Safety Branch from PRO FO1032/353; FO1032/618–621; F. S. V. Donnison, *Civil Affairs and Military Government North-West Europe 1944–46*, HMSO, London, 1961; Noel Annan, *Changing Enemies: The Defeat and Regeneration of Germany*, HarperCollins, London, 1996

Pages 263–4

Special Branch role from FO1032/1852

Page 264

Werewolf information from CAB81/128; Nigel West and Oleg Tsarev, *The Crown Jewels*, HarperCollins, London, 1998

Page 264

Information on Nursery from PRO FO1032/621; *The Times*, 1 April 1946; *Daily Telegraph*, 2 April 1946; *The Times*, 3 April 1946

Pages 265–66

Information on Operation Selection Board from Perry Biddiscombe, 'Operation Selection Board: The Growth and Suppression of the Neo-Nazi Deutsche Revolution, 1945–47', *Intelligence and National*

Security, Vol 11., No. 1, (January 1996); *Daily Telegraph*, 24 February 1947; *The Times*, 24 February 1947; PRO FO1032/621

Page 267

Huge number of Soviet agents infiltrated into the British and US zones from Michael Smith, *New Cloak, Old Dagger*, Gollancz, London, 1996

Page 267

Denazification handed over to the Germans from FO1032/1847

Page 267

Foley examining German files from information provided to the author in confidence

Page 267

Foley at Chelsea flat and opinions of the Russians from letter to Andy Foley dated 18 July 1948 in possession of Dennis Foley

Pages 267–8

General details of Foley retirement from interviews with Irene Berlyn, dated 10 January 1997; Beryl Price, dated 4 March 1997; Gwen Evers, dated 27 March 1997; Ernest Ruppel junior, dated 20 December 1996; Arthur Timmins, dated 10 January 1997

Page 268

Kay Foley quotes from *Sunday Mercury*, 7 May 1961

Page 269

Foley dinner with Colvin and Ebbutt and details of Colvin book from letter to Margaret Foley dated 17 August 1951; PRO

DEFE28/22; DEFE28/23; R. V. Jones, *Most Secret War: British Scientific Intelligence 1939–45*, Coronet, London, 1979; Ian Colvin, *The Unknown Courier*, William Kimber, London, 1953

Pages 269–70

Frank Foley on war from letter to Andy Foley dated November 1952 in possession of Dennis Foley

Page 270

Dennis Foley conversations with Frank Foley from interview with Dennis Foley dated 25 July 1997

Page 270

Foley death from *Stourbridge County Express*, 17 May 1958

Page 270

Tributes from Israel from CZA K11/391

Pages 270 71

Robert Weltsch letter from the *Daily Telegraph*, 14 April 1961

Pages 271–2

Emmy Hirschberg testimony from CZA K11/391

Page 272

Wim van Leer testimony from Wim van Leer, *Time of My Life*, Carta, Jerusalem, 1984

Page 272

Mossad kidnapping of Eichmann and use of Benno Cohn to

identify Eichmann from Isser Harel, *The House on Garibaldi Street*, Frank Cass, London, 1996

Pages 272–3

Benno Cohn testimony from transcript of Eichmann trial, Session 14, 25 April 1961

Bibliography

All About Shanghai: A Standard Guidebook, University Press, Shanghai, 1934

Andrew, Christopher, *Secret Service*, Sceptre, London, 1985

Annan, Noel, *Changing Enemies: The Defeat and Regeneration of Germany*, HarperCollins, London, 1996

Beeby, Dean, *Cargo of Lies: The True Story of a Double Agent in Canada*, University of Toronto, Toronto, 1996

Bower, Tom, *The Perfect Englishman*, Heinemann, London, 1995

Brook-Shepherd, Gordon, *The Storm Petrels*, Collins, London, 1977

Brown, Malcolm, *The Imperial War Museum Book of the Somme*, Sidgwick and Jackson, London, 1996

Bristow, Desmond (with Bill Bristow), *A Game of Moles*, Warner, London, 1994

Buchan, John, *A History of the Great War, Vol IV*, Thomas Nelson, London, 1920

Carr, E. H., *The Twilight of Comintern, 1930–1935*, Macmillan, London, 1982

Clarke, Dudley, *Seven Assignments*, Jonathan Cape, London, 1948

Clayton, Anthony, *Forearmed: A History of the Intelligence Corps*, Brassey's, London, 1993

Cohen, J. M. and M. J., *The Penguin Dictionary of Quotations*, Penguin, London, 1978

Cohen, J. M. and M. J., *The Penguin Dictionary of Modern Quotations*, Penguin, London, 1978

Collier, Basil, *Hidden Weapons: Allied Secret or Undercover Services in World War Two*, Hamish Hamilton, London, 1982

Colvin, Ian, *The Unknown Courier*, William Kimber, London, 1953

Colvin, Ian, *Flight 777*, Evans, London, 1955

Colvin, Ian, *Canaris, Chief of Intelligence*, George Mann, London, 1973

Court Repington, Lt-Col C., *After the War*, Constable, London, 1922

Cox, Geoffrey, *Countdown to War: A Personal Memoir of Europe 1938–40*, William Kimber, London, 1988

Davies, Phillip H. J., *Organisational Development of Britain's Secret Intelligence Service, 1909–1979*, University of Reading, Reading, 1998

Dear, I. C. B. (ed), *The Oxford Companion to the Second World War*, OUP, Oxford, 1995

Derry, T. K., *The Campaign in Norway*, HMSO, London, 1952

Dexel, Ephraim, *Shai: The Exploits of Hagana Intelligence*, Thomas Yosellof, London, 1959

Dilks, David (Ed), *The Diaries of Sir Alexander Cadogan O.M. 1938–1945*, Cassell, London, 1971

Donnison, F. S. V., *Civil Affairs and Military Government North-West Europe 1944–46*, HMSO, London, 1961

Douglas-Hamilton, Lord James, *The Truth about Rudolf Hess*, Mainstream, London, 1993

Dukes, Sir Paul, *The Story of ST-25*, Cassell, London, 1938

Eatwell, Roger, *Fascism: A History*, Virago, London, 1996

Edmonds, Gen Sir James E., *Military Operations France and Belgium 1918*, Macmillan, London, 1935

Friedlaender, Saul, *Nazi Germany and the Jews: The Years of Persecution 1933–39*, Weidenfeld and Nicolson, London, 1997

Friedrich, Otto, *Before the Deluge: A Portrait of Berlin in the 1920s*, Harper and Row, New York 1972

Fromm, Bella, *Blood and Banquets: A Berlin Social Diary*, Geoffrey Bles, London, 1942

Fry, Michael Graham, *Power, Personalities and Policies: Essays in Honour of Donald Cameron Watt*, Frank Cass, London, 1992

Gannon, Franklin Reid, *The British Press and Germany 1936–1939*, Clarendon Press, Oxford, 1971

Gilbert, Martin, *The Holocaust*, Fontana, London, 1987

Harel, Isser, *The House on Garibaldi Street*, Frank Cass, London, 1996

Henderson, Sir Nevile, *Failure of a Mission*, Hodder and Stoughton, London, 1940

Hinsley, F. H., *British Intelligence in the Second World War*, (Abridged Edition), HMSO, London, 1994

Hinsley, F. H. et al, *British Intelligence in the Second World War Vol I*, HMSO, London, 1979

Hinsley, F. H., and Simkins, C. A. G., *British Intelligence in the Second World War, Vol 4*, HMSO, London, 1990

Höhne, Heinz, *Canaris*, Secker and Warburg, London, 1979

Howard, Michael, *British Intelligence in the Second World War, Vol 5*, HMSO, London, 1990

Hutton, J. Bernard, *Hess: The Man and his Mission*, David Bruce & Watson, London, 1970

Irving, David, *Hess: The Missing Years 1941–1945*, Macmillan, London, 1987

Isherwood, Christopher, *The Berlin Novels*, Minerva, London, 1992

Jones, R. V., *Most Secret War: British Scientific Intelligence 1939–45*, Coronet, London, 1979

Jones, R. V., *Reflections on Intelligence*, Mandarin, London, 1990

Juenger, Ernst, *Storm of Steel*, Constable, London, 1994

Keegan, John, *The Second World War*, Viking Penguin, New York, 1990

Kersaudy, Francois, *Norway 1940*, Arrow, London, 1991

Kimche, Jon and David, *The Secret Roads*, Secker and Warburg, London, 1954

Kirkpatrick, Sir Ivone, *The Inner Circle*, Macmillan, London, 1959

Kramish, Arnold, *The Griffin*, Macmillan, London, 1986

Lacey, Greg, and Shephard, Keith, *Germany 1918–1945*, John Murray, London, 1997

Landau, Henry, *All's Fair: The Story of British Secret Service Behind German Lines*, Puttnam, New York, 1934

Landau, Henry, *Spreading the Spy Net*, Jarrolds, London, 1932

Lowenthal, Marvin, *The Jews of Germany*, Lindsay Drummond, London, 1939

Lycett, Andrew, *Ian Fleming*, Weidenfeld and Nicolson, London, 1995

MacDonogh, Giles, *Berlin*, Sinclair-Stevenson, London, 1997

McKay, C. G., *From Information to Intrigue*, Cass, London, 1993

Maslen, Geoffrey, *Burnham-on-Sea and Highbridge in Old Photographs*, Alan Sutton, Stroud, 1988

Masterman, J. C., *The Double Cross System in the War of 1939 to 1945*, YUP, London, 1972

Middlebrook, Martin, *The Kaiser's Battle*, Penguin, London, 1983

Morgan, K., *Harry Pollitt*, MUP, Manchester, 1993

Moss, Robert, *Carnival of Spies*, Hodder and Stoughton, London, 1987

Mosse, Werner E. (Ed), *Second Chance: Two Centuries of German-Speaking Jews in the United Kingdom*, J. C. B. Mohr, Tübingen, 1991

Mure, David, *Master of Deception*, William Kimber, London, 1980

Neuberg, A., *Armed Insurrection*, NLB, London, 1970

Ofer, Dalia, *Escaping the Holocaust: Illegal Immigration to the Land of Israel 1939–1944*, OUP, Oxford, 1990

Padfield, Peter, *Hess: The Führer's Disciple*, Papermac, London, 1994

Payne, Ronald, *Mossad: Israel's Most Secret Service*, Corgi, London, 1991

Powers, Thomas, *Heisenberg's War: The Secret History of the German Bomb*, Cape, London, 1993

Reed Olsen, Oluf, *Two Eggs on my Plate*, Companion Book Club, London, 1954

Reid, Margaret, and Rolstad, Leif C, *April 1940: En Krigsdagbok*, Gyldendaf Norsk Forlag, Oslo, 1980

Salmon, Patrick (Ed), *Britain and Norway in the Second World War*, HMSO, London, 1995

Shepherd, Naomi, *Wilfred Israel: German Jewry's Secret Ambassador*, Weidenfeld and Nicolson, London, 1984

Sherman, A. J., *Island Refuge: Britain and Refugees from the Third Reich 1933–39*, Frank Cass, London, 1994

Shirer, William L., *Berlin Diary: The Journal of a Foreign Correspondent 1939–1941*, Alfred A. Knopf, New York, 1941

Simpson, A. W. Brian, *In The Highest Degree Odious: Detention Without Trial in Wartime Britain*, Clarendon, Oxford, 1992

Smith, Michael, *New Cloak, Old Dagger*, Gollancz, London, 1996

Thurlow, Richard, *The Secret State: British Internal Security in the Twentieth Century*, Blackwell, Oxford, 1994

Van Leer, Wim, *Time of My Life*, Carta, Jerusalem, 1984

Valtin, Jan, *Out of the Night*, Fortress Books, London, 1988

Volkman, Ernest, *Espionage: The Greatest Spy Operations of the 20th Century*, Wiley, New York, 1995

Walker, Mark, *German National Socialism and the Quest for Nuclear Power, 1939–1949*, CUP, Cambridge, 1990

Watson, Fernando, *Olga*, Peter Halban, London, 1990

West, Nigel, *MI6: British Secret Intelligence Service Operations 1909–1945*, Weidenfeld and Nicolson, London, 1983

West, Nigel, and Tsarev, Oleg, *The Crown Jewels*, HarperCollins, London, 1998

Whitwell, John, *British Agent*, Frank Cass, London, 1996

Willoughby, Charles A., *Sorge: Soviet Master Spy*, William Kimber, London, 1952

Winterbotham, Frederick, *Secret and Personal*, William Kimber, London, 1969

Worth, Dr N., *Tourist's Guide to Somersetshire Rail and Road*, Edward Stanford, London, 1894

Young, Kenneth (Ed), *The Diaries of Sir Robert Bruce Lockhart*, Macmillan, London, 1980

Index

Abwehr 209, 253, 257, 267
Admiralty 181
aerial photography 201
agents, recruiting technique 18
Air Ministry 181
Aktivisti 53
aliyah 143
Allaverdi, Berlin 31–2
Allied Control Commission 261–7
    Public Safety Branch 261
    Special Branch 261, 263–4
Andalsnes 188
Andreasson, Carl Aage 210
Annan, Noel 262–3
Anschluss 104–7, 115–16, 160
appeasement, British policy of 95–7, 98,
    116–17, 139, 166, 217
Argentina 58, 272
Arian, Amalie 168–9
Arian, Dr David 168–9
Armistice 19
army career, Foley's 6–15
Artist 252–4
Aryanisation of German society 46–50, 70,
    73–5, 77–87, 91, 101–2, 104, 108, 111,
    137–8, 158, 163, 245
atomic weapons
    German research 140–1, 213–16
    Manhattan Project 214–16
Aue, Captain W.C.R. 98–9
Auschwitz concentration camp 93, 107

Austria 5, 58
    Anschluss 104–7, 115–16, 160
    anti-semitism 105–7, 115–16
    Jewish emigration 106–8, 146–8, 158, 160
Avigur, Shaul 144

Baeck, Rabbi Leo 63, 126–7
Baker, Josephine 32
Balfour, Arthur 45
Balfour Declaration 45–6
Barbarossa, Operation 209–10
Barbie, Klaus 265, 266
Beardsall, Private Frank 9 10, 12
Beaverbrook, Lord 235
Beer Hall Putsch 35, 37, 40, 71, 122
Belgium 58
    Jews 19, 200
Benes, Eduard 117
Bengeo Preparatory School, Hertford 6
Ben Gurion, David 143–4
Benton, Kenneth 252–3
Bergh, Sverre 212, 213
Berkhamsted 6–8
Berlin 210
    Allied Control Commission 261–7
    anti-Jewish riots 86–7
    arson attack on Reichstag 44, 52
    British journalists in 84–5, 103
    communism 26, 31, 41–2,
        51–2
    Golden Twenties 39

Jewish shops defaced and destroyed
114, 124
Kristallnacht 122–30, 136–7, 143–4,
158, 159
nightclubs 32–3, 39, 166
Passport Control Office 29–30, 46,
98–9, 170–1
Russian community 31–2, 52
Schieber 25–6, 262
Secret Service station opened 20–4, 29–30
Soviet spies 32, 51–2, 267
see also Germany
Berlin Olympics 97
Berlyn, Irene 173, 268
Beta 205
Bethe, Hans 68, 213
Bevan, Colonel Johnny 255
Bismarck 210
Blauer Vogel, Berlin 31
Bletchley Park, Government Code and
Cipher School 195, 197, 201, 206, 210,
238, 239–40
Blomberg, General Werner von 83, 104
Bolsheviks 217
in Germany 20, 23–4, 26, 31–2, 51, 52
Bond, James 252
Bonn 210
Borchardt, Hans 170
Bordeaux 198
Born, Max 68, 213
Bosch, Carl 68
Boyes, Admiral Hector 177–8
Braun, Wernher von 212
Brazil
communist coup 58–61
Jonny X 249
Lieutenants' Uprising 58
National Liberation Alliance (ANL) 59–60
Britain
anti-semitism 66, 160
appeasement, policy of 95–7, 98, 116–17,
139, 166, 217
Balfour Declaration 45–6
British subjects expelled from Germany
103
German invasion of Norway 190–6, 201
Germany's attempted alliance with 217–18
Jewish refugees 66–7, 107–10, 154–5,
158–60, 198, 200, 207–8
League of Nations Mandate,

Palestine 45–6, 97, 131–2,
167
planned German invasion 209, 210
refugees interned 207–8
war declared on Germany 174
British Medical Association (BMA) 160
Brooman-White, Dick 257
Browning, Lieutenant-Colonel Freddie 21
brownshirts see Sturmabteilung (SA)
Brutus 257
Buchenwald concentration camp 127–8,
130, 133
Bullecourt 9
Bund Deutscher Madel 264
Burnham, Somerset 4, 6

'C' 20, 21–2, 56
Cadogan, Alexander 220, 221, 229
Cambridge spy ring 234
Canada 249–50, 258
Canaris, Admiral Wilhelm 209, 217, 246
Capitalist Visa see
Kapitalistenzertifikat
Central Bureau for Jewish Emigration
144, 159
Centro-Soyuz 57
Chamberlain, Neville 116–17, 160,
166, 191–2
Chiang Kai-Shek 56
Cholmondley, Charles 250–1
Churchill, Sir Winston 84, 208, 220, 221,
222, 224, 227, 229–30, 233, 236
Clarke, Colonel Dudley 194
codes
Bletchley Park code-breakers 195, 197,
199, 201, 210, 238, 239–40
Enigma ciphers 195, 197, 238, 239–40, 241
MI6 emergency codes 188
Ultra decrypts 201, 206, 240
Cohn, Benno 44, 46–7, 97–8, 126, 131–2,
145, 272–3
Cologne 19, 20–1
Colvin, Ian 84, 156, 269
Comberti, Sabine 80–1
Comintern 51–2, 53, 55, 56–7, 58, 59–61
Commander of the Order of St
Michael and St George, Foley
created 208
communism
Brazil 58–61

Germany 20, 23–4, 26, 41–2, 44, 51–2,
    54, 109–10
India 52
OGPU 51–2
Red Hundreds 54–5
Shanghai 56–7
Spartakus League 23, 26, 54
Communist International *see* Comintern
concentration camps 50, 86, 89, 94, 111, 115,
    126, 151, 158, 163–5, 167, 232–3
    Auschwitz 93, 107
    Buchenwald 127–8, 130, 133
    Dachau 45, 105, 151
    Esterwegen 45
    Oranienburg 92, 254
    Sachsenhausen 45, 103, 164–5
    Theresienstadt 93, 160
    Treblinka 112
    wild 44–5
Confessional Church 102–3
Cooper, Duff, *Operation Heartbreak* 269
Copenhagen 52, 173–4, 182
Coq d'Or, Berlin 31
Council for German Jewry 153–4
courts of honour 94
Cowgill, Felix 234–5, 240–5, 246, 253, 254
Cripps, Sir Stafford 209
Crossbow, Operation 259–60
Cumming, Mansfield 20, 21–2, 23, 56
cut-outs 30, 177, 180
Czechoslovakia 58
    German invasion 166, 210
    Sudetenland 116–17

Dachau concentration camp 45, 105, 151
Daladier, Edouard 117
Dame Blanche, La 18, 20
Dansey, Lieutenant-Colonel Claude 199
D-day 256–8
dead-letter boxes 30
deGraff, Johann Heinrich *see* Jonny X
Delmer, Sefton 47
Denmark 5, 169, 182
Detter, Friedl 163–4
Deutsche Revolution 265–6
diplomatic bag, transmission of information
    by 30, 175
Dombass 187
Doran, E. 66
Dormer, Sir Cecil 175, 185–6, 194–5

Double-Cross System 236, 237–47,
    249–60, 267
Drexler, Anton 35
Dukes, Paul 21–2
Dunkirk evacuation 198
Dunstan, Patricia 247, 255, 256

Ebbutt, Norman 84, 85, 103, 269
Ebert, Friedrich 26
Ecoust-St-Mein 10–14
Edelweiss Pirates 264–5
Ehrhardt Brigade 27, 34
Eichmann, Adolf 144, 272
Einstein, Albert 68, 140, 213
Eismann, Colonel Hans 265–6
Ellersiek, Kurt 265–6
Emden 6
Enigma ciphers 195, 197, 238, 239–40, 241
Esser 47
Esterwegen concentration camp 45
ethnic German areas 36, 82
Ewert, Arthur 57, 59 61

Falkenhausen, General Alexander von 246–7
Farben, I G 107
Fawley Court 202
Fehr, Inge 74–5, 102, 123, 127, 137–8, 160
Fehr, Professor Oscar 74–5, 160, 207–8
Feldgendarmerie 44–5
Felix 18
Fleming, Commander Ian 198
flight tax *see Reichsfluchtssteuer*
Foley, Andrew Wood (father) 3–5, 6, 24, 63
Foley, Andy (brother) 3, 269–70
Foley, Bert (brother) 3
Foley, Dennis (great-nephew) 270
Foley, George (brother) 3
Foley, Isabella (mother) 3–5, 267
Foley, Kay (wife) 19, 24–5, 33–4, 45, 63,
    123, 126–7, 134, 157, 163, 166, 200, 225,
    267, 270
Foley, Margaret (sister) 3, 4
Foley, Ursula Margaret (daughter) 34, 63,
    200, 267, 270
Foley Mission 192–6, 197
Forbes-Robertson, Ann 148–9, 156, 158,
    166, 170
Forscher 252
Fortitude South 257
France 58

German invasion 210
German invasion of Norway 192–3
German reoccupation of the Rhineland
　96
Interallie resistance 257
mobile MI6 special intelligence
　unit 197–9
World War I 8–15, 19
Fred 258
Freikorps 26–7, 36
Frick, Wilhelm 86, 87
Friedenthal, Hans 231
Frisch, Otto 140, 213
Fritsch, General Werner von 104
Funk, Walter 104

Garbo 241–2, 257–9
Garby-Czerniawski, Roman see Brutus
Garcia, Juan Pujol see Garbo
Gauleiters 41, 85, 115
Gedye, Eric 104
Geheime Staatspolizei see Gestapo
Geneva 208–9
George VI, King 208
German police, liaison with 30, 31
German spies 161, 204, 237–47, 249–50,
　252–3
German Workers' Party 35–6
Germany 5
　Allied occupation 261–7
　anti-semitism 26–7, 34, 42–3, 70–1, 73–5,
　　77–87, 111–15, 124–30
　Aryanisation of German society 46–50, 70,
　　73–5, 77–87, 91, 101–2, 104, 108, 111,
　　112, 137–8
　Aryanisation of Jewish businesses 46–7,
　　73–4, 85, 94, 101–2, 104, 108, 113–15,
　　137, 158, 163
　churches and Hitler 102–3
　citizenship, qualification for narrowed 87
　communism 20, 23–4, 26, 31–2, 44, 51–2,
　　54, 109–10
　economy 25–6, 34–5, 42, 49
　hyperinflation 34–5, 37, 39
　Jewish emigration 45–6, 49, 63–75,
　　77–87, 89–95, 97–8, 133–5,
　　143–6
　Kristallnacht 122–30, 136–7, 143–4, 150,
　　158, 159
　non-Aryans, definition 48

non-German culture, Nazi campaign
　against 78
Nuremberg Laws 87, 89
rearmament 83–4
reparations 26, 34
rural areas 43, 78
war-time MI6 intelligence network
　209–16
see also Berlin
Gestapo (Geheime Staatspolizei) 50, 65–6,
　98–9, 103, 127, 133, 136, 144, 151, 170,
　204, 205, 252–3
Ginzberg, Pino 145
Gittins, Chris 268
Goebbels, Josef 40, 41, 43, 78, 115, 122–3,
　125, 136, 137, 225, 233
Göring, Hermann 70, 83, 104, 113, 138, 144,
　166, 215
Gotha 127
Goudsmit, Samuel 215
Graham, Colonel Gibson 223, 224, 230
Great Depression 42, 49
Greater Germany 36, 82
Greene, Hugh Carleton 124–5
Griffin see Rosbaud, Paul
GRU 51–3, 55, 56, 57, 61
Grynszpann, Herschel 121–2
Grynszpann, Mordechai 121
Grynszpann, Zindel 121–2
Gunnarside 214
Gustloff, Wilhelm 97
gypsies 45

Haakon VII, King of Norway 185, 196,
　201, 256
Haavara 91
Hagana 144
Hahn, Otto 68, 140–1, 213–16
Hamar 185, 186
Hamburg 5, 23, 210
　Red Hundreds 54–5
Hamilton, Duke of 218–20, 223–4
Hamlet 245–7, 257
Hampton, Victor 210
Handler, Arieh 157
Hankey, Maurice 49
Hardware 204
Haris, Tommy 257
Harrer, Karl 35
Harrow-on-the-Hill 17

Hassel, Odd 180
Haushofer, Albrecht 217–19, 226
Haushofer, Karl 217–18
Hehalutz 143, 144
Heisenberg, Werner 68, 213–16
Helldorf, Count Wolf Heinrich 115
Henderson, Sir Nevile 113, 114–15, 139
Hertfordshire Regiment 8
Hess, Rudolf 37, 217–36, 243
Heydrich, Reinhard 144–5
Highbridge, Somerset 3–4
Hilfsverein der Deutschen Juden 64–5, 109, 151, 155
Himmler, Heinrich 47, 72, 121, 264, 266–7
Hindenburg, Paul von 43–4, 72
Hirschberg, Emmy 271–2
Histadrut 144
Hitler, Adolf 48–9, 70, 71
    appointed Chancellor 44
    assassination attempt 209
    attempted alliance with Britain 217–18
    Beer Hall Putsch 35, 37, 40, 71, 122
    British appeasement 66, 95, 98, 116–17, 139, 166, 217
    imprisonment 37, 40
    leads Nazi Party 35–6, 37, 39, 40
    made supreme commander of the Wehrmacht 104
    Mein Kampf 37–8, 39, 77, 136, 218
    Night of the Long Knives 72–3, 82
Hitler Youth 78, 114, 124, 133, 156, 264–5
Hoare, Sir Samuel 107, 155, 160
Holburn, James 124
Horwell, Arnold 65
Horwitz, Arnold 146
Howard, Leslie 254–5, 269
Hungarian Jews 158
Hunter, Major-General Alan 222–3

Indian Communist Party 52
Inland Passports 102
Inns of Court Officer Training Corps 6–8
Intelligence Corps 15, 17–19
Inter-Allied Military Commission of Control 19, 20–1
International Transport Federation 175, 180
invisible inks 18, 30
Isherwood, Christopher, Goodbye to Berlin 64
Israel, Francis Edward Foley Memorial Grove 271–2

Israel, Wilfred 64, 66, 109, 115, 124, 170, 254, 269

Jacobi, Pastor Gerhard 102
Jakobsen, Sigurd 204
Janowski, Werner 249–50
Jebsen, Jonny see Artist
Jewish Agency 91, 143, 170, 254
Jews
    anti-semitism in Britain 66, 160
    anti-semitism in Germany 26–7, 34, 36, 38, 41, 42–3, 70–1, 73–5, 77–87, 125–30
    anti-semitism on mainland Europe 19
    artists 78–9
    Aryanisation of Jewish businesses 46–7, 73–4, 85, 94, 101–2, 104, 108, 113–15, 137, 158, 163
    Austrian 104–5, 106–8, 115–16, 146–8, 158, 160
    Belgian 19
    concentration camps 44–5
    emigration from Germany 45–6, 49, 63–75, 77–87, 89–95, 97–8, 109, 133–5, 143–6
    emigration to America 154–5, 158
    emigration to Britain 154–5, 158–60, 207–8
    emigration to Palestine 45–6, 63–4, 79, 109, 143–6, 149–50, 157, 164–5, 171
    emigration to Shanghai 150–2
    excluded from public areas 137–8
    excluded occupations 114
    exit permits 133–4
    France 198, 200
    Freikorps treatment of 26–7
    German passports confiscated 102, 104
    Hungarian 158
    Kristallnacht 122–30, 136–7, 143–4, 150, 158, 159
    medical profession, in 114, 159–60
    non Aryans, definition 48
    Norway 185, 200
    Polish 121–2, 143
    property confiscated 113, 137
    scientists 68, 140
    Star of David, forced to wear 46–7
    suicides amongst 106, 114, 124, 147, 160
    Zionist movement 45, 65, 92, 97, 131–2, 143, 167–8

Joint Intelligence Committee 182
Jones, R.V. 178–9, 216, 259–60
Jonny X 53–61, 63, 67, 249–50, 258
Jünger, Ernst 13, 14

Kahn, Berthold 91–3
Kahn, Clara 93
Kahn, Elsbeth 92–3
Kahn, Emma 93
Kahn, Hermann 92–3
Kahn, Hilde 92
Kahn, Paul 92
Kaiserschlacht 10–15
Kapitalistenzertifikat 79–80, 91–2, 94, 271
Karweik, Martyl 118–19, 176
Kelley, John (nephew) 63, 67, 69–70
Kelley, Joyce 68, 69
Kempka, Eric 72
Kendrick, Captain Thomas 106, 115–16, 147,
    222, 223, 225, 227–8
Kenney, Rowland 187
Kilmarnock, Lord 22
King-Salter, Lieutenant-Colonel E.J.C.
    193, 194
Kirkpatrick, Ivone 17–18, 117, 220–1,
    223, 228–9
Knight's Cross of St Olav, Foley awarded
    196, 245, 256
Koht, Dr Halvdan 186
Königsberg 210
Kon Tiki expedition 205
Kozis 41–2
Kramer, Ernst 128
Krauser 47
Kristallnacht 122–30, 136–7, 143–4, 150,
    158, 159

Lachs, Fred 158–9
Lachs, Richard 158
Lachs, Werner 158–9
Landauer, Georg 149–50, 231
Landau, Henry 18, 20, 29–31, 98, 203–4
Landgraf Café, Berlin 31
Law, Frank 128–9
League of Nations
    High Commission for Refugees 95
    Palestinian Mandate 45–6
Lee, Kay *see* Foley, Kay
Lee, Owen 19, 33, 200
Lee, Rita 173, 200, 267

Lee, Ruth 267
Lee, William 24–5
Leer, Wim van 125–6, 138–9, 141, 150, 272
Lenard, Philipp 119
Leon Café, Berlin 31
Lerwick 201–3
Liebknecht, Karl 23, 54
Lisbon 241–2, 245–6, 252–4
Locarno Pact 95–6
Locker-Lampson, Oliver 66
Lockhart, Robert Bruce 227
Londonderry, Lord 83
Ludendorff, Field Marshal Erich 37
Luftwaffe 83, 195
Luftwaffe Forschungsamt 215
Luxembourg 18
Luxemburg, Rosa 23, 54

McDonald, James G. 95
MacDonald, Ramsay 86
McEwen, David 156
Machtergreifung 40, 51, 70
Maclean, Gordon Thompson 254
Manhattan Project 214–16
Mao Tse-Tung 56
Masterman, J.C. 239, 243–6
Mayer, Hans Ferdinand 119–20, 176–7
Meitner, Lise 68, 140, 211–12, 213
Menzies, Sir Stewart 19, 178, 196, 199, 205,
    217, 220, 221–2, 228, 229–30, 232, 233–6,
    242, 246, 254
Messerschmitt Me-262 213
Meyer-Michael, Susanne 78
Meyer-Michael, Wolfgang 77–82
MIıc 18, 21, 22
MI5 219, 237, 238, 242–3
    blacklist of suspicious aliens 31
    refugees interned 207–8
    Twenty (XX) Committee
        238–47
MI6 52, 238
    A Sections 199
    counter-espionage 56
    emergency codes 188
    escape lines 139, 272
    G Sections 199
    intelligence network in war-time
        Germany 209–16
    Operations department 199
    Production sections 199

Scandinavian agents in Germany
  175, 180–1
Section V 56, 240, 242–4, 255
Section VX 244
ship-watching stations 204
Special Liaison Units 197–206
training school 202
Twenty (XX) Committee 238–47
Mills, Eric 89–90, 131, 133
Milorg 201
Mincemeat, Operation 250–2, 269
Mischlingen 119
Mitchell, Leslie H. 156, 180, 181, 183–4,
  185, 193, 195–6, 199, 201, 202–3
Moe, Kaare 183
Molotov-Ribbentrop Pact 169
Montagu, Ewen 240–1, 251, 269
  The Man Who Never Was 252
Moonbeam 258
Morgan, Brigadier Harold de Reimer 194
Mory 9–10
Mossad leAliyah Bet 141, 143–6, 167, 272
Mountbatten, Lord 251
Mullet 246–7, 257
Munich 23, 35
Munich Conference 117, 166
Mussolini, Benito 37
Mytchett Place 222–9, 235

National Socialist Party see Nazi Party
Nazi Party
  anti-semitism 36, 38, 41, 42–3
  Austrian 104–5
  Beer Hall Putsch 35, 37, 40, 71, 122
  Decree for the Protection of the People
    and the State 44
  Hitler as leader 35–6, 37, 39, 40
  homosexual members 156–7
  Machtergreifung 40, 51, 70
  membership 50, 263
  Night of the Long Knives 72–3, 82
  origins 35–6
  post-war attempts to re-establish 264–7
  post-war hunt for members 261–7
  rural areas 43
  Twenty-Five Point Programme 36, 40–1
  voted largest party in Reichstag 43–4
  see also Schützenstaffel (SS);
    Sicherheitsdienst (SD); Sturmabteilung
    (SA)

Netherlands 5, 58
  Jewish refugees from 200
Neumarkt 111
neutral countries 208, 241–2, 245–6
Newill, Commander J.B. 176, 185, 193,
  195, 199
Niemöller, Martin 103
Night of the Long Knives 72–3, 82
Noreuil 13
Norway 169, 174–84, 208
  agents in occupied Norway 201–6
  German invasion 181–4, 185–206
  gold reserves 185, 196
  government-in-exile 201
  Jews 185
  Milorg (resistance) 201–6
  mobilisation 187, 190
  refugees 201
  XU intelligence network 201, 205–6, 210,
    212, 215
Nuremberg Laws 87, 89
Nursery 264–5, 266

Ogilvie Forbes, Sir George 138
OGPU 51–2
Oldell 204–5
Ollen, Olle 213
Olsen, Oluf Reed 183, 201, 205
Olympic Games (1936) 97
Oranienburg concentration camp 92, 254
Oslo 173–84, 190, 204
Oslo Report 173–9
Oster, Colonel Hans 169–70
Owens, Arthur 237–8
Oyer 189–90

Palestina Treuhand-Stelle (Paltreu) 91
Palestine
  Arab unrest 91, 97, 167
  Balfour Declaration 45–6
  British Mandate 45–6, 97, 167
  Central Bureau for the Settlement of Jews
    in Palestine 149–50
  illegal emigration to 143–5, 149–50, 167–9
  Jewish immigration 45–6, 63–4, 67, 79,
    89–92, 97–8, 109, 131–2, 143–6, 157,
    164–5, 167, 171
  Mossad leAliyah Bet 141, 143–6
  Zionist movement 45, 65, 92, 97, 131–2,
    143, 167–8

Papen, Franz von 43–4
Passport Control Officers 20, 22, 24, 98–9
    Berlin 29–31, 46
    Scandinavia 175–84
Patton, General 258
Peenemünde research station 179, 212
Peierls, Rudolf 140
Peiler 204, 205
Petrie, Sir David 242
Philby, Kim 84, 200, 234–5, 240–1, 246, 253, 254, 257
Picton, Harold 86
Poitiers 5
Poland
    German invasion 166, 169–70, 174
    illegal emigration to Palestine 143
    Molotov-Ribbentrop Pact 169
    Polish Jews repatriated 121–2
    Polish refugees 264
political prisoners in Germany 44–5
Political Warfare Executive 227
Pollack, Hubert 44–5, 64–6, 109–10, 132, 141, 145, 154, 161, 170, 171, 185, 271
Pollack, Isidor 107
Popov, Dusko *see* Tricycle
Portugal 241–2, 245–6, 252–4
Powitzer, Gunther 163–5
Powitzer, Willi 164
Prager Diele Café, Berlin 31
Preis, Eli 118
Preis, Lotte 118
Preis, Ohniel 118, 123
Preis, Willi 118
Prestes, Luis Carlos 58–61
Price, Beryl 173, 268
Price, Ken 173, 268
priesthood, Foley's early training for 4–5
Protestant Churches in Germany 102–3
Prussian Academy of the Arts 77–8
Puppet 247

Quakers 125, 138, 272

Raaby, Torstein 205
Rabow, Albert 93
Rabow, Miriam 93
Rabow, Paula 93
radar, German experiments with 179
Rathenau, Walter 34
Rath, Ernst von 122

Red Army 23, 53
Red Hundreds 54–5
Rees, Colonel J.R. 226, 230
Reichsfluchtssteuer 79, 108, 113
Reichskulturkammer 78
Reichstag, arson attack 44, 52
Reichsvertretung de Deutschen Juden 63
Reichswehr 82
Reichswerke Hermann Göring AG 113
Reid, Margaret 132–3, 135–6, 170, 173–4, 175–6, 179–80, 183–92, 194–200, 208, 222
    awarded Krigsmedalje 196, 245
reparations 26, 34
Rhineland
    Allied occupation 19, 20–1, 26
    French separatist movement 19
    German reoccupation 95–6
    Inter-Allied Military Commission of Control 19, 20–1
Ribbentrop, Joachim von 70
Rjukan 214
Robertson, Lieutenant-Colonel Tommy 'Tar' 237–8, 239, 252
Röhm, Ernst 44, 45, 47, 71–2
Rolstad, General Leif 177–8, 192
Roman Catholic Church
    concordat with Hitler 102
    Foley's faith 4–5, 200, 272
Romania 58
Romberg, Heinz 94
Rorholt, Bjorn 205
Rosbaud, Hilde 109
Rosbaud, Paul 68–9, 109, 140–1, 170, 175, 180, 210–13, 216
Rosenbacher-Levy, Jacob 160
Rosenbacher-Levy, Sarah 160
Rothenberg, Franz 107
Roy, M.N. 52
Ruge, Major-General Otto 189–94, 196, 208
Ruhr, French and Belgian occupation 34
Rumbold, Lady 46
Ruppel, Anne-Marie 128–30
Ruppel, Ernest (junior) 127–30
Ruppel, Ernst (senior) 127–30, 268, 270, 275
Ruskin, John, *Sesame and Lilies* 188

Saarland, German reoccupation 82
Sachsenhausen concentration camp 45, 164–5
Sahm, Dr Heinrich 94
St Clair, Sheila 179

St John's Church of England Elementary
School 4
St Joseph's College, Poitiers 5
St Joseph's Roman Catholic School 4
Schacht, Hjalmar 104
Schieber 25–6, 146, 262
Schleicher, General Kurt von 44, 72
Schmidt, Wulf see Tate
Schuschnigg, Kurt von 104–5
Schutzenstaffel (SS) 45, 47, 72, 82, 106, 121,
164–5, 263–7
Scott, Lieutenant-Colonel Malcolm 222–3
Sea Lion, Operation 209–10
Secret Service 15, 17–18
'C' 20, 21–2, 56
Passport Control Officers 20, 22,
24, 29–31
Selection Board, Operation 265, 266
Semeshko, Gregory 57
Senator, Werner 64, 66, 89, 261–2
Serelman, Hans 89
Seyss-Inquart, Arthur 104
Shanghai
communism 56–7
Jewish immigration to 150–2
Russian community 56
Shetland Bus 203
Shirer, William 72, 82–3, 85, 95, 103
Sicherheitsdienst (SD) 144, 178, 253–4, 267
Sicily, Allied invasion 250–2
Siemens 119, 176–7, 179
Simon, Lord 227–30
Sinclair, Admiral Hugh 56, 116–17, 178
skoyter 201–3
Smallbones, R. T. 73
Smedley, Agnes 57
Smith, Gabriel 204–5
SNOW 237–8
Social Democratic Party (Germany) 42
Somme 8–9
Sonderkonto 79–80
Sorge, Richard 54, 55, 57
Soviet Union
German invasion 209, 210, 221, 231
German troops trained on Soviet
territory 52
GRU 51–3, 55, 56, 57, 61
Hitler's proposed alliance with Britain
against 217–18
OGPU 51–2

Soviet spies in Berlin 32, 51–2, 267
world revolution, intention of provoking
23, 31–2, 51–2
Spain 246, 251, 252
Spartakus League 23, 26, 54
Special Operations Executive (SOE) 201–2,
206, 232
Speer, Albert 214–15
Spender, Stephen 39–40
Stalin, Josef 209
Steptoe, Harry 57
Stockholm 156, 208, 210
Stonyhurst College 5
Stourbridge 173
Strasser, Gregor 40, 41
Strassmann, Fritz 68, 140
Streicher, Julius 85
Stresemann, Gustav 35
stringers 237
Sturmabteilung (SA; Brownshirts) 36–7,
41–5, 70, 71–2, 86–7, 91, 106–7, 113, 122,
124, 125, 147–8
Stürmer, Der 41
Sudetenland 116–17
Sueffert, Fritz 140
Supreme Headquarters Allied Forces in
Europe (SHAEF) 256
Sweden 169, 174, 208
Switzerland 208
Szymanska, Halina 209, 217

Tate 237
Theresienstadt concentration camp 93, 160
Third Country Rule 22, 67, 83–4
Thomas, Edward 181, 182
Thomson, Sir Basil 23
Thümmel, Paul 210
Thurnheer, Walther 235
Times, The 84, 85, 103
Transfer Agreement see Haavara
Treblinka concentration camp 112
Tretis 30
Tricycle 252–4, 257
Tuaillon, Louis 77
Turnbull, Isabella see Foley, Isabella
Turner, Cobden 119, 176–7
Twenty (XX) Committee (Club) 238–47,
250, 251, 254, 256, 257, 259–60

Ultra decrypts 201, 206, 240

United States of America 154–5, 158, 171
Université de France, Poitiers 5
Uranverein (Uranium Club) 213–16

Valtin, Jan 52, 53
V-bombs 179, 212, 259–60
Versailles, Treaty of
    German army, restrictions imposed on 52,
        71, 72–3
    German reaction to 26, 35
    reparations 26, 34–5
    Rhineland 19
Vienna 115–16, 210
    British Passport Control Office 146–8
Vigne, Commandant Bertrand 193
Vivian, Colonel Valentine 56, 61, 199,
    269, 270

walk-ins 53
Wallinger, Major Ernest 17
Wall Street crash 42
War Office 17, 181
Watchdog 250
Weber, August 136–7
Weber, Maria 136
Weber, Paula 135–7, 179–80
Wehrmacht 82–3, 104, 195
Weimar Republic 34, 39, 42, 153
Weizsäcker, Carl von 214–16
Weller, Marjorie 146–7
Welsh, Eric 199, 204
Weltsch, Robert 47, 270–1

Werewolf 264, 266–7
Wertheimer, Adele 111–12
Wertheimer, Leopold 111–12
Wertheimer, Simon 111–12
Weserübung, Operation 181
Westbureau 52, 53
White, Dick 237, 239
Wiesbaden 113–14
Winterbotham, Frederick 102
wireless transmitters
    Foley Mission 175, 185–6, 190–3, 195
    MI6 Special Liaison Units 197–206
Wittlich 125
World War I
    army career 6–15
    bullet wound damages left lung 13–14, 15
    Foley's escape from Germany 5–6
    Intelligence Corps 15, 17–19 Mory 13
Wormwood Scrubs prison 239

XU intelligence network 201, 205–6, 210,
    212, 215
XX Committee see Twenty Committee

Yishuv 46
Youth Aliyah 157, 171

Zentralausschuss für Hilfe und Aufbau 64
Zimmels, Max 145
Zionist movement 45, 65, 92, 97, 127,
    131–2, 141, 167–8, 231
    Mossad leAliyah Bet 141, 143–6, 167